**Red Rock Canyon**
National Conservation Area

5 miles

N

95

Lee Canyon Road

156

Red Rock Canyon
Conservation Area
Boundary

Lucky Strike Mine

158

Kyle Canyon Road

157

Tule
Springs

White Beauty
Mine

95

Mount
Charleston

**Griffith Peak**
**11,053'**

S
p
r
i
n
g

La Madre Mine

Sandstone
Quarry

Las
Vegas

Summerlin Parkway

W. Charleston Blvd.

Rainbow Blvd.

**Scenic**
**Drive**

R
e
d

R
o
c
k

Rheastone
Quarry

D0879292

M
o
u
n
t
a
i
n
s

Mountain
Spring

160

Mormon Road - Old Spanish Trail

Potosi Mine

160

Blue Diamond Highway

**Mount**
**Potosi**
**8512'**

Snell Press
Las Vegas, Nevada
www.snellpress.com

Library of Congress Control Number: 2012907823

ISBN-13: 978-0-9855771-0-0

**Front cover:** A strawberry hedgehog blooms atop a band of Chile Sandstone in Pine Creek Canyon.

**Facing page:** A winter storm breaks over the Calico Hills and Turtlehead Peak.

**Contents page:** Aztec Sandstone is found in elaborate shapes at Brownstone Canyon

**Back cover (left to right):** A Frémont cottonwood turns golden in the fall at the village of Blue Diamond. A ram bighorn sheep near White Rock Spring. The summit of Rainbow Mountain dusted in show. Sunrise in the Mojave Desert.

**Page 6:** Thin clouds roll over the Red Rock Escarpment, as seen from the High Point Overlook.

MIX
Paper from
responsible sources
FSC® C019704
www.fsc.org

### Warning! Read before using this book.

Every effort has been made to ensure that this book is as up to date as possible at the time of publication. Some details, however, such as telephone numbers, hours of operation, prices, display materials, and travel information are liable to change. Neither the author nor the publisher accepts responsibility for any consequences arising from the use of this book, or for any material on third party websites, and cannot guarantee that any website address in this book will be a suitable source of information.

Some of the activities described in this book can be extremely dangerous. The information, descriptions, and difficulty ratings within this book are entirely subjective and based on opinions gathered from a variety of sources. Always use judgement rather than the opinions presented here. The author assumes no responsibility for injury or death resulting from the use of this book.

Certain plants and animals have been described as being useful to Native Americans and others. Never consume or otherwise take any plant or animal part(s) without proper knowledge, training, and oversight by a qualified person. Allergic reactions, severe illness, and death can be caused from doing so. Additionally, collection of plants within the Red Rock Canyon Conservation Area is not allowed. See page 10 for additional information.

Certain descriptions have been recorded for historical purposes only. The inclusion of an area or trail in this guide does not imply a right of use. Trail designation, access and

# Red Rock Canyon
## *Visitor Guide*

# Climate and Weather

Although every season offers a distinctive experience, most visitors choose to come during the fall and spring.

*Winter storms, like this one that dusted Bridge Mountain with snow, are a treat to see. Most of the time, however, Red Rock has warm, agreeable weather*

### ► Climate

Red Rock Canyon is located within the Spring Mountains west of Las Vegas, Nevada. The region is in the southern tip of the Great Basin and within the northeastern region of the Mojave Desert, one of the driest places in North America.

The little precipitation that does occur is in the form of late summer thundershowers and winter storms. Mountainous regions, such as Red Rock, receive considerably more precipitation than lower valley regions.

The mountains are also cooler; the canyons of Red Rock are typically 10°F cooler than the Las Vegas Valley. Temperatures range from oppressively hot in the summer to bitterly cold in the winter. Due to low humidity, the air does not hold heat well. Between night and day, temperatures can vary drastically. Similarly, temperatures vary between shade and sun, especially noticeable on cold winter days.

### ► Weather

A number of websites provide weather forecasts. The National Weather Service provides reliable information. Search for Blue Diamond, NV at www.weather.gov

to get the most accurate forecast.

### ► When to Go

Generally, September to May is considered the best season for visiting Red Rock. August is still rather warm, with highs reaching above 100°F. December and January can be cold, and storms periodically cover Red Rock with a thin blanket of snow. However, during December and January, it is also common to have spells of beautiful, cloudless days with temperatures in the mid 60s.

A bloom of wildflowers typically peaks in early May, but from late March until September wildflowers can be found.

During summer thunderstorms, flash floods, while infrequent and often localized, can pose a hazard. The narrow, rocky canyons allow little infiltration, and runoff quickly forms into powerful torrents.

### ► What to Wear

Although personal preferences vary and each activity has its own requirements, below are what most find comfortable:

**Spring:** Pants and a T-shirt or long-sleeved shirt with a sweater on hand.

**Summer:** Shorts and a T-shirt, a sun hat, and sunscreen.

**Fall:** Pants and a T-shirt or long-sleeved shirt with a sweater and hat on hand.

**Winter:** Pants, long-sleeved shirt, sweater, jacket, and hat.

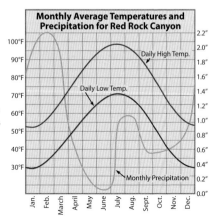

# Accommodations

Whether roughing it in the desert or being pampered in a five-star hotel, the area offers somewhere to stay for all tastes.

### ► Developed Camping

In the early 1980s, the idyllic Willow Springs was the spot to go for camping at Red Rock Canyon. Centrally located, it provided short hikes to areas of interest and had a communal feel. Since then, the campground has relocated many times, from a beautiful location east of Mount Wilson, to the east slope of Fossil Mountain near Blue Diamond village, and finally to its present location.

The most accessible developed campground in the vicinity of Red Rock is out of sight from SR-159, on the east side of Blue Diamond Hill (see map, inside back cover). Managed by the Bureau of Land Management, the **Red Rock Canyon Campground** has a 14-day limit and sites cost $15 per night. Sites are available on a first-come, first-serve basis; reservations are not accepted. Each site can accommodate two vehicles, has a fire ring, picnic table, and access to water and toilets. Showers and utility hookups are not available. Although there is a resident caretaker, theft has been a problem in recent years. For site availability and additional information, call (702) 515-5371.

**Directions:** From its junction with the CC-215, continue west on West Charleston Boulevard for 3.3 miles. Turn left onto Moenkopi Road, which leads 1.2 miles to the campground. If traveling from Red Rock, Moenkopi Road is on the right, 0.5 miles past Calico Basin Drive.

### ► Primitive Camping

Camping is not allowed along the dirt roads near Black Velvet and Windy Canyons, or anywhere in Calico Basin. However, a few primitive camping options are available:

A permit is required to camp along Rocky Gap Road (a scenic 4x4 road that connects Willow Springs and Lovell Canyon) and anywhere above 5000' in areas south of the La Madre Mountains within the Red Rock Canyon National Conservation Area. Call (702) 515-5050 for further information. Camping is subject to a 14-day limit and fires are not allowed. Also, camping within ¼ mile of springs or riparian areas is not allowed.

Sites in Lovell Canyon (on the west side of the Red Rock Escarpment) do not require a permit, but are still subject to the 14-day limit. The easiest access is from Lovell Canyon Road, 3.2 miles west of Mountain Springs.

*With facilities for all group sizes, from couples and smore-making families to mini armies, the Red Rock Canyon Campground fills up fast in the fall and spring. Therefore, it's best to have a backup plan.*

### ► Four-walled Options

Bonnie Springs, an 'old Nevada' themed hotel, is a good option. It is centrally located off SR-159, northwest of Blue Diamond, and has reasonable rates (See page 144). Call (702) 875-4191 for more information.

Las Vegas offers a myriad of options, from $20-a-night motels to luxury resorts.

Temporary house rentals in Las Vegas are becoming increasingly available from private owners and real estate managers; check the internet for information.

# The Land and its Use

▶ **Land Ownership**

Owned by the Federal Government, Red Rock Canyon National Conservation Area (RRCNCA) is administered by the Bureau of Land Management (BLM). Currently encompassing more than 196,000 acres, the conservation area was designated in 1990 to conserve, protect, and enhance the land for current and future generations. Because the conservation area receives over one million visits each year, there is a great potential for harmful impacts to its ecology and cultural resources.

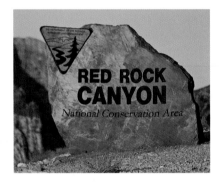

To better care for the land, certain areas have been designated as 'wilderness areas' with special restrictions. Additionally, the conservation area is operated under a management plan that sets forth rules, which outline acceptable land uses. Described below are some of the rules, restrictions, and special considerations that visitors need to know and observe.

▶ **Getting Around - The Scenic Drive**

Whether sightseeing or out for a hike, the most straightforward way of getting around is by automobile. Several State Routes and dirt roads traverse the conservation area (see map, page 1 and inside back cover).

The Scenic Drive is a two-lane, one-way loop that provides access to the Calico Hills and Red Rock Escarpment. While the scenery is stunning, please take care while driving. The paved road is winding, narrow, has soft shoulders, and is sometimes congested. Speed limits vary from 15 mph to 35 mph. Parking areas are provided along the Scenic Drive but are occasionally full. When no parking spaces are available, do not park off the pavement; continue to the next designated parking area.

Since 1998, the BLM has collected fees for use of the Scenic Drive (see box, opposite page). Fees are used to improve visitor services and maintain facilities at Red Rock Canyon. The Scenic Drive opens at 6:00 am and is closed at night (see table below). The Red Rock Overlook on SR-159 is open for one additional hour. The BLM strongly enforces the closing time of the Scenic Drive, and fines are around $150 for failing to exit. Late exit and overnight passes are available for certain uses; call (702) 515-5350 for information, and (702) 515-5050 to reserve a pass.

▶ **Water**

Drinking water is available at the visitor center. Natural water sources, such as springs within the park, are not fit for drinking and are reserved for wildlife.

▶ **Rest Room Facilities**

Along the Scenic Drive, pit-toilet-style restrooms are located at Calico II, Sandstone Quarry, White Rock Trailhead, Willow Springs, Ice Box Canyon, Pine Creek Canyon, and Oak Creek Canyon. Pit toilets are also located at the Late Night Parking Area near SR-160 and at Red Spring. The BLM maintains flush-toilet rest rooms at the Red Rock Canyon Visitor Center.

▶ **Trail and Dirt Road Use**

The dirt road and trail system at Red Rock Canyon is used by hikers, mountain bikers, horseback riders, and motorized vehicles. Trails and roads have been designated for each user group, and some paths are shared (see page 170 for more information on shared-use trails). Motor vehicles are prohibited on all trails north of SR-160 and south of La Madre

| Hours of Operation | |
|---|---|
| **Visitor Center** | |
| 8:00 am to 4:30 pm | |
| **Scenic Drive** | |
| October | 6 am to 7 pm |
| Nov. - Feb. | 6 am to 5 pm |
| March | 6 am to 7 pm |
| April - Sept. | 6 am to 8 pm |

Mountain, although they are allowed on certain dirt roads in this area. Trails designated for mountain bikes can be found in the Cottonwood Valley Trails (see map, page 190).

### ▶ Handicap Accessibility
While the visitor center is fully handicap accessible, most hiking trails are not. Wheelchair-accessible trails can be found at Willow Springs, the visitor center, and the Red Rock Overlook.

### ▶ Group Use
Depending on the group size and activities planned, a group-use permit may be required. Contact the BLM at (702) 515-5350.

### ▶ General Rules
- The use of firearms is illegal at the RRCNCA, unless in the act of hunting, which is only allowed south of SR-160 and north of La Madre Mountain during set seasons.
- Fires are prohibited outside of BLM camping areas unless in a grill or stove designed for such use. However, additional fire restrictions are often in effect from May to October. To find out if these restrictions are in effect, call (702) 515-5350.
- Collection of downed vegetation for firewood or any other purpose is not allowed.
- Painting, marking, carving, or defacing natural and man-made features is prohibited.

### ▶ Wildlife Viewing
One of the great things about Red Rock is the diverse array of wildlife. However, some of these species are considered sensitive or endangered. Others, such as burros and rodents, are prone to becoming tame and dependent on human support. Feeding, injuring, harassing, or disturbing any form of wildlife is prohibited. Burros are a treat to see, but special considerations should be followed for safe viewing (see box, page 12).

### ▶ Wilderness Areas
The Rainbow Mountain and La Madre Mountain Wilderness Areas are located in the RRCNCA. These areas are covered under the

Wilderness Act, a set of federal laws meant to protect critical areas. The Wilderness Act does not allow the use of motor vehicles or equipment. However, small electronics and cameras are allowed. Because cell phone service can be unreliable, leaving trip plans with someone before coming to Red Rock is recommended.

## Park Fees and Passes

*While access to certain areas within Red Rock Canyon is free, a fee is charged to enter the Scenic Drive and visitor center.* **Fees can be paid by cash or check only.**

- The fee for a **Scenic Drive Day Pass**, which includes access to the visitor center, is $7.00. This pass is good for one vehicle (car, truck, van, etc.) for one day. If traveling by motorcycle, bicycle, or on foot, the fee is $3.00. A receipt is issued, which must be shown to enter again later in the day.
- A **Red Rock Annual Pass** is available for those planning to visit multiple times. The cost is $30.00.
- The **America the Beautiful Pass** is accepted and costs $80.00. This annual pass is honored by the National Park Service, U.S. Forest Service, and certain other agencies. For U.S. citizens over 62, this pass costs $10.00. The pass is free for those who are permanently disabled.

### ▶ Cultural Resources
The Archaeological Resource Protection Act of 1979 (ARPA) applies to Red Rock Canyon. It states that "No person may excavate, remove, damage, or otherwise alter or deface or attempt to excavate, remove, damage, or otherwise alter or deface any archaeological resource located on public lands or Indian lands." Additionally, it is prohibited to make rubbings of rock art or apply substances, such as chalk, to make them more visible.

It is the BLM's responsibility to protect archaeological sites. To this end, they continually monitor sites, enforce ARPA, a federal law, and close areas to visitors if they deem there is a lack of respect for cultural resources. If any undocumented archaeological resources are encountered, they must be left in place and the BLM notified at (702) 515-5350.

### ▶ Mineral and Fossil Collecting
Collecting or defacing any rock or fossil is prohibited within the RRCNCA.

# Is it Red Rock Canyon or Red Rocks?

Historically known as Cottonwood Valley, the official name given to the cliffs and canyons west of SR-159 by the U.S. Board on Geographic Names is 'Sandstone Bluffs.' However, most groups use the term *Red Rocks* or *Red Rock Canyon*.

The name Red Rock Canyon, used by many organizations and government agencies, is rather misleading. It suggests that there is only one canyon, when in fact, there are some nine major canyons. Therefore, many outdoor recreational groups refer to the place simply as Red Rocks.

In this book, the terms *Red Rock* and *Red Rock Canyon* apply to the east side of the Spring Mountains, from SR-160 to the La Madre Mountains, and *Red Rock Escarpment* refers to the sandstone bluffs that extend from SR-160 to White Rock Spring (see map, inside back cover).

## ▶ Pets

While pets are allowed at Red Rock Canyon, their activities are quite restricted. Pets must not be left unattended, allowed to run at large, or make excessive noise, and are required to be leashed with a 6' or shorter leash in developed areas. Waste from pets must be removed and disposed of properly.

Red Rock Canyon is not an appropriate place to set free an unwanted animal. If they manage to survive, dogs, cats, fish, and reptiles not native to the region will severely disrupt the ecosystem.

## ▶ Red Rock Canyon Organizations

The BLM partners with two nonprofit organizations to provide visitor amenities and maintain the conservation area:

The **Red Rock Canyon Interpretive Association** works to enhance the recreational, educational, and interpretive programs at Red Rock Canyon. This group operates the gift shop at the visitor center, prints brochures and fliers, and has a staff of knowledgeable naturalists who direct programs and hikes in the conservation area. To learn more, visit www.redrockcanyonlv.org.

The **Friends of Red Rock Canyon** assist the BLM in developing and supervising a volunteer program for graffiti removal, trash pickup, trail maintenance, staffing the information desk, monitoring cultural sites, and other tasks. Each year, on average, they provide over 16,000 volunteer hours for tasks critical to the health of Red Rock Canyon. Check their website at www.friendsofredrockcanyon.org for events and volunteering opportunities. Volunteers may also sign up and find out about events and training at www.getoutdoorsnevada.org.

## ▶ Spring Mountain Ranch State Park

The Spring Mountain Ranch State Park, described on page 138, lies within the RRCNCA but has a separate entrance fee. Specific rules that visitors are asked to follow while in the park are listed below:
• Drive only on established roadways.
• Park in designated areas.
• Keep pets on a leash no longer than 6' in length.
• Do not collect plants, animals, or minerals.
• Dispose of litter in appropriate receptacles.
• Observe closed areas and all signs.
• Do not climb trees.

## Interacting with Burros

*Because feeding encourages these feral animals to congregate on roadways, where many have been killed and injured by vehicles, the BLM makes the following recommendations:*

• Drive carefully and be cautious when you see animals on or near the road. They may step out in front of your car unexpectedly.
• Observe feral burros from a distance. The safest place is from your car.
• Pick a safe place to stop and pull completely off the roadway.
• Refrain from the temptation to feed or water these hardy desert creatures. If you have food in an open container, seal it if an animal approaches you.
• Keep an eye on your dog: Burros intentionally trample dogs, just as they would coyotes.

**leave no trace™**
CENTER FOR OUTDOOR ETHICS

Initially conceived by the U.S. Forest Service in the 1960s, Leave No Trace is an ethical program rooted in scientific studies and common sense that aims to reduce human impacts on the environment. The Leave No Trace Seven Principles pertaining to Red Rock Canyon have been reprinted with the permission of the Leave No Trace Center for Outdoor Ethics. For more information, visit www.LNT.org.

## Plan Ahead And Prepare

- Know the regulations and special concerns for Red Rock Canyon.
- Prepare for extreme weather, hazards, and emergencies.
- Schedule your trip to avoid times of high use (fall and spring).
- Visit in small groups when possible. Consider splitting larger groups into smaller groups.

## Travel And Camp On Durable Surfaces

- Durable surfaces include established trails, dirt and paved roads, and developed campsites.
- Walk single file in the middle of the trail, even when it is wet or muddy.
- Keep campsites small. Focus activity in areas where vegetation is absent.
- Avoid places where impacts are just beginning.

## Dispose Of Waste Properly

- Pack it in, pack it out. Pack out all trash, leftover food, and litter.
- Deposit solid human waste in catholes dug 6 to 8 inches deep at least 200 feet from water, campsites, and trails. Cover and disguise the cathole when finished.
- Pack out toilet paper and hygiene products.
- Wash yourself or your dishes at least 200 feet away from dry washes or water sources and use small amounts of biodegradable soap. Scatter strained dishwater.

## Leave What You Find

- Preserve the past: examine, but do not touch, cultural or historic structures and artifacts.
- Leave rocks, plants and other natural objects as you find them.
- Avoid introducing or transporting nonnative species.
- Do not build structures, furniture, or dig trenches.

## Minimize Campfire Impacts

- At developed campsites and picnic grounds, use established fire rings or barbecue stands.
- Keep fires small. Only use wood gathered from outside the conservation area.
- Burn all wood and coals to ash, put out campfires completely, then scatter cool ashes.

## Respect Wildlife

- Observe wildlife from a distance. Do not follow or approach them.
- Never feed animals. Feeding wildlife damages their health, alters natural behaviors, and exposes them to predators and other dangers.
- Protect wildlife and your food by storing rations and trash securely.
- Control your pets, or leave them at home.
- Avoid wildlife during sensitive times: mating, nesting, raising young, or winter.

## Be Considerate Of Other Visitors

- Respect other visitors and protect the quality of their experience.
- Be courteous. Yield to other trail users.
- Step to the downhill side of the trail when encountering horses.
- Take breaks and camp away from trails and other visitors.
- Let nature's sounds prevail. Avoid loud voices and noises.

# Geologic History
### *of Red Rock Canyon*

The landscape of Red Rock Canyon tells a story that goes back hundreds of millions of years. It is a story of vibrant tropical seas, vast sand dunes, and most recently tremendous tectonic activity and erosion.

From 540 to 250 million years ago, southern Nevada was submerged under a tropical sea. Animal life flourished in this warm sea. The skeletons of these creatures were dissolved into seawater and deposited on the sea floor to create the massive layers of white and gray limestone cliffs visible today.

Beginning roughly 200 million years ago, the region was dominated by vast sand dunes that have become the colorful Aztec Sandstone at Red Rock.

Later, the region was under enormous compressional stresses that were relieved by extensive tectonic activity. The stresses on the earth were so great that the massive layers of limestone were pushed above the sandstone. Since then, erosion has been the major factor shaping the stunning landscape we see today.

## ► Precambian

The oldest rocks in southern Nevada are thought to have been formed by island arcs that were pushed into the edge of the continent by a rift in the sea floor (Figure 1.1). These rocks, composed of gneiss and schist, likely form the bedrock of the Spring Mountains and Red Rock Canyon but are exposed only at the northern tip of the range.

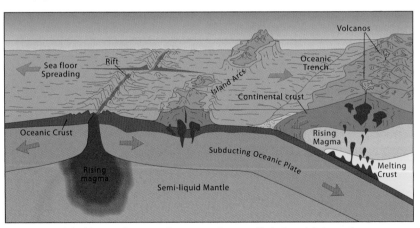

**Figure 1.1.** *The oldest rocks in southern Nevada were likely formed through fundamental plate-tectonic processes involving sea-floor spreading and subduction: A 'hot spot' of rising magma filled the space created by two oceanic plates moving away from each other. The oceanic plate was forced below the continental plate. Island arcs carried by the oceanic plate crashed into the continent adding to the continental crust.*

| Geologic Age | | | Prominent Rock Types and Formations at Red Rock Canyon |
|---|---|---|---|
| Cenozoic | Quaternary | Holocene — present / 10,000 ya | **alluvial deposits** - Poorly-cemented, gravelly conglomerate sometimes with extensive caliche. *Example Location*: Along the broad wash north of SR-159, east of Calico Basin. |
| | | Pleistocene — 1.8 Mya | |
| | Tertiary | Pliocene | *no formation present* |
| | | Miocene | |
| | | Oligocene | |
| | | Eocene | |
| | | Paleocene — 65 Mya | |
| Mesozoic | Cretaceous — 146 Mya | | |
| | Jurassic — 202 Mya | | **Aztec Sandstone** - Red, orange, white, sometimes yellow and purple sandstone often with dark varnish. *Example Location*: The colorful cliffs of the Calico Hills and Red Rock Escarpment. |
| | Triassic | | **Chinle Sandstone** - Deep-reddish-orange sandstone. *Example Location*: Cliff bands below the Red Rock Escarpment. |
| | | | **Shinarump Conglomerate** - Dark brown, sometimes yellowish conglomerate with round cobbles of varied color. *Example Location*: Underfoot on the Overlook Trail, Spring Mountain Ranch. |
| | | | **Virgin Limestone** - Thin-layered, yellowish-to-gray limestone with patchy layers of chert. Some layers show rippling indicative of a river depositional environment. *Example Location*: Southwest of SR-159, between Blue Diamond and Oliver Ranch. |
| Paleozoic | Permian — 251 Mya | | **Kaibab and Toroweap Formations** - Kaibab is gray-to-yellowish-gray limestone and dolomite with many brown chert beds. Toroweap is similar but less cherty. *Example Location*: Blue Diamond Hill Trails area (see page 188). |
| | | | **Permian redbeds** - Red and yellowish-orange sandstone. *Example Location*: The east side of Blue Diamond Hill. |
| | Pennsylvanian — 299 Mya / 318 Mya | | **Bird Spring Formation** - Yellowish-gray, brownish-gray, and gray limestone and dolomite with sometimes extensive beds of brown chert. It forms ledge-and-slope terrain, which indicates a changing environmental setting where deposition took place. *Example Locations*: East of Mount Potosi in Cottonwood Valley, the east flanks of Mount Charleston including much of the terrain north of La Madre Mountain, and in Lovell Canyon. |
| | Mississippian — 359 Mya | | **Monte Cristo Formation** - Forms prominent, white-to-gray limestone cliffs with sparse layers of brownish chert . *Example Locations*: The cliffbands surrounding the White Rock Hills and the gray rock northeast of Gateway Canyon. |
| | Devonian — 416 Mya | | **Sultan Limestone** - Dark, organic-rich limestone and dolomite. *Example Locations*: The summit and backside of Turtlehead Peak and the 30' to 40' tall cliffbands south of Blue Diamond village. |
| | Silurian — 444 Mya | | **Mountain Springs Formation** (*no formation during the Silurian*) - Grainy-textured dolomite in thin and thick layers of light-gray to pinkish-gray color. Formation includes conglomerate-like beds where caves and sinkholes have collapsed. *Example Location*: The cliffs below the summit of Turtlehead Peak. |
| | Ordovician — 488 Mya | | |
| | Cambrian | | **Nopah Formation** - Banded like the Bonanza King, but more prominently. Formation has lenses of yellowish-brown chert. The base is composed of shale, suggesting a river delta depositional environment. *Example Location*: Between the Calico Hills and Turtlehead Peak. |
| | | | **Bonanza King Formation** - Light- and dark-gray banded limestone and dolomite indicative of tidal deposition. Small worm and animal burrows are often visible in the rock. *Example Location*: Immediately above (west) of the Keystone Thrust. |
| Precambrian | Proterozoic — 542 Mya / 2500 Mya | | *no formation exposed* |
| | Archean — 3850 Mya | | |
| | Hadean | | |

*Alluvial deposits*

*Aztec Sandstone*

*Chinle Sandstone*

*Shinarump Conglomerate*

*Kaibab Formation*

*Monte Cristo Formation*

**Figure 1.2.** *Time scale with rock types and formations found at Red Rock Canyon. Mya stands for million years ago.*

# ► Paleozoic Era

Beginning in the late Proterozoic and throughout most of the Paleozoic, southern Nevada was part of a continental shelf situated near the equator and dominated by warm, tropical seas similar to the present-day Caribbean (Figure 1.4). These shallow seas supported growing populations of marine life. The trilobites were one of the first organisms to flourish and underwent a population explosion in the Cambrian Period. Later in the Paleozoic,

snails, seashells, sponges, sea lilies, trilobites, mollusks, plankton, jellyfish, worms, coral, fishes, and even sharks lived in huge reef environments (Figure 1.3).

These marine organisms lived for millions of generations in the sea covering southern Nevada. When each animal died, the calcium carbonate of its skeleton dissolved into the ocean or was fossilized by silicate minerals. Because calcium carbonate is more soluble in cold water, it tends to precipitate out of warm water, like that of the tropical sea of the time. On the sea floor the calcium carbonate collected with other sediments and, with time, solidified into rock. The abundance of marine life in the Paleozoic was so great that the dissolved and fossilized remains of the animals has formed massive layers of rock over 23,000' thick in the Spring Mountains.

There were, however, phases where the sea advanced or receded, changing the depth of the sea floor and the depositional environment. These changes, along with the appearance and extinction of certain animals, have led geologists to distinguish a number of rock formations from the Paleozoic. At Red Rock Canyon, some of these formations can be readily identified and lead to insights about the environment and animals living during certain time periods. Figure 1.2, found on page 15, presents brief descriptions of the prominent rocks and formations. A geologic map of Red Rock Canyon is found on page 23.

Southern Nevada was located within a tectonically stable, slowly-sinking basin throughout the Paleozoic. However, on the east coast of America, during the Devonian and Mississippian Periods,

**Figure 1.3.** *Life forms that inhabited the Caribbean-like shallow sea environment of southern Nevada approximately 400 million years ago during the Devonian Period of the Paleozoic Era: 1. Trilobites, 2. Sea lilies (Crinoidea), 3. lungfish (Fleurantia sp.), 4. Colonial rugose coral, 5. Colonial tabulate coral, 6. Solitary rugose coral, 7. Massive Stromatoporoid, 8. Dendroid Stromatoporoid, 9. Encrusting Stromatoporoid, 10. Sponge, 11. Algae (faint green). More information on the fossil remains of these animals is found on page 104 (photograph by Jeanette McGregor, Courtesy of the Nevada State Museum, Carson City).*

*Figure 1.4. The Southwest during the Cambrian period, 510 million years ago. Nevada was situated south of the equator and covered in warm, shallow seas that later supported extensive reefs.*

Gondwana (a land mass of South America, Africa, India, and Australia) collided with the North American continent to form Pangea. This collision led to the uplift of the Ancestral Rocky Mountains centered in Colorado and the Appalachian Mountains; the latter were then comparable to the present-day Andes. The Ancestral Rocky Mountains will become important later, because it is believed that the sand grains which compose the Aztec Sandstone came from these mountains.

With the formation of Pangea complete, early in the Permian Period, the ocean began to subside from the west coast of the continent. During the Permian, shallow seas persisted intermittently at Red Rock Canyon, leading to many different depositional environments for sedimentary rocks: Where seas persisted, limestone was formed. Gypsum was formed in areas such as Blue Diamond Hill where sea water evaporated. In higher terrain, sedimentary rocks derived from erosion, such as siltstone and sandstone, were deposited. Outcrops of these varied rock types can be found on Blue Diamond Hill and in the hills around the village of Blue Diamond.

At the end of the Permian Period

(251 million years ago), the largest mass extinction ever known occurred. Over a few million years 96% of marine species and 70% of terrestrial vertebrates disappeared from existence. There are several proposed causes for the extinction event, including both catastrophic events and gradual processes. Most of the marine creatures, such as certain seashells, sea lilies, and mollusks, were severely reduced. Some, such as trilobites, and rugose and tabulate corals were completely destroyed. In the oceans, pre-extinction biodiversity levels did not occur until 100 million years later.

## Mining in Paleozoic Limestone

In the Spring Mountains, lead-silver-zinc ores are found along faults in the Paleozoic carbonate rocks. Gold-copper ores, however, are formed in the contact zone between intrusive granitic formations and surrounding sedimentary rocks. Because there are no intrusive granitic formations exposed at Red Rock, there is no gold or copper to be found.

# ► Mesozoic Era

Beginning in the Middle Triassic, southern Nevada lay in the Chinle River Basin, a broad, lowland bordered to the south and west by volcanically-active mountain ranges and to the east by the Ancestral Rocky Mountains. The erosional debris from these ranges was transported into the basin by many branching streams and later by winds.

At Red Rock Canyon, the Shinarump Conglomerate and the Chinle Sandstone were deposited from this erosional debris; both are visible below the towering cliffs of the Red Rock Escarpment. The thin layer of purplish-brown Shinarump Conglomerate often includes specimens of petrified wood (see photo, page 107) created by the replacement of cellular material with silica derived from volcanic ash put forth by the volcanic ranges to the west and south. The Chinle Sandstone is a bright, orange-red band of sandstone (see photo, page 69).

Beginning in the Late Triassic, a rift formed east of the Appalachian Mountains and forced the North American continent to move northwesterly at a relatively fast rate of 3" per year. The floor of the Pacific Ocean was thrust into the west coast of the continent causing the formation of the Sierra Nevada Range and the uplift of the Chinle River Basin.

The now-elevated terrain of Nevada, northern Arizona, and Utah became a desert. The winds scoured the dry mudflats and floodplains of the Chinle River Basin turning sediments into airborne sand. During the Early Jurassic, these shifting quartz sands were trapped in a vast landscape by the bordering mountain ranges, sorted and rounded by the northern trade winds, and deposited in the largest sand dunes ever to exist in North America (Figure 1.5). The formations from these events are now stunning landscapes of sandstone cliffs, sometimes thousands of feet high: the Wingate Sandstone near Moab and Canyonlands, the Navajo Sandstone of Zion National Park, and the Aztec Sandstone of Red Rock Canyon.

The terrain and climate in the Early Jurassic were similar to the present-day Sahara Desert. Periods of annual monsoons fed patches of vegetation and isolated oases. This vegetation allowed insects and small, mammal-like reptiles to survive. Larger animals also roamed the dunes; *Grallator* tracks from Red Rock Canyon indicate

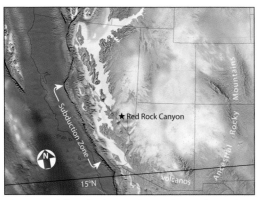

*Figure 1.5 (above). The Southwest during the Early Jurassic Period, 180 million years ago. Extensive sand dunes were trapped by the newly-formed Sierra Nevada Range to the west, a volcanic mountain belt to the south, and the Ancestral Rocky Mountains to the east. The sand from these dunes has been compacted into the dramatic sandstone cliffs and formations at Red Rock Canyon.*
*Figure 1.6 (below). Some of the many forms of Aztec Sandstone. Left: Various concretions, penny for scale. Center: A distinct red-white color separation. Right: Turtle-shell-like surface caused by weathering and erosion in the Calico Hills.*

*Figure 1.7. At times in the Early Jurassic, the vast sand dunes that covered Red Rock received annual monsoon rains, which fed isolated oases. Large-dog-sized dinosaurs and some of their prey, such as these squirrel-like creatures, roamed the dunes and made footprints in the moist sand. Their fossilized footprints are known as* Grallator *and* Brasilichnium *respectively (painting by Ariel Milani Martine).*

the presence of a two-legged, carnivorous dinosaur that likely stood 3' tall and 10' long (Figure 1.7, see also page 107).

The sand dunes that these animals called home were a uniform, bright-red color. Today, however, the Aztec Sandstone displays many hues of red, as well as whites, yellows, and even purples; sometimes with sharp distinctions between the colors. The change in color began after the sands were compacted and cemented into sandstone.

Initially, each sand grain had a thin coat of the iron-rich mineral hematite ($Fe_2O_3$), likely derived from the mountains that surrounded the dunes. When exposed to air and water, hematite rusts and becomes red. In the Late Cretaceous, southern Nevada was in the foothills of the Sierra Nevada Range, exposed to a relatively wet climate. Aquifers formed and transported groundwater through the small pores between the sand grains. The groundwater, slightly acidic from contact with organic-rich materials, dissolved the

hematite coatings, leaving the sandstone bleached white. However, the groundwater was only able to do this in certain spots, because the porosity and the structure of the sandstone varies by location. The resulting color differences are stunning to see, especially in the Calico Hills where fantastic color patterns occur.

The groundwater transported the dissolved hematite to other parts of the sandstone where it was deposited. Depending on the conditions of deposition, the hematite could recrystallize into globules and give the rock an orange color, or form very high concentrations in concretions (see next page).

The yellows and purples in Aztec Sandstone result from a second phase of groundwater movement that occurred during the Miocene. In this phase, groundwater conditions were different, and goethite ($FeO(OH)$) was dissolved and transported. When deposited, small crystals of goethite give a yellow color and larger crystals give a purple color.

*Visitors and locals alike enjoy the vibrant contrast of colors in the rock and sky.*

# Aztec Sandstone at Red Rock Canyon

*The sandstone that makes Red Rock Canyon so colorful has a wide range of unique attributes. Some of those attributes are described here.*

## ► Concretions

There are, generally-speaking, two types of concretions at Red Rock Canyon: red dots and brown rock balls. Both are caused by the mineral hematite, which can be either color.

Red dots form where the clay minerals, which cement the sand grains together, have been concentrated into a sphere. Because of its lower porosity, the sphere 'holds on to' hematite while groundwater bleaches the surrounding sandstone.

Brown rock balls form when hematite precipitates out of groundwater through a complicated chemical process that organizes the iron-rich mineral into spherical layers.

**Figure 1.8.** *Concretions resulting from hematite deposition. The surrounding white sandstone has eroded exposing the harder, iron-rich deposits.*

## Why are the rocks red?

180 million years ago, vast sand dunes covered the Southwest. Initially, every sand grain had a thin coat of the iron-rich mineral hematite, likely derived from the surrounding mountains. When exposed to the elements, hematite 'rusts' or oxidizes to a red color. As the sand was buried and compacted, the rusting of the iron continued, deepening the red color. Later, groundwater movements dissolved the hematite coating from some rocks, leaving them less red or bleached white. The groundwater transported the hematite to other places in the sandstone where it was deposited to form other shades of red and orange or concretions.

# ► Desert Varnish

Unlike some other Jurassic-age sandstones in the Southwest, the Aztec Sandstone of Red Rock is heavily varnished. Varnish forms from windblown clay that is chemically altered into a thin, brown, or black coating through a complex process involving the underlying rock, water, sunlight, and possibly microbes. The speed at which varnish forms depends on local conditions but is on the order of hundreds to thousands of years.

Using a stone chisel, Native Americans pecked away the varnish, revealing the lighter-colored underlying stone to create petroglyphs. At Red Rock, some petroglyphs are so old that varnish is forming over the artwork.

# ► Cross Bedding

A distinctive feature of Aztec Sandstone is cross bedding. Whereas most sedimentary rocks are deposited in horizontal beds, much of the sandstone at Red Rock displays bedding planes that abruptly stop and change direction. These cross beds are caused by changes in the prevailing wind direction, which then changes the leeward (depositional) side of the dune.

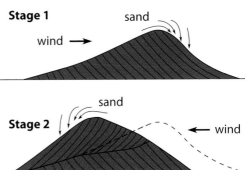

**Figure 1.9.** Cross bedding in sand dunes resulting from changes in wind direction. The area below the dotted line in Stage 2 represents sand that has been eroded.

# ► Strange Forms

The beautiful fins, spires, arches, caves, slot canyons, tanks, and elaborately sculpted shapes that now exist at Red Rock have been created by erosion and weathering of the rock.

Rainstorms are a major force in this process. Heavy rainfalls can tear through washes with incredible intensity and transport house-sized boulders. On a smaller scale, rainwater breaks down the cement that holds sand grains together. Areas of softer rock are then eroded, while harder stone remains intact. Although each rainfall may have a small effect, the process has occurred for millions of years to create the shapes we see today.

**Figure 1.10.** Rainwater and runoff erode areas of softer rock leaving unique shapes of weather-resistant stone.

*Figure 1.11. The results of the Keystone Thrust are dramatically displayed west of the White Rock Hills where older, gray limestone and dolomite are positioned above younger Aztec Sandstone. Bedding layers in the sandstone were folded as the upper block was thrust over.*

# The Keystone Thrust
### *A brilliantly displayed geologic feature*

Typically, layers of sedimentary rock are exposed in the same way they were deposited, with the youngest layers above the oldest layers. At Red Rock Canyon, however, we find 540-million-year-old limestone and dolomite above 180-million-year-old sandstone. The reason for this is a world-famous fault called the Keystone Thrust, which is conspicuously displayed above the Red Rock Escarpment.

When the sand dunes, which became the Aztec Sandstone, were deposited, some 180 million years ago, they sat atop many layers of sedimentary rock that had formed earlier. The bulk of the underlying layers was made up of billions of tons of limestone and dolomite deposited in the Paleozoic from 540 to 250 million years ago.

Awesome forces are required to move such an enormous quantity of rock. These forces were generated by the collision of the North American continent with the sea floor of the Pacific ocean. This collision, which began in the Triassic, intensified during the Cretaceous, causing the sea floor to push the leading edge of the continent eastward, resulting in huge compressive forces being placed on the continental crust. To alleviate the stress, thrust faults (see Figure 1.12) formed east of the Sierra Nevada Range. One such thrust fault, the Keystone Trust, forced layers of Paleozoic limestone and dolomite, hundreds of feet thick, over Jurassic-age Aztec Sandstone for many miles. After thrusting subsided, the layers were likely intact and extended many miles east of their current manifestation. They have since been eroded back to display the distinct thrust fault we see today.

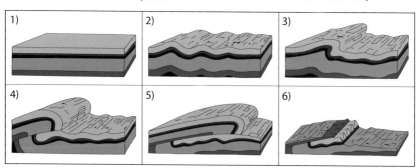

*Figure 1.12. Sequence of the Keystone Thrust: 1) Initial state: sedimentary rocks deposited horizontally atop one another. 2) Compressive forces caused the rock to fold forming a washboard-like surface. 3) An area of weaker rocks allowed a fold to overturn. 4) Additional compressive stresses caused the rocks to break along the overturned fold allowing the upper block to begin sliding eastward over the lower block. 5) The upper block continued to slide eastward; the total displacement of the upper block was about 65 miles. 6) Current state: both the upper and lower blocks have been eroded back to reveal a dramatic thrust fault.*

**La Madre Mountains**

8092'

5740'

4920'

Turtlehead Peak
6323'

4100'

White Rock Hills
4962'

Calico Hills

4714'

Calico Basin

Scenic Drive

E s c a r p m e n t

Bridge Mtn.
7003'

5447'

Visitor Center

159

Mount Wilson
7070'

Blue Diamond Hill

**Red Rock Canyon**
*Geologic Map*

contour interval = 165'

|←——— 1.5 miles ———→|

**Formations**
*see page 15 for descriptions*

☐ Quaternary alluvium

■ Aztec Sandstone

■ Chinle Sandstone and
Shinarump Conglomerate

☐ Triassic siltstone and limestone

☐ Virgin Limestone

☐ Kaibab and Toroweap Formations

☐ Permian redbeds

☐ Bird Springs Formation

☐ Monte Cristo Formation

☐ Sultan Limestone

■ Mountain Springs Formation

■ Nopah Formation

■ Bonanza King Formation

Spring
Mountain
Ranch

R e d   R o c k

E s c a r p m e n t

Blue Diamond

6236'

Mountain Springs

160

# ► Cenozoic Era

During the Early Cenozoic, the Spring Mountains were in the foothills of the Sierra Nevada Range. Erosion was exposing the Aztec Sandstone from underneath the hundreds of feet of limestone and dolomite that had been thrust over it. Sometimes landslides slid as far as six miles with rocks from many formations jumbled together. Other times the layers of rock cleaved off and slid as a unit. Likely because of the uniform composition of the Aztec Sandstone, canyons were eroded into the Red Rock Escarpment at roughly equivalent distance intervals.

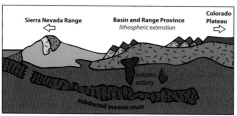

**Figure 1.13.** *A simplified cross-section of the Western United States, late in the Cenozoic Era. In response to extensional forces, faults formed in the Basin and Range Province allowing ranges to spread apart.*

About 19 million years ago, in the Early Miocene, a process of tectonic extension began to pull the Sierra Nevada Range away from the Colorado Plateau (Figure 1.13). In response, north-south faults formed throughout the Great Basin and further south. These faults allowed blocks of crust to tilt like books that fit loosely on a bookshelf, creating the distinctive north-south mountain ranges common throughout Nevada.

The Las Vegas Valley was pulled apart causing the Spring Mountains and Red Rock Canyon to move as much as 70 miles northwestward while the Colorado Plateau, to the east, remained fixed. The new terrain created from this extension is continually being filled with millions of tons of gravel and sediment from storm-water runoff.

In the last 2½ million years, much of this runoff occurred during periods of El Niño-type weather when northern latitudes were covered by glaciers. During the latest glaciation, which reached its maximum extent 18,000 years ago, the Spring Mountains received considerable amounts of snow. However, it is unclear if Mount Charleston was covered by a glacier. The Las Vegas Valley was cooler and received roughly 35% more precipitation than today. It was dotted with ponds and wetlands supporting a diverse plant ecosystem, including cattail and many other succulents. Surrounding these wetlands, fields of grasses and sagebrush grew. The gently sloping alluvial fans above were dominated by Joshua tree, Utah juniper, ponderosa pine, and limber pine (*Pinus flexilis*) woodlands.

In the Late Pleistocene, a 50-pound giant condor (*Teratornis merrami*) with a 12' wingspan scanned the Las Vegas Valley for the corpses of mammals that would look quite unfamiliar to us today. In the wooded hillsides, two species of ground sloths (*Nothrotheriops shastensis* (Figure 1.14) and *Megalonyx* sp.) ate the leaves of Joshua trees and Mormon tea (*Ephedra* spp.). Sizable herds of American camel (*Camelops hesternus*) roamed the grasslands adjacent to marshy areas in the Las Vegas Valley. Also in the grasslands were large-headed llama (*Hemiauchenia macrocephala*), two species of horse (*Equus* spp.), and two species of bison (*Bison latifrons* and *B. antiquus*). These grassland inhabitants depended on speed to elude predators such as: the American lion (*Panthera leo atrox*), which weighed as much as 900 pounds; the giant jaguar *(Panthera onca augusta)*, which lurked in the shrubs; and packs of dire wolves (*Canis dirus*). The Columbian mammoth (*Mammuthus columbi*) lived here in herds. It stood 11' tall, weighed as much as six tons, and had spiraling tusks 7' long. Unlike the woolly mammoth (*Mammuthus primigenius*), the Columbian mammoth was better suited for a warmer climate. It had exposed skin like African elephants (*Loxodonta* spp.) of today and only a few patches of hair.

This cooler, wetter environment, studded with megafauna, was encountered by the first humans to see Red Rock Canyon.

**Figure 1.14.** *A Shasta ground sloth browses near Mount Wilson. In the Late Pleistocene, Red Rock likely was visited by megafauna such as American camels, American lions, dire wolves, ground sloths, and Columbian mammoths. The reasons these animals went extinct by 8000 BC is a subject of debate, but probably involve climate changes that caused the area to become hotter and drier (painting © Bradley W. Giles).*

# Native American History
### in Southern Nevada and at Red Rock Canyon

For thousands of years Native Americans have lived in southern Nevada and used Red Rock Canyon for its abundant water, plants, and animals as well as a place of spirituality.

The scant evidence of the earliest people to use the area some 11,000 years ago makes it difficult to determine the extent of their use and occupation. However, many scholars believe that these people were nomadic, roaming the West in search of big game.

Later peoples appear to have been more sedentary, following seasonal rounds within the Las Vegas Valley and Spring Mountains.

Circa AD 500, a new way of life tied to trade emerged that focused on such crops as corn, beans, and squash. This allowed for a surge in populations and the creation of more sophisticated tools and facilities.

For reasons not entirely known, the civilization vanished from southern Nevada in the 12th century and later inhabitants relied on seasonal hunting and foraging rounds. These people, the Southern Paiutes, were those Euro-Americans found living in the Las Vegas Valley and Red Rock Canyon when they began to arrive in the 1800s.

## ▶ Paleoarchaic Peoples
*Roughly 9500 BC to 8000 BC*

The first people to leave traces of their presence in southern Nevada were here between 9500 BC and 9000 BC. Current understanding suggests that people in the Southwest and Great Basin at this time were skillful in using native plant and animal resources. They lived adjacent to Pleistocene lakes and marshes, where they used stone (obsidian and chert) projectile points, scrapers and knives, bone tools, and awls; tools that suggest a tendency towards hunting. The Clovis point (Figure 2.1), a characteristic artifact, was lashed to a wooden shaft and thrust, likely with an atlatl (Figure 2.3), into large mammals such as bison, mammoth, and possibly ground sloth and American camel. Such close range combat required a team of men and involved a great amount of effort, risk, and time. But groups would profit greatly from a kill: skins for clothing and shelter, meat for consumption and storage, bones for tools, sinew for cord,

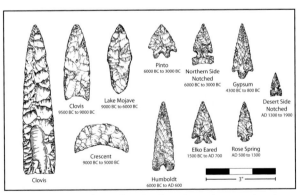

**Figure 2.1.** *Chronology of projectile point styles associated with peoples known from southern Nevada. Rose Spring-style points were used with the advent of the bow and arrow; the example shown here was found in the Moapa Valley.*

**Figure 2.** *It is highly likely, but not proven, that paleoarchaic people hunted American camel in southern Nevada during the late Pleistocene. The techniques a group would employ are similarly unknown, but it is possible that a higher degree of skill and cunning was used than an all-out attack with spears and bludgeons as shown here at Tule Springs with the Spring Mountains in the background (painting by Jay Matternes courtesy of National Geographic Stock).*

and so forth. Although artifacts from these people are known from Tule Springs and the Las Vegas Wash, the number of artifacts discovered in the Las Vegas Valley is scant. This suggests that the region was used temporarily for gathering resources during extensive foraging trips away from 'home' encampments such as Pleistocene Lake Mojave, and China Lake in California. At these lakeside sites, and elsewhere in the Great Basin, many artifacts have been found, including curved stone tools called crescents. Crescents are associated with lake and marsh environments in the Great Basin, and may have been used as part of a projectile weapon for water fowl or to prepare plants for eating.

By roughly 12,000 years ago, the climate had begun to undergo widespread changes. What had been a cool, wet environment was becoming warm and dry. Many ponds and marshes in the Las Vegas Valley were evaporating, and ecosystems were dying off or relocating to higher elevations. The megafauna, such as the Columbian mammoths, giant ground sloths, giant jaguars, American lions, American camels, horses, and llamas; as well as many smaller mammals and certain specialized birds, were not able to adapt as fast as the climate was changing and became extinct by 8000 BC.

An environment slightly more hot and arid than today followed, forcing native peoples to rely more on seeds and foraging than on the rich resources provided by the shallow-water ecosystems of the past. By 7000 BC, the climate was similar to that of today. Creosote had moved into the valley floor and juniper and sagebrush grew on the flanks of the Spring Mountains. An intermittent stream, fed by numerous springs, ran from the Tule Springs area through roughly the US-95 corridor of today, and out to the Lower Las Vegas Wash. Along the stream were small riparian ecosystems and stands of mesquite trees; both provided a rich resource base for native peoples.

# ► **Desert Archaic Peoples**

*Roughly 8000 BC to AD 500*

After the Pleistocene megafauna went extinct, foraging people archaeologists call the Desert Archaic developed a way of life better suited for the hotter, drier climate. The term Desert Archaic is a broad catch-all for foraging cultures in the Southwest from roughly 8000 BC to AD 500. Within this time span, distinct cultural groups existed in a pattern that roughly coincides with changes in the climate.

**Figure 2.3.** *Technique used to throw a spear using an atlatl. For more than eight thousand years this technique was passed down from generation to generation.*

In southern Nevada, the people moved with the seasons, following food resources by wintering in the valleys and summering in the uplands. In the spring, succulent plants were gathered; in the fall, seeds of mesquite and pinyon pine nuts were gathered, consumed, and stored for winter.

Depending on the locality and nearby resources, dwellings were simple and quickly fashioned, varying from rock outcrops with little improvements to brush shelters and sunshades. The atlatl was used extensively with smaller projectile points (Figures 2.1 and 2.3). Snares and nets, made from human hair and yucca fibers, were employed. Deer and sheep were not daily staples; instead, hunters focused on jackrabbits, cottontails, woodrats, quails, desert tortoise, and to a lesser extent, chuckwalla, snakes, and other small reptiles. Mats, cloths, and sandals were expertly woven. Baskets were used for foraging and transporting. Milling stones (manos and metates, see Figure 2.4), for seed and plant processing typically stayed at the resource sites and were not transported seasonally. In sites of winter habitation, underground cists were used to store foodstuffs. Trade of specialty items, such as shell beads from coastal California, also occurred.

Around 4500 BC, the intensity of the aridity and heat generally decreased, and populations responded favorably. This increase in population is evidenced by an increase in the number of archaeological sites, as well as a greater similarity in artifacts dating to after 4500 BC. Petroglyph creation also increased, and a dominant style of the period is abstract curvilinear designs, which rarely include representations of people (Figure 2.6, top left).

Evidence of the Desert Archaic people has been found near springs throughout the Las Vegas Valley. The Gypsum Cave site, located northeast of Las Vegas, was visited as early as 7300 BC. A unique projectile point style was discovered there and attributed to a time period from 4300 BC to 800 BC (Figure 2.1).

The same people who made these projectile points used upland sites at Red Rock Canyon, such as Willow Springs and Calico Basin, for seasonal hunting and gathering.

**Figure 2.4.** *Stones used for grinding seeds and plant material—like this mano and metate, which is likely from a later period—saw increased use by the Desert Archaic people and indicate a more permanent occupation.*

# ► Cultivators: Anasazi and Patayan Influences

*Roughly AD 1 to AD 1150*

Roughly 2500 years ago, while the Desert Archaic people were moving through their ancient seasonal rounds in southern Nevada, peoples in more fertile areas of the Southwest were becoming less transient, creating permanent dwellings and using more sophisticated tools. Over generations, these people changed their way of life and culture.

Groups were cultivating plants, but not farming year-round. Maize, domesticated by advanced civilizations in what is now Mexico, was traded northward and appeared in the Las Vegas Valley by 300 BC. During the spring, people planted seeds of sunflower, maize, and squash in fertile lands irrigated by creeks and springs. Then continued their seasonal migration to the uplands following the new growth of plants and the appearance of animals. Returning in the fall, they harvested and stored for the winter.

They used many of the same tools as the Desert Archaic people. Some items, like baskets, were highly modified and are used to characterize their culture today. The cultivation of plants allowed them to settle more permanently, and around AD 1, they constructed pit houses in the Four Corners region. These dwellings, typically 6' deep and 12' wide, provided substantially better insulation in the summer and winter, as well as better protection from storms and wind.

## ► Anasazi

In the Four Corners, ceramic technology arrived from the south around AD 400 and was adapted to the local environment. With the advent of pottery, these people became known as the Anasazi.

The pottery allowed for different cooking methods and foods to be utilized. Cooking dry beans, for example, would have been labor, time, and fuel intensive when using pitch-lined baskets and fire-heated rocks, but practical using a clay vessel that could be placed on the fire.

Now, instead of an entire band of people traveling to the higher elevations during summer foraging and hunting seasons, groups of specialists in the

*Figure 2.5. Anasazi artifacts from southern Nevada: A decorated black-on-white ceramic bowl, a corrugated ceramic vessel, and shell beads traded from California. The introduction of corn (initially much smaller than the ears shown here) from cultures to the south allowed some peoples to abandon their seasonal gathering and hunting.*

band would perform these duties, while others tended crops. The bow and arrow found widespread use at the same time as farming, roughly AD 500, possibly in response to the vermin attracted by crops. Interestingly, the atlatl was still used for centuries alongside the bow and arrow, and then continued to be shown in petroglyphs, perhaps as a symbol of the hunting ritual.

Over time, pit houses became more elaborate, multi-roomed, lined with slabs of stone and clay, and were arranged in groups, like a small community. Seeds, vegetables, and dried meat were stored in small rooms.

*continued on page 33*

# Rock Art at Red Rock Canyon

For several thousand years native peoples in southern Nevada and the West created drawings on rock walls, shelters, and boulders. These drawings consist of representational and abstract symbols that can provide insight into native lifeways and rituals.

## Pictograph vs. Petroglyph

*Petrogylphs* are pecked or, less frequently, scratched into the rock. Pecking was accomplished with a hammerstone alone or hammerstone and chisel. *Pictographs* are painted onto the rock using organic and mineral substances as paint.

## Who Made It?

The Desert Archaic people, people with ties to the Anasazi, and the Southern Paiute all made rock art at Red Rock. One of the difficulties with assigning cultural affiliation to panels and glyphs is that the methods of dating rock art are not precise. Nevertheless, certain styles have been broadly associated with cultural groups at Red Rock. These associations can sometimes be supported or refuted based on other factors, such as patination (desert varnish takes many hundreds, sometimes thousands, of years to form), the archaeological record (horses, for example, are only known from historic times), and superposition (later groups sometimes placed their art on top of that of previous groups). Some examples of styles linked to cultures can be seen on the facing page.

## What Does It Mean?

Despite the widespread existence of rock art in the West, there is no generally accepted explanation regarding the meaning or function of rock art in Native American culture. While some assert that rock art was merely 'indian doodling' or graffiti, the frequent recurrence of certain symbols, as well as our ability to distinguish styles, strongly suggests that there is some meaning or reason for the rock art to be there. The three most prevalent theories on the significance of rock art are discussed below.

### • Hunting-Magic Theory

Pioneered in the early 1960s, this theory makes a connection between what is depicted (sheep, people hunting, weapons of the hunt) and site location (near hunting resources) to suggest that rock art was used for rituals to increase success in gathering food resources. Opponents argue that this theory only applies to a narrow set of sites and provides no insight into the many abstract or non-hunting-related symbols. Another question unanswered by this theory is why are there few small mammals depicted, which were frequently hunted, while sheep symbols appear often.

### • Rock Writing Theory

The idea that gylphs and images are a form of writing used to communicate stories, record events, and give directions has led many to attempt to decipher the markings. Notably, LaVan Martineau developed the hypothesis that certain glyphs are based on a system of sign language known to be used during historic times between native peoples of different tongues. Although bolstered by accounts from native people, his translations deal with specific time periods and rock art styles, and do not always agree with the archaeological record.

### • Power/Vision Association Theory

This theory suggests that abstract rock art panels portray images that were seen in the mind's eye of shamans as well as images of shamans themselves. Native accounts agree that rock art sites were places where power, or *puha*, could be acquired and functioned as vision quest sites. The theory also suggests that these rock art sites were separate from habitation sites and were visited only by shamans and those on vision quests. Archaeological evidence, however, shows that many sites, which appear to be used for shamanistic or vision quest purposes, were also habitation sites.

**Figure 2.6.** *Examples of rock art from Red Rock Canyon.* **Top left:** *Pictographs of an abstract curvilinear style possibly associated with a Desert Archaic group.* **Top right:** *The desert varnish atop this panel, combined with the style of the symbols, suggests creation by a Desert Archaic group.* **Middle left:** *This panel, from Willow Springs, shows repeated triangular symbols, like the pictograph at top right, which have been associated with the Anasazi.* **Middle right:** *An Anasazi-styled pictograph panel. The location of this panel, in a rock alcove with good acoustics, suggests it was used for storytelling or religious rites.* **Bottom left:** *Southern Paiute charcoal drawings of Anglo travelers, possibly depicting their migration to California in the late 1800s.* **Bottom right:** *The lack of patination and depiction of men wearing hats in other glyphs at the site suggest that this panel was created within the last 500 years.*

## Where can I see Rock Art at Red Rock Canyon?

The two best places for viewing rock art are Red Spring and Willow Springs.

**Red Spring:** Along the base of the hillside adjacent to the boardwalk are a scattering of boulders that have an array of petrogylphs. See page 161 for more details.

**Willow Springs:** In addition to the 'Painted Hands' pictograph located immediately north of the picnic tables, there is a trail that leads to a petroglyph panel, which is on the opposite side of the wash. See page 174 for more details.

**Figure 2.7 (above).** *A possible scene circa AD 1000 near Little Red Rocks, northeast of Calico Basin. For tens of generations, people harvested and roasted hearts of Utah agave (page 109) at Red Rock Canyon. The agave hearts were placed in a pit lined with limestone rocks, then smothered with hot ashes and baked overnight. The cooked hearts were chewed for their sweet flesh as well as dried for later use. Today, the remains of roasting pits can be found at Willow Springs (painting © Bradley W. Giles).*

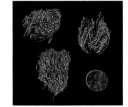

**Figure 2.8 (right).** *Agave hearts have inedible fibers at their centers that were chewed then spit out and discarded, like the ones shown here.*

*continued from page 29*

## ► Virgin Anasazi

In the Moapa Valley of southern Nevada, a group of people used new technologies from the Four Corners. Labeled the Virgin Anasazi, they irrigated fields with water from the Virgin and Muddy Rivers and made textiles, pit houses, and pottery of a design remarkably similar to that of the Anasazi. However, they did not adopt the ceremonial kiva or change their styles of pottery and shelter in the same way, raising questions as to their Anasazi identification. It has been suggested that they were a different people, possibly descendants of a Desert Archaic group, who adopted the Anasazi technology that fit with the climate and natural resources of southern Nevada.

Regardless of their cultural affiliation and heritage, these people created gravity-fed irrigation channels to increase crop yields. Cotton, first grown around AD 700, was well suited to the climate and was cultivated in the fertile land along the Virgin and Muddy Rivers. Within communities, specialized groups seasonally foraged and hunted, but many stayed at the pit houses year-round. The permanent residents tended the plots of cotton, maize, beans, squash, and other wild plants. The triad of maize, beans, and squash were usually planted together, with the cornstalk providing support for the climbing beans and shade for the squash. The squash vines provided ground cover to limit weeds, and the beans provided nitrogen to fertilize the soil.

The Virgin Anasazi were active in extensive trade networks, thought to reach into Mexico and Central America, as well as in the Four Corners region. Suggestive of the surplus these people had for trade, there were often four storage rooms to each habitation room in their pueblos. In addition to staples such as foodstuffs, cotton, pottery, and baskets, salt and turquoise from local mines were valued commodities.

## ► Patayan

The Patayan, contemporaneous to the Anasazi, settled along the Colorado River, Southern California, and west-central Arizona (Figure 2.9). These people shared many of the same technological advancements as their northerly neighbors, such as pit houses, farming, and pottery, but did so in their own distinctive style.

While Anasazi ceramics were typically white or gray with black designs, the Patayan ceramics were buff-colored and painted with red designs, indicative of different clays and process of manufacture. The dead were typically cremated, whereas the Anasazi performed burials. A mortar and pestle was used for milling instead of the mano and metate. The Patayans also created intaglios. These large (sometimes 25 yards across) images were made by clearing rocks from the ground surface to represent people, animals, and supernatural beings that would have been visible from above.

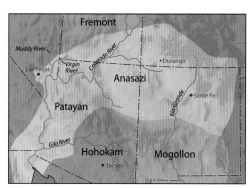

***Figure 2.9.*** *Cultural territories, circa AD 1000. Although people in southern Nevada associated with the Anasazi and Patayan cultures, it is not completely understood to what degree. Given its location along the Colorado River, with access to the coast of California, southern Nevada naturally was a hub of ancient trade.*

Patayan farming along the Colorado was based, not on diversion of water for irrigation, but on inundation resulting from spring flooding of the Colorado River (today the Colorado is dammed, and flooding to this scale does not occur). The degree of flooding varied from year to year, and the Patayan people, like the Virgin Anasazi, varied their reliance on hunting and foraging. Because their farming sites

## Turquoise

Prized as an ornament and highly valued in trade, turquoise was mined in this region as early as AD 400. The chief mining area, Halloran Springs, California, was controlled by people with ties to the Anasazi. Later, the Chemehuevi, a group related to the Southern Paiutes, warred over the area with immigrants who attempted to control the mines.

changed from year to year and subsequent floods have destroyed much of the archaeological record, substantially less is known of the Patayans than of the Anasazi.

### ▶ In the Las Vegas Valley

In the Las Vegas Valley, Anasazi and Patayan influences became mixed.

Both the Corn Creek Dunes and the Lower Las Vegas Wash contain pit-house structures dating from before 750 AD.

*Figure 2.10. An Anasazi-inspired petroglyph located near Red Spring. While some interpret this symbol to be a fringed shaman blanket or medicine bag, others contend it represents stalks of maize.*

Big Springs (today's Springs Preserve) supported a five-room pueblo-type structure where seed crops and Virgin Anasazi pottery have been found. Whether these people were truly Anasazi, or another culture that used the technology of the Anasazi, is not known for certain. Many sites at Red Rock Canyon, especially along the northern end of the Red Rock Escarpment, testify to their activities, but no pit houses or pueblos have been found.

Sites like Red Spring likely served as base camps for foraging and hunting. Indeed, bedrock grinding surfaces attest to the area being used to process seeds and plants. These people could have crossed Calico Basin to collect agave and desert tortoise, which were roasted in mounds (Figure 2.7), or traveled up the wash along the Calico Hills, headed to the White Rock Hills and Willow Springs in search of rabbits, sheep, or quail.

While roasting pits like those near Willow Spring and White Rock Spring are known from late Desert Archaic times (as early as 1600 BC) and from later groups, it is during this period, roughly AD 500 to 1100, that their use flourished at Red Rock Canyon.

Based on the types of pottery found, the Patayan influence appears to be stronger in southern parts of the Las Vegas Valley, such as the Duck Creek Wash and Lower Las Vegas Wash. For example, near the Las Vegas Wash there is an intaglio of a human roughly 40′ wide.

### ▶ Exodus

Around AD 1100, the Virgin Anasazi began to abandon their homes. While there are a number of plausible theories that attempt to explain this departure, the actual events are unknown and could involve a combination of factors, such as prolonged drought leading to crop failures, hostilities with neighboring groups, a breakdown of trade networks spurred by the collapse of the Toltec Empire in Mexico, and disease caused by crowded conditions.

Ultimately, those Anasazi who survived dispersed into family groups and lived much like their hunting and foraging, seasonally-migrating ancestors.

# ► Southern Paiutes

*Into modern times*

In southern Nevada, after the Anasazi abandonment, a people less reliant on agriculture used many of the same areas known by the Anasazi. The culture of these people has come to be known as Southern Paiute. The Southern Paiute maintain that they have lived in this area since time began and refer to Mount Charleston and the entire Spring Mountain Range as *Nuvágantu*, their birthplace and spiritual center.

Southern Paiutes lived in family groups of 10 to 15 that moved seasonally between low valley areas and higher, mountainous regions, following the ripening of a wide variety of seeds, roots, berries, and plants. Garden plots were also cultivated near water sources but generally did not serve as year-round habitation sites. Hunting of large game occurred when practical but was typically secondary to the seasonal foraging rounds. If a group had excess food, it was shared with neighboring groups.

Within each group, a headman was chosen who led the others to foraging areas and advised in social matters. The members were not bound by his decisions, and his leadership role was defined by their acceptance to follow.

Each group had a territory that they customarily used and cared for described by a 'song trail.' Song trails were elaborate oral maps used not only to delineate the land but also to characterize it and man's relation to it. Each song, and the area it represented, was passed down from generation to generation and could only be sung by those who used its territory.

Within the groups, gender roles were faithfully followed. All gathering, food preparation, and basket making were woman's work. Fashioning weapons and hunting was strictly the domain of men, but the packing of a kill back to camp could be done by women. Fashioning of garments, however, was the job of men who sewed together rabbit skins to keep the family warm in winter. Such strict roles made marriage a necessity, but the practice did not have the stigmas and moral overtones of today. If either partner was unhappy with a union, it was dissolved. And it was common for a man or woman to have three or four partners over the course of a lifetime.

**Figure 11.** *A family group of Southern Paiutes poses in front of their wikiup wearing traditional fringed-hide shirts and dresses, and basketry hats. Southern Paiutes had a highly-evolved social structure and spiritual belief system that was being severely disrupted when this photo was taking in 1870.*

Many family groups came together to participate in certain activities, such as pine nut harvests, agave roasts, and rabbit drives. These communal activities were accompanied with songs, dances, and story telling. In these ancient myths, moral and historical messages were conveyed through animals that played roles as spiritual beings. The animals exemplify the traits of humans and implore a sense of humility.

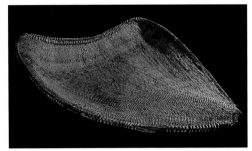
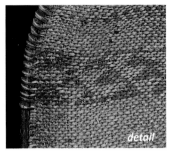

*detail*

*Figure 12. Because of their mobile way of life, Southern Paiutes favored baskets over more fragile, heavier pottery. They were master basketmakers who fashioned many different types for foraging, winnowing, roasting, transporting, and other tasks. Shown here is a winnowing tray used to separate seeds from husks.*

They are sometimes strong and proud, and other times pitiful or vile. For example, the coyote is a popular character. His mischievous deeds result from an incessant desire to have sex. Mankind acts out the part of the coyote, often giving into selfish ambitions, and is therefore relegated to live in this realm, below the supernatural.

Early on, Southern Paiutes recognized an interconnectedness between water flows, rocks and soil, plants, animals, and the cycles of life. They created a system of beliefs that reflected their desire to maintain the balance of nature's systems. Central in this belief system is the idea of *puha*. Puha is an energy force or power that came into being during Creation and was placed in all elements: air, water, rocks, minerals, plants, animals, geographic places, the sun, the moon, thunder, clouds,

## Place Names of the Las Vegas Paiutes

While many place names have been lost, ethnographer Isabel Kelly recorded these in the 1930s. They have been interpreted by members of the Las Vegas Paiute Tribe and Dr. Catherine Fowler. The names have been written by the author of this book for an English speaker to pronounce with spaces between the syllables. Interpretations are in quotations.

**eye vah tain ah:** "*at the base of white mountain,*" Spring Mountain Ranch.

**eye voo vee:** "*possibly white sandstone,*" the Red Rock Canyon area.

**kai bag a roo pats:** "*mountain spirit water,*" a spring on the east side of the Spring Mountains.

**kah eeg:** "*playground,*" Cottonwood Spring (present-day Blue Diamond).

**koon ah bee:** "*big wash,*" Kyle Canyon.

**mut nwee ta pats:** "*bull roarer spring,*" Wheeler Camp Spring.

**new vah ghan tu:** "*having snow,*" Mount Charleston/Spring Mountains. The source of *puha* for Southern Paiutes.

**see goot seeb:** "*navel,*" a water catchment in the La Madre Mountains.

**so su wa:** "*the star cluster Pleiades,*" La Madre Mountains.

**too hoo ta mu:** "*dark saddle,*" Mountain Springs.

**so ah ree ou wahv:** "*Joshua tree valley,*" Upper Las Vegas Valley.

**yew wah ghan tu:** "*having plains,*" Las Vegas Valley.

and wind. It enables these elements to be alive and have a will; therefore *puha* is most concentrated in living things. Furthermore, it exists in a network and flows between elements based on the desires of the those with the most *puha*.

Humans can hold substantial amounts of *puha*. Thus, people are responsible for maintaining its balance in the universe. If this balance is disrupted, *puha* flows away and sickness, misfortune, natural disasters, and death occur. Southern Paiutes used ceremonies including round dances and tool offerings in addition to an innate respect for all around them to maintain this balance of *puha*.

Not all people are born with the same amount of *puha*, and each person's capacity to hold and use *puha* is different. In the past, a rite of passage was required to become and adult: for males a vision quest, and for females a first menses ceremony. Males typically went to special places apart from everyday life, to be guided by a spirit helper or shaman through isolation and sensory deprivation, physical stress, drumming or dancing, and ingesting hallucinogens in order to become attuned to, and gather, *puha*.

The shaman was a person who had a special connection with *puha* and lived apart from the normal social groups, often in caves of concentrated *puha*. They used their powers to affect weather, animals, and illnesses. Not all shamans could wield their power appropriately and those who did not consistently bring health and well-being were killed or banished.

## ► At Red Rock Canyon

It is possible that all reaches of Red Rock Canyon had family groups and associated song trails. It is easy to imagine song trails in certain locations: from Cottonwood Spring to Mountain Springs, from Calico Basin to Willow Springs and into the La Madre Mountains, and from the Corn Creek area into the forests of Mount Charleston. However, only brief snatches of the songs remain, and the archeological evidence is too fragmentary to validate such seasonal paths.

Nevertheless, Spring Mountain Ranch, Willow Springs, and Red Spring would have been favorite spots, providing ample water

**Figure 13.** *A Southern Paiute staple, the seeds and pods of mesquite trees were ground into a flour to be made into cakes or added to soups.*

and abundant resources in certain seasons.

The population question, like the extent of occupation, is difficult to answer. In 1872, Lt. George Wheeler estimated that there were some 200 Southern Paiutes living a 'life of leisure' between the Las Vegas Valley and Cottonwood Springs (present-day Blue Diamond). Considering that this population had survived the devastating diseases, slave raids, and displacement of earlier decades, some have suggested that the Las Vegas Valley and eastern Spring Mountains may have supported 500 to 800 Southern Paiutes.

After 1872, Euro-Americans continued to encroach on lands Southern Paiutes had used for countless generations. Native people were able to maintain some of their old lifeways but increasingly were forced into Western society. By 1905, with the arrival of the railroad, the best land and water rights were controlled by Anglos. Southern Paiutes were pushed aside and subjected to a number of injustices. Today, the Las Vegas Paiute Tribe owns 10 acres near downtown Las Vegas and a reservation east of Mount Charleston, where they operate thriving smoke shops and a golf course.

# Euro-American History
## at Red Rock Canyon

*Captain John C. Frémont leads his scouting party to a spring after crossing the Spring Mountains in May 1844. Frémont did not have wagons with his party, but the report he published set the stage for their use and made cross-country travel through the Southwest and Red Rock accessible for many (painting by Mervin Corning).*

## ► Arrival of Europeans
*Early explorers and new ways of life, circa 1540 to 1829.*

Long before actual face-to-face contact occurred, European colonization had profound impacts on the Southern Paiutes. Spanish conquistadores began to explore the Southwest as early as 1540. Spain sought to expand its empire and desired immediate wealth in the form of silver and gold to support wars in Europe, the Catholic Church, and aristocratic extravagance.

In 1598, these desires brought conquistadores from Mexico up the Rio Grande to near present-day Santa Fe, where they occupied a Pueblo village and set up the first European colony in the Southwest. The natives retaliated but were massacred by the Spaniards, who killed 800 men, women, and children, and took another 500 captive. To elicit fear and obedience in those who still threatened

them, the Spanish cut off one foot of every male adult captive. Through torture and occasional alliance with natives, they received reports of gold. Following these leads, they explored east to Kansas and west to the Colorado River, where they sighted the Grand Canyon.

Failing to find coffers filled with silver and gold, as they had in their lucrative conquests of the Aztecs and Incas in South America, the Spanish focused on expansion of their empire. They converted native peoples into Spanish Catholic subjects and established new farms and missions in present-day New Mexico, Arizona, and coastal California.

In the mid-1770s, the Spanish made two attempts to find an inland supply route to link their territories. One party, led by Father Francisco Garcés, traveled from Yuma, Arizona up the Colorado River to Mohave settlements near present-day Bullhead City. With Mohave guides, the party then followed an ancient trade path west through the Mojave Desert to the mission in Los Angeles.

The second party, led by Fathers Dominguez and Escalante in 1776, began in Santa Fe and headed northwest to avoid the hostile natives known to reside in south-central Arizona. They made it as far west as Cedar City, Utah, when they decided to return because winter was approaching. Although they had not been able to reach the California coast, the priests were happy to have found many potential Catholic converts and a safe route of travel.

As the Spanish made inroads in the Southwest, slave trading became one of the first direct influences on the Southern Paiutes. By the late 1700s, the Spanish colonies in the Americas had a long-established tradition of using native women and children as slaves for domestic tasks. Large Ute bands, highly mobile thanks to Spanish horses, traveled across southern Nevada, raiding Southern Paiute groups, and transporting their human captives to the Spanish colonies in California and Santa Fe, where they were traded into servitude. Although slave raids surely dwindled the Southern Paiute populations, smallpox and measles, to which the native people had no immunity, are thought to have had an even more devastating effect. Because of the paucity of documentation and artifacts before the early-to-mid 1800s, the extent of the decimation from disease and slave raids can only be inferred; estimates for the century between 1750 and 1850 report a 65% to 90% decrease in population.

In the 1820s, following Mexico's independence from Spain, southern Nevada and most of the Southwest became part of Mexico. New routes of trade opened and taxes on goods were reduced. Trapping for furs and trading was profitable, and likely brought the occasional Mexican or Anglo through southern Nevada.

The little that nonnatives knew of the region prior to 1830 was based largely on hearsay and speculation. For example, many maps of the period reference a 'Buenaventura River,' which flowed westerly from the Wasatch Mountains of Utah, through the Sierra Nevada Range, and into the San Francisco Bay. The economic importance of such a river was a factor that led Jedediah Smith to form a trapping expedition in 1826 that went down the Virgin River from Utah into the Colorado River Valley. Smith traveled westward from the Colorado River through the Mojave Desert, following a path similar to the one that the Father Garcés party had traveled in 1776.

## Fur Trappers and Horse Thieves

With the decline of the fur trade in the late 1830s, livestock raids became a viable venture for many trappers and mountain men. Old Bill Williams, among others, led well-planned raids that occasionally gathered thousands of horses from Spanish and Mexican settlements in California. After driving the beasts through some of the harshest stretches of the Mojave Desert, Old Bill and his men sometimes brought the surviving horses to the springs east of the Red Rock Escarpment. They set up camp at present-day Spring Mountain Ranch and rested the weary horses before selling them in Utah and New Mexico.

*'Old Bill' Williams*

# ► The Old Spanish Trail – Mormon Road

*The longest, most arduous pack mule route in the history of America had an alternate route through Red Rock Canyon that was used extensively by Mormon settlers traveling by wagon to California.*

*Most autumns, from 1829 until the late 1840s, a small handful of pack mule trains traversed southern Nevada along paths of the Old Spanish Trail en route to California. In the spring, the traders retraced their paths, driving horses and livestock back to Santa Fe. Here, muleskinners coerce a mule, overloaded with goods, to get back on the trail.*

In 1829, after the journeys of Father Garcés, Dominguez-Escalante, and Jedediah Smith, the growing knowledge of feasible routes through the Southwest led New Mexican merchant Antonio Armijo to organize a commercial pack train of 60 men and 100 mules to travel from Santa Fe to Los Angeles. Crossing southern Nevada in the winter, they followed the Virgin and Colorado River drainages south, camped at the Lower Las Vegas Wash, then left the Las Vegas Valley by crossing the Black Mountains south of Henderson. They were successful in reaching the Spanish missions along the coast of California. The following spring, they retraced their path back to Santa Fe, establishing what is known today as the Old Spanish Trail.

The trail, known as the "longest, most arduous pack mule route in the history of America," was typically used by pack mule trains (not wagons) that left New Mexico in the fall carrying woolen blankets and shawls that were exchanged in California for horses, mules, silk, and other foreign goods. While the exact route of the trail varied from party to party (see map, inside front cover), most parties did not follow in Armijo's footsteps and took a route across the Spring Mountains roughly following today's SR-160.

It is likely that the routes through Red Rock Canyon began to be used in the early 1840s. In fact, one of the earliest recorded names for Cottonwood Spring, Spring of Quintana, may have been given by a prominent Mexican merchant.

Depending on their cargo, traders may have taken different routes through Red Rock Canyon. When driving horses or cattle, the northern route along the Red Rock Escarpment, with its multiple springs and grazing options, was likely preferred, while the route south of Blue Diamond Hill (Las Vegas Springs to Cottonwood Springs to Mountain Springs) would have been more direct for those with fewer livestock.

In the early 1840s, the United States military, aware of growing tensions with Mexico, was concerned about its lack of knowledge regarding basic geography in the Southwest. To survey the territory, the U.S. selected John C. Frémont and a former fur trapper, Kit Carson, to lead a party. In 1843, they left Salt Lake City and traveled westward through the Great Basin, crossed the Sierras, then headed south down the Central Valley of California. They returned by way of the main route of the Old Spanish Trail, which took them from the southern Pahrump Valley, over the Spring Mountains at Mountain Springs, and down into Red Rock Canyon, then known as Cottonwood Valley (see map, inside front cover). Regarding Red Rock Canyon, Frémont wrote in his journal: *"The ridge is extremely rugged and broken, presenting* on this side [east] *a continued precipice, and probably affords very few passes."* Frémont literally put the route through Red Rock Canyon on the map, which was published with a report of the journey in 1845.

The Mexican-American War erupted in 1846 and led to America gaining the territory from Texas to California in 1848. The same year, trading along the Old Spanish Trail reached a standstill when California imposed a 20% import duty on trade goods. However, gold was discovered in the Golden State leading to a large-scale immigration: the California gold rush of 1849. While the majority of these immigrants traveled by sea or took the northern route through the Great Basin, some hopeful prospectors came through Red Rock Canyon via the Cottonwood Springs route.

Mormons were also on the move and intended to settle the State of Deseret, which they envisioned to be all of the Great Basin, southern California, and the Colorado Plateau, where they would be able to practice their religion without persecution. Beginning in the late 1840s, the Mormons, who had heard of Frémont's

## Southern Paiute Impacts

In addition to facilitating slave raids, the Old Spanish Trail brought thousands of livestock animals through the region each spring and fall. The livestock consumed much of the vegetation and fouled the springs that the Southern Paiutes relied upon, forcing them to change their way of life. They began to favor less-accessible upland territory to avoid travelers and occasionally took livestock for food.

journey, used wagons on the sections of trail that traversed Red Rock Canyon for transporting supplies and people between California and Salt Lake City. With use, the trail became a well-established wagon road, known today as the Mormon Road.

The road received frequent use by wagons into the 20th century. And with the advent of the automobile, many sections were re-graded and later paved, such as SR-160 southwest of Blue Diamond, which was completed in 1937.

*Men work to repair a wagon at Cottonwood Springs (today's Blue Diamond village). The second phase of the trail, known as the Mormon Road, was used primarily by family groups in wagons emigrating to California from Utah. These travelers stopped at Cottonwood Springs to camp or repair equipment after making the day-long journey from Las Vegas Springs, located at today's Springs Preserve.*

# ► Mining in the Spring Mountains

*Note: Mine sites are located on the maps found on the inside front and back covers.*

Since 1856, when the Mormons made the first recorded excavation of underground ore in Nevada at Mount Potosi, the Spring Mountains have played a major role in the mining history of Nevada, producing gold, silver, lead, zinc, and copper, as well as gypsum and stone for building construction.

## ► Mormon Settlement

The Mormons were well organized and efficient in establishing a settlement and way station at Las Vegas to service the Mormon Road in 1855. Settlers were carefully selected or 'called' by church leaders based on their skills and experience. Within the group of 29 that came to Las Vegas were farmers, blacksmiths, carpenters, laborers, and a bishop-leader: William Bringhurst. In the first few months, they had cleared acres of mesquite for gardens, built a small adobe-brick fort near the Las Vegas Creek, and forged a rough road to Mount Charleston for timber.

*Nathaniel Jones, shown here at age 24 while enlisted in the Mormon Battalion. Ten years later, in 1856, he spearheaded the first lode mine in Nevada at Mount Potosi, just south of the Red Rock Escarpment.*

The Southern Paiutes in the area did not rebel against the Mormons, who had effectively usurped the land. In fact, the Mormons were able to convert some to Mormonism, and used many to help farm the gardens. In conducting a census of the area, it is reported that Bringhurst was informed by a Southern Paiute named Coonakibats of lead ore on the eastern flanks of Mount Charleston. In April 1856, Bringhurst sent samples of the ore to Salt Lake for analysis.

On news that the assay reported a 90% lead content, Brigham Young sent Nathaniel Jones to begin mining operations a month later. Jones assessed the site and determined that there was not enough ore to warrant mining, which

likely contributed to friction between him and Bringhurst. The Mormons continued the search and traveled to the west side of the Spring Mountains, about three miles south of Mountain Springs, where a large quantity of ore could be more-easily worked. In September, a smelter on the site, known today as the Potosi Mine, was fired up to extract the lead, but the furnace proved unable to withstand the heat. While Jones returned to Salt Lake for a horse-powered bellows furnace, members of the Las Vegas Mission were able to produce only 1000 pounds of lead from more than 9000 pounds of ore. When Jones returned in December, they were able to produce 9000 pounds of lead in five weeks, but the smelting proved too difficult, likely because of the high zinc and silver content in the ore, of which the Mormons were unaware.

In addition to the lackluster performance of the mine, the Las Vegas Fort was plagued by leadership conflicts, tension with the Southern Paiutes, who occasionally stole crops, and social problems within the group; reasons which led to its dissolution early in 1857.

## ► Boom and Bust

The mining fever, which was spreading from California in the late 1850s, brought renewed interest in the Potosi Mine, and it was re-opened in 1860, this time for silver. When this news made it to California, miners rushed to the 'Las Vegas Silver Mines,' and at one point over 30 people were arriving daily. The need for fresh produce to supply the miners led to farming and ranching at the present-day Spring Mountain Ranch and the abandoned Mormon Fort.

*Before steam-powered tractors arrived, the primary means of transporting ore was in horse-drawn wagons. Here, circa 1908, a team takes a load of ore from the Potosi mine through Red Rock Canyon to a rail station south of Las Vegas.*

Although Potosi was a productive lode, there were not enough prospects for the booming mining population, and many searched elsewhere in the region. One such man, Octavius Decatur Gass (after whom Gass Peak is named), staked 16 claims in the gold mining district of Eldorado Canyon. The claims were not especially profitable, and in 1865 he moved into the Mormon Fort. Gass would go on to become a pioneer in the settlement of Las Vegas.

Despite optimistic reports that the Potosi district would rival the famous Comstock Lode of northern Nevada, by the late 1860s, many mining claims at Mount Potosi had been abandoned, and most miners moved on to Goodsprings or Ivanpah, California. Goodsprings, located immediately south of Red Rock Canyon, would go on to become one of Nevada's premier districts, producing 32,000 ounces of gold by the turn of the century.

Whereas the veins of lead-silver-zinc ores in this region are found along the faults of Paleozoic-age carbonate rocks (see page 16), the gold-copper ores exist along the contact zone between intrusive granite and the surrounding sedimentary rocks. Because Red Rock has no intrusive granitic formations exposed, there is no gold or copper to be found.

While many were drawn by the boom of the Goodsprings district, some continued to prospect at Red Rock and the slopes of Mount Charleston, where the Tersharrum and Fairview claims were made in 1870, the latter striking a vein of silver ore valued at $1,200 per ton. Today, this ore would be valued at over $37,000 per ton. By 1871, 15 prospects had been identified in the Spring Mountain district. One of the first to be mined was the La Madre Mine in 1870.

### ► La Madre Mine

Located near La Madre Spring on the west side of the White Rock Hills, the La Madre Mine had two shafts, which followed veins of silver. The mine proved unprofitable because the costs required to transport the ore using pack mules and horse-drawn wagons were too high and it was abandoned in 1883.

In 1907, with transportation available through the newly-built San Pedro, Los Angeles, & Salt Lake Railroad, the mine was reopened by W.E. Hawkins and J.R. Hunter. While Hawkins had his hands full running a general merchandise store in Las Vegas and serving as a Clark County Commissioner, Hunter set up a base camp at Cottonwood Ranch (today's Blue Diamond village) to work the mine. With help from hired hands, Hunter pushed the shafts to a depth of 100'. The ore they extracted was shipped by railroad and smelted for silver and zinc.

After Hunter left Las Vegas to serve as a State police officer in 1908, Hawkins, a Republican, put political differences aside and sold part ownership of the mine to Frank A. Doherty, a Democrat, and Arthur J. Frye, who was well-known for hosting parties with his wife at their Las Vegas residence. Because Doherty lived in Searchlight and served as Clark County Recorder and Auditor, the task of working the mine fell to Frye, who set up a camp near La Madre Spring. Frye and his wife made extended stays at the camp to work the La Madre Mine and other smaller prospects in the area before he moved to California in 1912. Hawkins went on to become mayor of Las Vegas in 1913.

Today, a stone-walled, timber-roofed shelter still exists below the mine site and is regularly visited by hikers.

*Today, falling into steep mine shafts poses a serious hazard for kids and adults.*

*Near the La Madre Mine is a cabin presumed to have been used by Hawkins and his partners. The low timber roof is thought to have been added to the structure by later groups.*

## ► Arrival of the Railroad

At the turn of the century, the Las Vegas Valley had roughly 30 nonnative residents. Searchlight was better populated and was emerging as a gold mining camp. After Senator William A. Clark announced that

Las Vegas would be a junction point on his railroad, materials and people arrived in mass to the valley. In late January 1905, the San Pedro, Los Angeles & Salt Lake Railroad began making trips between Los Angeles and Salt Lake City.

With the railroad came canvas lodging houses, wood-framed saloons, banks, a newspaper, numerous general stores, an ice-producing facility, and many jobs related to the railroad and freight industries. Soon, private lots were sold, and by the end of 1905, substantial development, including many stone and wood-framed dwellings, existed near present-day Fremont Street.

When the railroad arrived in 1905, most major mineral-resource sites had been identified in the Spring Mountains, and efforts focused on locating the veins and extracting the ore. One exception, re-discovered in 1906 by Jacob Holcomb, was the Lucky Strike Mine, which Coonakibats, a Southern Paiute, had pointed out to the Mormons in 1855. Near the mine, located on the east flank of Mount Charleston near the border of the Red Rock Canyon Conservation Area, there were soon 12 more claims staked, all showing good signs of lead. After extraction, the ore was loaded onto wagons and hauled by horse teams to a rail stop at Corn Creek, along the Las Vegas and Tonopah Railroad. From there, it was sent to Salt Lake City for smelting. Mining likely continued at the Lucky Strike until the early 1920s when the lack of demand drove down the price of metals.

Responding to the increased demand due to World War I, the Potosi Mine saw renewed interest when zinc mining began in 1913. An aerial tram improved production and helped it become Nevada's largest zinc producer before production waned and the operations ceased in 1928. Today, the Potosi Mine and its small townsite, located nearby, are abandoned.

*At its peak, as many as 30 men worked to extract and transport the beautiful red and white sandstone from Sandstone Quarry. The quarry was never exceptionally profitable and ran, off and on, from 1905 to 1912.*

## ► Sandstone Quarry

Inspired by the nearly inexhaustible supply of red and white sandstone—intended to be used for building construction in Los Angeles and San Francisco—the Lyon-Wilson Construction Company began quarry operations at the Sandstone Quarry adjacent to today's Scenic Drive in the spring of 1905, shortly after the completion of the railroad.

Rough dirt tracks were blazed from Las Vegas and a number of buildings were constructed at the quarry site, including sleeping quarters for some of the 8 to 30 men employed at any given time. To extract the stone, 10-ton blocks were created using channeling and blasting machines. Derricks and hoists were used to load the blocks onto wagons that were hauled to the Las Vegas railroad station by the 'Big Devil Wagon,' a massive steam-powered tractor that burned 400 gallons of crude oil per day.

Using such enormous quantities of fuel was expensive, and transportation of the stone proved to be a major obstacle in turning a profit. Less than one year after starting up, the quarry, with pressure from another quarry located closer to the railroad, was forced to cease operations.

In 1909, with new sources of capital, operations again began extracting stone using similar methods. The company hoped that a railroad spur would be built to the site, but settled on getting the county to help grade a 60'-wide dirt road on which they could drive a 35,000 pound tank-like tractor for hauling the stone. The improvements proved insufficient to keep the quarry profitable and by 1912, it was again closed.

In all, only a small amount of stone was extracted, but some did end up in San Francisco and Los Angeles. After operations ceased, the quarry was a popular spot to picnic for early Las Vegans. Today, it continues to be a favorite place to visit, and much evidence remains of the mining activities.

*The Big Devil Wagon, which appeared like the relic pictured here, was used to haul the stone down to Las Vegas, circa 1906.*

# ► Homesteading and Ranching

From the late 1800s until the mid 1900s, Red Rock Canyon was used primarily by ranchers. The land was publicly owned, and under the Homestead Act of 1862, each man could claim 160 acres to be his with a $15.00 fee and five years of residence, improvement, and cultivation. However, following the Taylor Grazing Act of 1934, many restrictions were placed on homesteading and rangeland.

*Cottonwood Ranch, the predecessor to Blue Diamond, was in the 1910s a productive fruit and vegetable farm run by Vincent Matteucci (not pictured) whose wife is wearing an apron, second from the left.*

Although ranchers owned only specific parcels, they ranged and watered their cattle throughout the valley east of the Red Rock Escarpment, using the springs from Calico Basin to Cottonwood Spring. Such widespread grazing was necessary to maintain a herd, because the vegetation provided little fodder. When new grass growth was available at the spring-fed meadows that dot Red Rock, these sites were favored and, not surprisingly, were where ranches first became established.

## ► Sandstone Ranch

Known today as Spring Mountain Ranch, the Sandstone Ranch commanded ownership of the most profuse springs, and for roughly 100 years after it was established in 1876, it played a key role in setting the stage for ranching activities at Red Rock. A history of the ranch can be found on page 139.

## ► Cottonwood Ranch

Southern Paiutes were returning to the fertile grounds around Cottonwood Spring in the late 1800s after travelers along the Old Spanish Trail had displaced them earlier in the century. Lt. George M. Wheeler, under direction from the U.S. Congress, began surveys of the Southwest in 1869 and reported that some 200 Southern Paiutes were harvesting the wild grapes that grow at Red Rock and raising corn, pumpkins, and squash near Cottonwood Springs.

In 1903, the San Pedro, Los Angeles & Salt Lake Railroad acquired the water rights and 80 acres of land surrounding Cottonwood Spring. Five years later, Charles P. Ball, who owned a freight-shipping business in Las Vegas, made a vacation camp at the spring with his wife and children. The next year, they leased this land from the railroad and farmed a wide array of crops, from tomatoes, cabbage, sugar cane, and domestic grapes, to figs and peaches. The railroad was happy to have a tenant to maintain the property, a contingency of their ownership, and charged Mr. Ball only $1.00 per year to lease the land.

Ball, however, was occupied with various duties for the Las Vegas Chamber of Commerce, and other tenants occupied the ranch. Vincent Matteucci, his wife Mary, and their six children, moved into an adobe near the spring and were soon harvesting vegetables. Each week during harvest season, the family would load the crops into a horse-drawn wagon, which Vincent would drive downtown to sell the produce. Shortly after Mary died of influenza pneumonia in 1920, Vincent moved to California where he had family. Ranch operations sputtered in the 1920s with various absentee tenants.

In 1924, Matteucci and his partner, Peter Buol, sold their mining claims to the bluff north of the ranch to Blue Diamond Materials Company. In the early days of the Blue Diamond Mine, the ranch provided a shady retreat for the workers with its tall cottonwoods and earth-lined swimming hole. During this period, chickens, rabbits, and pigs were raised on a small scale until a company town for the mine was built at the ranch in 1941.

### ▶ Morgan Ranch

Round about the turn of the century, when William C. Morgan was crossing the Las Vegas Valley on horseback to deliver mail between the Moapa Valley and a railroad station in the Ivanpah Valley, a Southern Paiute by the name of Indian Ben made his home near the spring that now bears his name (see map, inside back cover).

*Vera Krupp, who purchased the Spring Mountain Ranch in 1955, ranged her cattle from Calico Basin down to the slopes of Mount Potosi and improved many springs at Red Rock for cattle use.*

Morgan, a free-spirited character, is often remembered in the romantic sense of a Western pioneer. Indeed, by 1915, when he began ranging cattle at Red Rock, he had already won the title for breaking wild horses to harness at the 1893 Chicago World's Fair and formed his own 'Bronco Bill's Wild West Show,' which toured the eastern states and Midwest in 1901. By 1921, at the age of 52, Morgan had acquired 320 acres around Ben's Spring and was running a vibrant ranch with numerous horses and many head of cattle.

As Morgan and his wife grew older they spent less time at the ranch and more time at their home in Las Vegas. In the late 1930s, Chauncey B. Oliver became aware of the property and in 1944, exchanged land on the slopes of Mount Charleston with Morgan for the ranch.

Mr. Oliver, educated at the University of Illinois, was an industrious man receiving nine patents between 1933 and 1962. He was attracted to Nevada to avoid the income taxes imposed by other states. The Morgan Ranch became the Oliver Ranch, which Mr. Oliver and his wife used as a vacation property until the early 1970s. During this time, they made a number of improvements to the property, including a full-sized concrete-lined swimming pool and several stone-walled structures that still stand today. Mrs. Oliver's family were Western pioneers, and an inscription on one of the stone buildings attests to an 1881 Apache attack, which her mother, with little help at the age of 17, fought off at their New Mexico ranch.

The Oliver Ranch, incorporated into the conservation area in 1993, was slated in 2003 to become an expansive facility funded by public land sales for elementary school kids to learn about science and ecology. However, it was determined that the project was not feasible.

## The CCC at Red Rock Canyon

Initiated in the early 1930s as a work relief program by the federal government, the Civilian Conservation Corps (CCC) undertook projects related to recreational development, flood control, range management, and archaeology.

At Red Rock Canyon in 1941, the men of company 2557, from Ohio, Indiana, and Kentucky focused on rangeland and grazing projects. They built short pipelines to carry water into troughs for watering cattle at Willow Spring, White Rock Spring, Lone Grapevine Spring, and others. In Brownstone Canyon, they built a small dam to collect water for similar purposes. Their largest project at Red Rock was the construction of Rocky Gap Road to connect the Roberts Ranch in Lovell Canyon with Willow Springs and the Las Vegas Valley.

## ► Red Spring - Calico Basin

Although James B. Wilson, owner of the Sandstone Ranch, and his adopted sons grazed and watered their cattle in Calico Basin, the first documented resident was Ella M. Mason in the mid 1910s.

Miss Mason arrived in Las Vegas shortly after the railroad was completed and ran a boarding house downtown. By 1915, she and her daughter had moved out to the grassy meadow near Red Spring and established a small ranch. They stayed and worked the land for seven years; then, through the provisions of the Homestead Act, earned title to the land. The details of their departure are unknown.

The Small Tract Act of 1938 opened up plots of land within Calico Basin for purchase and residential developments. However, it was not until the late 1960s that the area saw extensive development.

## ► Pine Creek Canyon

Horace Wilson, a stone mason who came from Indiana to reside in southern Nevada, first became acquainted with Red Rock Canyon while horseback riding through the area. Stunned by the beauty of Pine Creek Canyon, arguably one of the most picturesque of all the canyons of Red Rock, Horace and his wife, Glenna, decided to file on the land and build a homestead near the grassy meadow at the mouth of the canyon in 1922.

At this time, a rough dirt road, which was continually getting washed out, ran roughly along today's SR-159. To access their ranch, the Wilsons blazed a road into the canyon by dragging objects, such as trees and sections of fence, from the bumper of their automobile. Today, the road is being reclaimed by nature, but parts of it serve as the hiking trail into Pine Creek Canyon.

At the homestead, the Wilsons built a two-story, red-adobe-brick house with a large fireplace and an ample veranda. In the nearby meadow, they irrigated crops, such as alfalfa, sweet potatoes, melons, wild grapes, and berries; string beans grew so well they could sell the excess. They also planted an orchard of apple and apricot trees, some of which are still alive today.

In the mid-20s, the homestead was a popular spot for their friends to spend the day, and cars would line the dirt road leading to the home. The Wilsons' occupation, however, was rather short. In 1929, the couple sold the homestead to Leigh Hunt, who, at the time, was the single largest land holder in Las Vegas. The arrangement made good financial sense for the Wilsons, as they then paid rent to Hunt until his death in 1933. After Hunt's death, the couple moved back to Las Vegas. In the decade after the Wilsons' departure the homestead fell into disrepair. Careless visitors destroyed the orchards, shot up water tanks, and a group of kids accidentally burned down the house.

Today, only a concrete foundation of the house remains (see photo, page 182) and the property is part of the conservation area.

*The idyllic Pine Creek Canyon was one of the last places to be homesteaded before the laws changed in 1934. Horace and Glenna (right photo) built a lovely house at the mouth of the canyon and often hosted weekend picnics for their Las Vegas friends.*

# ► Bootlegging at Red Rock Canyon

A substantial number of Las Vegans, like many people across America from 1920 to 1933, thought Prohibition was unreasonable and secretly violated it. In fact, liquor flowed copiously throughout Las Vegas. Speakeasies flourished downtown, and later along Boulder Highway. Many bars were boarded up, but patrons knew to simply enter through the back door. Stills of all sizes could be found throughout the region; some were located in the back rooms and hidden closets of businesses and homes, others were on private ranches and estates, and many were hidden in the mountains east and west of town.

Some of these mountain stills were operated near springs at Red Rock Canyon where bootleggers used the water to make their mash and wood to fire a still. With a gallon of booze selling for $10.00 ($130.00 today), bootleggers stood to make handsome profits if they could avoid being arrested or fined.

While most law enforcement officials at the local level were willing to turn a blind eye for a fair price, there were others, mostly Federal Prohibition Agents, intent on enforcing the law. The agents would often pose as out-of-towners to 'locate and sample' the booze and even went as far as opening their own bar, called Liberty's Last Stand, located at 10 Stewart Street. Most of the time, however, word of impending raids spread quickly, allowing those involved to avoid arrest.

There were, however, successful raids in the region: agents arrested 11 bootleggers in 1923, and eight were taken by the U.S. Marshall in 1926. In 1929, agents focused on the Mayor of Las Vegas, the Police Commissioner, as well as the mountains west of town including Red Rock Canyon. Bill Morgan's Ranch, located at today's Oliver Ranch, was a prime target. Bill's brother, Reese, was a member of the Las Vegas Police Force, and Bill just happened to be away from the ranch when agents made the raid. He escaped arrest, but the agents destroyed two of his stills. Reportedly, the apricots Bill Morgan used to make brandy came from the Spring Mountain Ranch, where evidence of a still has also been found.

*Set up in downtown Las Vegas, Liberty's Last Stand was a profitable bar run by Federal Prohibition Agents and used to ferret out the region's bootleggers.*

Most of those who operated at Red Rock did well to hide their activities. In the 1920s, Las Vegas extended only as far west as Valley View Blvd., and Red Rock was a distant wilderness. While on a hunting trip with a friend at Red Rock, J.D. Smith, a dentist from Las Vegas, came upon a 'great big still' and the operator of the still, *who had a gun*. Smith recognized the bootlegger; he had pulled the man's tooth the day before. Laughs abounded and the men shared a drink of the hooch.

Other operations may have never been discovered, but place names, such as Moonshine Spring and Bootleg Spring, attest to their activities. Bootleggers often hid their mash and stills in inaccessible caves or buried them underground.

One of the last Federal sting operations, in May 1931, used the information gathered from Liberty's Last Stand to arrest 108 people and shut down numerous bars. The sting discovered a well-connected outfit at Indian Springs where John J. Russell and Jack Cunningham ran an operation producing roughly 225 gallons of liquor per day, using the largest still known in Nevada at the time.

# ► Blue Diamond Hill – Gypsum Mining

In 1925, the Blue Diamond Materials Company began to extract large quantities of gypsum from the bluff between Red Rock Canyon and Las Vegas, known as Blue Diamond Hill (see map, inside back cover). Before operations took place, extensive surveying identified the best deposits, and a large capital investment was made to purchase heavy equipment and construct the necessary rail lines, haul roads, and tramway.

The gypsum occurs in beds and lenses 12' to 20' thick, often with limestone resting above. Depending on the terrain, both room-and-pillar and open-pit methods were used

*Gypsum (CaSO$_4$·2H$_2$O) typically is a soft, white or clear mineral formed by the evaporation of seawater. It is used to make wallboard, plaster, and cement in the construction and housing industries.*

to extract the mineral. With the room-and-pillar method, the limestone above remains in place, whereas it must be removed and discarded to mine an open pit.

In the first years of the mine, men used air-powered rotary jackhammers to drill arrays of 15'-deep holes into the gypsum.

Each hole was packed with black powder and dynamite, then all were blasted simultaneously, creating blocks of rubble that muckers loaded by hand onto ore carts. On average, each mucker loaded 20 tons of gypsum in a day, for which he was paid $4 ($50 today). Other workers, such as the drillers, equipment operators, and mechanics were only slightly better paid.

The ore carts were pulled by a locomotive to the 'crusher' located at the south rim of the bluff. The crusher pulverized the blocks, so the gypsum could be transported down the steep bluff via a gravity-powered aerial tramway that functioned much like a ski lift. From the base of the tramway, the gypsum was taken by train to a processing facility near Los Angeles.

Within a few years, the mine was producing 200 tons of gypsum per day and employing some 30 people. Two

*The village of Blue Diamond began as a company town for the miners and supervisors who worked at the nearby gypsum mine. Construction of the town began in 1942 and continued throughout the 1940s. Here, in 1946, houses have been framed on Allegro Street. When the town was privatized in 1959, homes sold for between $4,000 and $6,000. In 2008, the average home value in Blue Diamond was $400,000.*

camps were established atop the bluff, complete with cookhouse, bunkhouse, apartments, school, and three houses. The camps provided for basic needs: food, water, and shelter, but other facilities such as a hospital, post office, and stores for specialty goods required a long drive into Las Vegas. Cottonwood Spring, located in today's Blue Diamond village, was a popular spot for the families. There, they were able to escape the scorching summer heat at an earth-lined swimming pool fed by the spring and shaded by tall cottonwoods.

*Prior to 1941, nearly all mine workers lived atop the bluff. Every afternoon, workers and their families gathered at camp while the blast charges were detonated at the end of shift.*

The demand for gypsum decreased significantly during the Great Depression, but by 1941, business was back up. The company built a processing plant for wallboard manufacture on site and signed a long-term lease to build a company town at Cottonwood Ranch (see page 46). Construction of a handful of inexpensively-built tract homes began in 1942 for use by married supervisors and key employees. A trailer park in the village housed some workers, but many stayed at a camp atop the bluff. Throughout the 1940s, the town, named Blue Diamond, added more homes, a post office, village store, and a new school.

By the mid 1950s, following the post World War II construction boom and improved mining technology, the mine increased production to 900 tons per day and was employing around 350 people. Management changed in 1959 when the Flintkote Corporation purchased the mine.

The new company did not want the burden of running a company town and began selling the homes in Blue Diamond. By 1966, the last of the properties had been sold to private parties.

## Where are the Diamonds?

The name Blue Diamond comes from a phrase one of the mining company's original owners used to describe another of their mines: "*The quality of our lime is like a blue diamond among gems.*"

In 2003, despite an estimated 20 years of gypsum reserves left in the ground, the property was sold to housing developers. Today, the mine is no longer active, although the processing facility, located about one mile east of Blue Diamond village, still receives shipments of gypsum and produces wallboard.

*Left: As technology improved, muckers were replaced with heavy equipment. Circa 1960, a shovel loads gypsum for transport to the crusher. Center: A room and pillar mine. Right: The crusher pulverized large blocks of gypsum for transport down the steep bluff in an aerial tramway, which was replaced with a conveyer belt in the 1980s.*

*Residential development in Calico Basin with the Calico Hills and Red Rock Escarpment behind.*

# ► Modern Times

After the arrival of the railroad and the establishment of the town of Las Vegas in 1905, people began to frequent Red Rock Canyon, Spring Mountain Ranch, and Mount Charleston for recreation. Mount Charleston, which had been the primary source of lumber for Las Vegas and the surrounding mines, became a forest preserve in 1906. At Red Rock, the land was being grazed by cattle, and the need for protection of the area was not recognized for many decades.

## ► Getting Special Status

The first step in setting the lands of Red Rock Canyon aside came in 1936 when Franklin D. Roosevelt included them within the Desert Game Range—today's Desert National Wildlife Refuge—primarily for the protection of bighorn sheep. This meant that no new settlement would be allowed, but the land could still be managed for mining and grazing, which were not restricted.

Following World War II, the burgeoning Las Vegas population had more resources and free time. The roads that have become today's SR-159 and SR-160 were substantially improved, and the availability of Jeeps encouraged widespread exploration. Ranching still occurred, but picnicking, camping, hiking, and hunting were making inroads. The attitude that Red Rock Canyon should be protected, however, was slow to develop until the 1960s.

In 1961, following a rejection by the National Park Service (NPS) to include Red Rock Canyon in the U.S. park system, local residents, the Nevada Outdoor Recreation Association, and the Sierra Club began to rally for protection of the area. Although they pushed for National Monument status, a myriad of governmental organizations on the county, state, and federal levels worked to determine how best to designate and manage the place. While the NPS was unwilling to take on the responsibilities, the BLM had no experience managing a combined recreation and conservation site of this scale and public apprehension was voiced regarding BLM oversight.

When the dust settled in 1967, 62,000 acres were designated *Red Rock Canyon Recreation Lands*, thus giving the BLM its first big recreation land management project.

## ► Plans for a Park

After Red Rock was designated as recreation land in 1967, the BLM was required to formulate a Recreation Management Plan (RMP) which, after help from the NPS, they unveiled in 1968. The RMP called for extensive development on a scale comparable to Yosemite National Park. Included in the RMP were multiple administrative areas, a paved 'Crestline Scenic Drive' above the Red Rock Escarpment, a Scenic Drive similar to today, over 800 picnic spots, six campgrounds, a motel-restaurant at Spring Mountain Ranch, a trailer park in Calico Basin, and a dump just north of Blue Diamond. Although the Sierra Club and other local environmental groups suggested significant revisions, the BLM made no changes to the RMP. By 1970, however, funding could only be secured for half of the Scenic Drive, from the present-day visitor center to Willow Springs.

In the late 1960s and early 1970s, the environmental movement grew substantially, and by the time the Scenic Drive was completed to Willow Springs in 1972, public opinion was strongly in favor of less development in the few unspoiled spaces America had left. So many people were unhappy with the road cuts and impacts from the Scenic Drive that an environmental impact statement (EIS) was demanded for developments proposed in the RMP. The BLM responded by developing an EIS and altering their management plan to include far less development and an emphasis on services, not facilities.

## ► Rheastone Quarry

In 1950, Tilgham (TP) Rhea, a foreman at the Blue Diamond gypsum plant, met and married Mabel Grace Randall. The couple settled briefly in Blue Diamond, giving them time to have their first child and TP the opportunity to explore Red Rock Canyon.

At the base of Mount Wilson, TP found a deposit of exquisitely colored and remarkably hard sandstone—a superb building material—and began envisioning a quarry and homestead where he could raise his family. The plan would have to wait while he and his wife were on a two-year sojourn in California where they had their second child. Upon their return in 1955, TP secured a job at a manganese plant in Henderson and filed the mining claims to his find with the BLM.

He graded a road out to Bee Hive Knoll, where the stone was located, and built a cabin from which to work the claims, but he was hesitant to solicit the capital needed to get the quarry up and running. In the late 50s, a family friend purchased some necessary machinery and provided funds for operating costs. Soon, the quarry had as many as ten people working to extract and process the stone, some of whom lived at the site; others, like TP, commuted from points in the Las Vegas Valley.

Shortly after the operation successfully filled an order for shipment to Fresno, California in 1961, the investor dropped out, leaving TP to choose between raising his family or operating the quarry. TP kept his vision alive, working many jobs to save

*Tilghman Rhea and his son, Buddy, take a break while loading stone for a shipment to California in the fall of 1961. The quarry, located below Mount Wilson, saw a burst of activity in the late 50s and early 60s.*

money for the quarry, but put his family first. To this end, the quarry served as an ideal spot to take his kids. It was their private family retreat tucked up against the Red Rock Escarpment.

In 1971, while working in rural Nevada, TP died unexpectedly of a heart attack at the age of 55. Mabel tried to rebuild the cabin, which had been vandalized, and fence off the property—tasks the BLM required to maintain the claims—but could not. And in 1973, one of the last major private inroads made, in what is now the Red Rock Canyon National Conservation Area, reverted to the BLM.

## ▶ Oil and Gas Drilling

Despite the land management changes of the previous decade, in the late 1970s, Red Rock Canyon once again found itself on the verge of more developments. As America's desire to free itself from a dependence on foreign oil increased, the West became a hot spot of oil and gas exploration. By 1979, wildcatters had filed for lease rights throughout the entire Red Rock area.

*Since the early 1980s, encroaching housing developments have been a hot topic for both local residents and conscientious visitors who have seen Las Vegas grow at alarming rates.*

The environmental assessment, which was now required to allow such leasing, reported that drilling for oil and gas would have major negative impacts to the area. Most citizens were confidant that the BLM would deny the leases. Some citizens, however, were vehement in their support, suggesting "Drill for oil at Red Rock, or Yellowstone, or anywhere and get those Arabian shackles off of us!"

In 1980, the BLM decided, because many of the negative impacts could be mitigated, to allow leasing and exploratory drilling on 30% of land at Red Rock. To the relief of many who were shocked with the decision, none of the lessees made exploratory wells and their option to do so expired in 1990.

## ▶ Encroaching Developments

As the population of the Las Vegas metropolitan area doubled in each decade of the late 20th century, more and more people found a need for the recreation opportunities at Red Rock. However, the suburban sprawl that they were trying to escape followed them to the mountains.

As early as the 1950s, Las Vegas businessmen, notably the eccentric billionaire Howard Hughes, and later, car dealer Fletcher Jones, began acquiring land in and around Red Rock. While the Nevada Division of State Parks curtailed Jones' plan to build housing for 2000 people with their purchase of the Spring Mountain Ranch in 1974, the Howard Hughes Corporation began work on a 25,000 acre master-planned community called Summerlin in 1984.

Initially, the plans for Summerlin called for development of a 5000-acre parcel that would end only 200' from the Red Rock Canyon Visitor Center, which was built two years prior in 1982. But through the work of local citizens and the Nature Conservancy, the lands were acquired by the BLM in 1988. Despite the victory, the Howard Hughes Corporation still owns much of the land immediately east of Red Rock Canyon and just north of SR-159, and would likely be developing it if not for the housing market collapse of 2008.

The threat of housing developments at the gates of Red Rock Canyon helped lead U.S. Senator Harry Reid and U.S. Representative James Bilbray to introduce legislation for the *Red Rock Canyon Recreation Lands* to become the *Red Rock Canyon National Conservation Area*. The new designation, which occurred in 1990, affords increased protection of the area and adds the objective of conservation into the mission of the BLM.

## ▶ SNPLMA

Enacted in 1998, the Southern Nevada Public Lands Management Act (SNPLMA) directs funds from the sale of public lands around Las Vegas to be used for a variety of government projects, chiefly in Clark County, including: water treatment, city parks, trail maintenance, land acquisitions to protect species of conservation concern, and capital improvements, such as government offices, schools, fire stations, and campground renovations.

The act has opponents who argue that it promotes urban sprawl and decreases the buffer between Las Vegas and places like Red Rock while not appropriately directing funds, such as the BLM's refusal to acquire private land atop Blue Diamond Hill. However, it has provided substantial funding for improvements at Red Rock Canyon, including restoration and boardwalk construction at Red Spring, improved campground facilities, the Late Night Parking Area, acquisition of private land holdings in Calico Basin, and partial funding for the new visitor center, which was completed in 2010.

## ▶ Homes on the Hill

In March 2003, Jim Rhodes purchased some 2500 acres atop Blue Diamond Hill—once the site of the Blue Diamond Gypsum Mine—with the intention of constructing a high-density residential development. Rhodes, however, was not the first to propose developing the hill. Less than one year prior, plans were drawn up for 8400 homes by John Laing Homes.

John Laing Homes' proposal of roughly 21,000 people, nearly 1.5 times the population of Boulder City, living atop the hill sparked a passionate outcry from citizens and legislation on the county and state levels to lock in the rural zoning, which would prevent such high-density development. Despite a public relations campaign by Rhodes, the state legislation to freeze the rural zoning, authored by Dina Titus, was signed into law in May of 2003.

U.S. Senators Harry Reid and John Ensign wanted the land out of private hands and suggested that the county purchase it using SNPLMA funds, an option that failed due to the cost of transforming the mine-shaft-riddled property from a liability to a public place.

In 2009, after years of legal battle, Rhodes got a federal judge to overturn the State's rural zoning freeze. He then put pressure on the county to approve his preliminary building plan, which they did in 2011. The plan has a number of contingencies, and the fate of Blue Diamond Hill remains uncertain.

## What's in a Name? - Red Rock Canyon Place Names

**Black Velvet Canyon:** A term used by rock climbers in the 1970s to describe a wall in the canyon. It refers to the quality of the rock, luxurious like velvet, and the intoxicating effects of the wall, like Black Velvet Whiskey.

**Calico Basin/Hills:** Named for resemblance of the colorful patterns in the rocks to calico-patterned fabric.

**Cottonwood Valley:** A 19th and early 20th century term describing the valley east of the Red Rock Escarpment. Today, only the southern portion to Cottonwood Pass is so named. It comes from the prevalence of Frémont cottonwoods in the area.

**First Creek:** The first year-round water source encountered when heading north from Sandstone Ranch, today's Spring Mountain Ranch.

**Ice Box Canyon:** Modern term referring to the generally cooler temperatures in the canyon.

**Kraft Mountain:** After Ozzie Kraft, a Vegas swimming pool builder in the 1950s, who owned a place below the mountain that was later demolished.

**La Madre Mountain:** Presumably after the La Madre Mine described on page 43.

**Mount Wilson:** After James B. Wilson, who established a ranch southeast of the mountain.

**Turtlehead Peak:** Modern term referring to the mountain's resemblance to the head of a turtle.

# Movies
### filemd at Red Rock Canyon

The gorgeous scenery of Red Rock Canyon has been showcased in numerous commercials, TV shows, music videos, and full-length films.

Whether it be Deepak Chopra filming *How to Know God*, an adventure-race reality TV show, scenes from an episode of *The Sopranos*, various car commercials, or a promo for Criss Angel's *Believe* show (during the filming of which the modern-day illusionist failed to use his magic before receiving a black eye from a 2000-pound Brahman bull), Red Rock Canyon has been featured in a wide array of film and video productions.

Described below are the full-length movies that have been filmed at Red Rock Canyon, Spring Mountain Ranch State Park, and Bonnie Springs.

**3000 Miles to Graceland** (*Action, February 2001*). A gang of ex-convicts (Kevin Costner, Kurt Russell, and others) use an Elvis convention as guise for a Las Vegas casino robbery. The ensuing police chase and inter-gang strife lead to plenty of gun fights, explosions, helicopters, and mayhem. Before the heist, the gang rides along SR-159 and pulls over

*Sonny Steele (Robert Redford) performs some on-the-fly animal husbandry with a top racehorse at the Sandstone Quarry in **The Electric Horseman**.*

east of Mount Wilson.

**The Aliens are Coming** (*Science Fiction TV Movie, March 1980*). Aliens plan to take over the Hoover Dam while Dr. Scott Dryden (Tom Mason), a sweet talking scientist, tries to track them down. At Red Rock, Dryden flies in a helicopter near Willow Springs in search of a UFO and finds evidence of a landing near the visitor center.

**Anywhere But Here** (*Drama, November 1999*). Adele (Susan Sarandon), a grandiose dreamer, and her reserved daughter (Natalie Portman) drive to Los Angeles in search of something more than their mundane, Midwestern lives but find that living with each other is a challenge in itself. En route to California, the duo have a quarrel on SR-159 and pull over east of Calico Basin.

**Bells of San Angelo** (*Western, May 1947*). Set near the Mexican border, Roy Rogers (himself), teams up with the local sheriff and the beautiful Lee Madison (Dale Evans) to get to the bottom of some peculiar business practices at a silver mine. Filmed extensively along what has become SR-159, in the Calico Hills, and at Spring Mountain Ranch, which was then being leased by Chet Lauck.

**Domino** (*Action/Drama, October 2005*). A bored Beverly Hills girl (Keira Knightley) enters the chaotic world of professional bounty hunting under the tutelage of Ed Moseby (Mickey Rourke). She learns the ropes and unknowingly becomes involved in a sensational plot that quickly escalates out of control. Scenes were filmed at Bonnie Springs and along SR-159.

**The Electric Horseman** (*Drama, December 1979*). Former rodeo champion Sonny Steele (Robert

*Gonzo journalist Raoul Duke (Johnny Depp) has a bizarre encounter with a cop at the High Point Overlook on the Scenic Drive in **Fear and Loathing in Las Vegas**.*

Redford) is now wearing a suit of lights to sell a corporation's breakfast cereal. Jaded, he makes off with a $12-million-dollar horse that the corporation mistreated. Eager to get the scoop on his plans, a clever reporter (Jane Fonda) is on his trail, along with the police. After stealing the horse, Steele begins to nurse him back to health at the Sandstone Quarry.

**Fear and Loathing in Las Vegas** (*Drama, May 1998*). Spurred by taking a barrage of illicit drugs, Raoul Duke (Johnny Depp) and Dr. Gonzo (Benicio Del Toro) journey to Las Vegas to probe the limits of their minds for an understanding of American culture circa 1971. Duke eludes a cop along SR-159 and finally pulls over at the High Point Overlook on the Scenic Drive.

**The Gauntlet** (*Drama, December 1977*). Ben Shockley (Clint Eastwood) is a past-his-prime cop assigned to escort a 'nothing witness' from Las Vegas to a 'nothing trial' in Phoenix. He quickly discovers that the witness, Gus Mally (Sondra Locke), is a sharp hooker who everybody—including the Vegas mob bosses—is trying to kill. Many scenes were filmed at Red Rock Canyon, which serves as the Arizona border. On the run, the pair stop to make a call at the Village Market in Blue Diamond. Later, in a moment of movie magic, Shokley and Mally head towards Oak Creek Canyon and end up in the Valley of Fire.

**Get Him to the Greek** (*Comedy, June 2010*). Aaron Green (Jonah Hill), a record-company intern, is given 72 hours to accompany rock star Aldous Snow (Russell Brand) from London to Los Angeles for a comeback concert. The prudish Green must negotiate an anything-goes atmosphere of hedonism to deliver Snow and keep his job. As the duo leave Las Vegas for LA, a scene takes place along SR-159.

**Girls' Night** (*Drama, June 1998*). In this somber story of life and death, two middle-aged friends, played by Brenda Blethyn and Julie Walters, head to Las Vegas to let loose amid bad news and good. While in Vegas, the women get a personal horseback tour of Red Rock Canyon from Cody (Kris Kristofferson), a cowboy who shows them the Calico Hills near the Sandstone Quarry and below Calico II.

**High Roller: The Stu Ungar Story** (*Drama/Biography, May 2003*). Stu Ungar (Michael Imperioli) tells the story of his life to a stranger in his room: playing high-stakes gin rummy at 14, escaping the mob at 20, winning big-money poker tournaments in the early 80s, living the Vegas lifestyle with its hookers and cocaine, and losing

*Lucky (Stella Stevens) discusses plans for a casino robbery at Old Nevada in Bonnie Springs during the opening scenes of **Las Vegas Lady**.*

his family and money. A few scenes were filmed at the Red Rock Overlook.

**Las Vegas Lady** (*Drama, June 1975*). Under the direction of a mysterious character, a trio of girlfriends, led by Lucky (Stella Stevens), plan to steal half a million dollars from Circus Circus. As the complex plan unfolds, troubles arise and threaten the girls' lives. The opening and finale of the movie were filmed at Old Nevada in Bonnie Springs.

**Megaforce** (*Action, July 1982*). Under the premise of preserving freedom and justice, a phantom army of super-elite fighting men, led by Ace Hunter (Barry Bostwick), uses high-budget toys to battle it out with the forces of tyranny and evil. The opening scenes were filmed at Sandstone Quarry, east of Brownstone Canyon, and along the road to the White Rock Trailhead.

*Despite a 20-million dollar budget, the 1982 action film **Megaforce** was a box-office blunder. In it, the good guys have a secret underground base somewhere near Sandstone Quarry.*

**The Mexican** (*Action/Romance, March 2001*). Jerry Welbach (Brad Pitt) heads south of the border alone, after a fight with his girlfriend, Samantha Barzel (Julia Roberts), to recover an antique pistol for his mob boss. The process of getting the gun back to America quickly escalates into a gripping foray for both Welbach and Barzel. James Gandolfini, who plays a mob hit man, kidnaps Barzel and they drive through Red Rock Canyon along SR-160 and SR-159.

**Mission: Africa (aka Commando Squad)** (*Action, 1968*). Five American soldiers undertake a cross-country mission to destroy a secret German outpost that is developing a super-explosive for use in WWII. A battle sequence was filmed at Red Spring and features footage of the ruins of Ella M. Mason's homestead.

**Next** (*Action, April 2007*). The FBI needs the help of Cris Johnson (Nicolas Cage), a man with the ability to see a few minutes into the future, to stop a criminal group intent on blowing up Los Angeles. Reluctant to help, he is tailed in action-packed pursuit by the FBI and the criminals as the chance to save LA hangs in the balance. There is a brief scene that was filmed along SR-159 with the Calico Hills in the background.

**Over the Top** (*Action/Drama, February 1987*). At the request of his dying wife, Lincoln Hawk (Sylvester Stallone) reconnects with his son after a 10-year absence. The mature boy must decide If he will live in the rough-and-tough world of his father—long haul trucking and arm wrestling—or in the high-and-mighty domain of his grandfather. Hawk enters Nevada along SR-159 through Red Rock Canyon driving his aging truck, and in the final scene leaves along the same road.

**Play it to the Bone** (*Drama, January 2000*). Longtime friends Vince Boudreau (Woody Harrelson) and Cesar Dominguez (Antonio Banderas) are worn-out middleweight boxers who travel to Las Vegas for a fight that could restart one of their careers. With their friendship, love lives, and well-being at stake, they duke it out in a climactic

*Tom Cruise and Dustin Hoffman stop in the village of Blue Diamond to do their laundry in the 1988, Academy Award winning **Rain Man**.*

fight. The final scene was filmed along SR-159, east of the Red Rock Escarpment.

**Race to Witch Mountain** (*Action/Family, March 2009*). A Las Vegas cabbie, Jack Bruno (Dwayne Johnson), picks up two human-looking aliens who are being chased by an evil alien and the federal government. To assist the unassuming aliens, Bruno must help them return to their spacecraft. A brief scene was filmed along SR-159.

**Rain Man** (*Drama, December 1988*). Charlie Babbitt, a slick car dealer played by Tom Cruise, discovers he has an autistic brother, Raymond (Dustin Hoffman), who has inherited their father's fortune. Despite pressing business, Charlie embarks on a cross-country road trip, trying to understand his brother and tap into the inheritance. En route to LA, the Babbitt brothers make a stop for laundry in Blue Diamond, then cruise down SR-159 near Mount Wilson.

**Rat Race** (*Comedy, August 2001*). An eccentric casino owner (John Cleese) gives six guests the chance to win $2 million in a race from Las Vegas to New Mexico. Along the way, each of the contestants runs into an array of outlandish difficulties. There are a couple of brief scenes of a mini-van driving on SR-159 through Red Rock.

**The Road Killers** (*Action, May 1994*). A family road trip to San Diego takes a turn for the worse when a band of irreverent delinquents intent on gratuitous terrorizing and killing are encountered. Scenes were filmed immediately east of Mount Wilson, where the band holes up in a run-down house; and along SR-159, east of the Red Rock Escarpment and near Calico Basin.

**The Stalking Moon** (*Western, December 1968*). Abducted by Apaches, a white woman (Eva Saint Marie) and her half-Apache son are recovered by the U.S. Army. Looking for a peaceful retirement, Sam Varner (Gregory Peck) must decide if he will protect them from a fierce Apache, Salvaje, the boy's father or let them fend for themselves. Filmed extensively in Pine Creek Canyon.

*American soldiers fight off a German attack at Red Spring in **Mission: Africa**.*

# Wildfire
### *at Red Rock Canyon*

Frequent and extensive wildfires in the Mojave Desert is a new phenomenon that threatens to transform some plant communities into grasslands.

### ► Past Conditions
In the past, at Red Rock Canyon and throughout the Mojave Desert, wildfires were small and infrequent. Chance lightning strikes caused wildfires, but they did not spread very far because of the large spaces between shrubs and trees.

*Many native plants and animals are poorly adapted to survive the increasing frequency and intensity of wildfires fueled by invasive grasses at Red Rock Canyon.*

### ► Current Conditions
Nonnative grasses, such as red brome (see page 134), are thriving in many habitats and becoming the dominant vegetation in some plant communities. These grasses fill in the spaces between larger, shrubby plants and provide fuel for wildfires to spread.

Today, when a wildfire catches, it typically burns hundreds, sometimes thousands of acres instead of only a few. After wildfires, nonnative grasses out-compete native plants for water, soil nutrients, and sunlight, leaving the landscape more like a grassland, which exacerbates the problem.

Additionally, despite the hard work of fire crews, accidents and careless acts do happen. The human presence is causing about half of the wildfires in the Mojave Desert today.

### ► What Can We Do?
The BLM has undertaken efforts to inhibit the spread of invasive grasses. They also aid native vegetation rehabilitation in burned areas through seed-drops and the planting of native shrubs.

Visitors can help by following the guidelines below:
• Stay on the designated roads and trails. Seeds of invasive grasses and weeds can 'catch a ride' on shoes, socks, and car tires. Staying on trails allows the BLM to monitor invasive grasses and weeds and apply treatment to protect the native vegetation.
• Stay out of burned areas. The soil is extremely fragile after a fire has occurred. The roots of the vegetation have lost their integrity, and hillsides are more susceptible to erosion. The desert crust that helps reduce erosion will slowly recover unless it is broken by foot or vehicle traffic.

## Recent Fires Impacting the Conservation Area

| Name | Location | Cause | Date | Acres Burned |
|------|----------|-------|------|--------------|
| Rainbow Fire | North side of Pine Creek Canyon | Lightning | June 2005 | 150 |
| Goodsprings Fire | E. of Mt. Potosi, N. of Goodsprings | Lightning | June 2005 | 31,600 |
| Loop Fire | Northern segment, Scenic Drive | Lightning | July 2005 | 920 |
| First Creek Fire | First Creek Canyon Trail, near SR-159 | Lightning | June 2006 | 50 |
| Picnic Fire | East side of Lovell Canyon | Lightning | July 2006 | 1200 |
| Scenic Fire | Southern segment, Scenic Drive | Lightning | Sept. 2006 | 900 |
| Bonnie Springs Fire | South of the Red Rock Overlook | Lightning | July 2007 | 390 |

# Springs
## *at Red Rock Canyon*

With some 53 springs, Red Rock Canyon is a relatively lush oasis that draws plants, animals, and humans.

### ► Why So Many Springs?

One of the special aspects of Red Rock and the Spring Mountains is an abundance of springs, which allow a wide variety of riparian plants and animals to flourish. The reason for this profusion of water is twofold: the geology of the area and the relatively large amount of precipitation the Spring Mountains receive.

The line of springs found along the base of the Red Rock Escarpment (see map, inside back cover) is caused by a layer of impermeable, tight-grained siltstone of the Chinle Formation that directs groundwater to the surface. Other springs, such as La Madre Spring and Rainbow Spring, are known as hanging aquifers. These are similarly caused by areas of impermeable rock, typically lenses of dense shale and carbonate rock.

### ► Plants and Animals

Springs allow special ecological environments to flourish. Many plant species that are rare in the Mojave Desert can be found near the springs at Red Rock. Springs also draw wildlife: bighorn sheep hardly ever venture more than two miles from a water source. Some species, such as Northern Pacific tree frogs and red-spotted toads, spend their entire lives in and around certain springs.

### ► Historical Significance

In addition to giving water to sustain life, the Southern Paiute believe that springs hold powerful concentrations of a spiritual life force called *puha* (see page 35). When Euro-Americans began to travel through Red Rock Canyon, the Southern Paiutes were forced to abandon many well-traveled springs and retreat into the mountains.

One of the first springs to be utilized by Euro-Americans was Cottonwood Spring, located at present-day Blue Diamond. The spring was an important stop along a route of the Old Spanish Trail in the 1840s and later, the Mormon Road (see page 40). The profuse springs at present-day Spring Mountain Ranch, which still put forth a tremendous amount of water and support a man-made lake, allowed James B. Wilson to establish the first Euro-American settlement at Red Rock Canyon in 1876.

*Tucked against the Calico Hills, Ash Creek Spring supports numerous riparian plants.*

In the early 20th century, ranching took hold at Red Rock despite the sparse and meager forage. Some springs, such as Red Spring and Mormon Green Spring, were privately developed for small-scale ranch operations. Others, such as Willow Spring and White Rock Spring, were developed to water cattle by the Civilian Conservation Corps in the early 1940s (see page 47).

### ► Some Special Springs to Visit

Red Spring and Willow Springs (see pages 161 and 174) are great spots to experience springs at Red Rock. Both have a rich history including Native American rock art and ranching developments. They also host unique plants and animals.

For a more tranquil setting, consider visiting First Creek Spring (see photo, page 67). Nestled amid Shinarump Conglomerate and velvet ash trees, the spring attracts numerous bird species and occasionally has a small waterfall. The hike to the spring is described on page 186.

# Plant Communities
*at Red Rock Canyon*

Certain species of plants and animals are found only in particular plant communities. Understanding these communities makes it easier to locate various species at Red Rock.

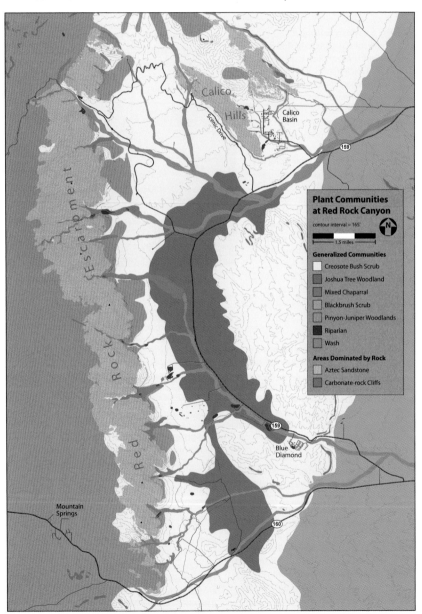

# Creosote Bush Scrub

This community typically is found below 4,000' and covers the bulk of southern Nevada. Soils are generally gravelly and occasionally rocky. The dominant shrub, **creosote bush**, usually is accompanied by **white bursage**. Creosote bushes are well spaced, with bare ground between them, due partly to chemicals secreted by their roots that deter other plants from growing. They have their own insect fauna, some of which are camouflaged to look like parts of the plant.

Cacti and yucca species are present in this community, but occur more sporadically than in the blackbrush scrub. The sugar-rich fruits of all cactus species are an important food source for **desert cottontails, white-tailed antelope squirrels, deer mice, kangaroo rats**, and many bird species. While deer mice and kangaroo rats are nocturnal, only the latter are highly adapted to the arid environment. Small-mammal populations fluctuate depending on food resources, such as profuse spring blooms.

In winters of abundant and regular precipitation, spring blooms are spectacular. Notable flowers include the vibrant yellow **desert marigold,** deep red **desert paintbrush**, lavender **desert larkspur**, and the delicate, white flowers of **California evening primrose**, which is found in sandy soils.

**Catclaw**, a thorny tree, appears where rocky areas concentrate runoff. Its branches are favored perches for a wide array of songbirds, such as **black-throated sparrows** and **gnatcatchers**. **Phainopeplas** arrive in the spring to feed on the berries of **mistletoes**, which draw their water and nutrients from catclaws.

In disturbed areas, invasive grasses, such as **red brome**, choke out the diverse native species and provide less nutritious fodder for herbivores like the **desert tortoise** and many mammals. Because these dry grasses carry fires to areas that rarely burned in the past, they threaten to change this plant community into an open grassland (see page 60).

### • At Red Rock Canyon
Look for this plant community in and around Calico Basin where it mixes with the blackbrush scrub, at the Red Rock Campground, and along SR-160 near its junction with SR-159.

*Most areas of creosote bush scrub at Red Rock Canyon are not as sparsely vegetated as the rest of the Mojave Desert. Here, east of the Calico Hills, creosote bush is accompanied by white bursage and Nevada jointfir.*

## ▶ Joshua Tree Woodland

In southern Nevada, this community is restricted to upland alluvial fan areas between 2,000' and 4,500'. The woodlands receive 6" to 15" of rain annually and are seldom 'woody' in the sense of an eastern forest. Instead, widely-spaced Joshua trees, up to 30' tall, are surrounded by an understory of **blackbrush**, **winterfat**, **spiny menodora**, **Apache plume**, **paper bag bush**, **buckwheat**, **Mojave yucca,** and **banana yucca**. Cacti can be common in this plant community, especially **pencil cholla,** **buckhorn cholla**, **silver cholla**, and **beavertail cactus**, which is a favorite of the **desert tortoise**.

### • At Red Rock Canyon
A nice stand of Joshua trees exists along SR-159 between the Red Rock Canyon Visitor Center and the village of Blue Diamond. There is also a healthy woodland north of SR-160, east of the Red Rock Escarpment, where mountain bike trails bob and weave around the beautiful trees.

*Stands of Joshua trees delight visitors and provide opportunities for perch-hunting birds, as well as woodpeckers, which probe the trees for grubs.*

## ▶ Mixed Chaparral

This community is characterized by dense, nearly impenetrable thickets of a variety of shrubs, including **scrub oak**, **manzanita**, **silktassel bush**, and **yerba santa**. The least friendly of the bunch, scrub oak has stiff branches protruding in all directions and holly-like leaves that are tipped with spines. In contrast, the branches of manzanita have an exquisite red exterior that is smooth to the touch.

With greater than 80% shrub cover, considerable leaf litter and dead plant material, this is a favored habitat of **spotted towhees** and **Gambel's quail**. When shrub density decreases, small cacti, such as **plains pricklypear** appear.

**Bobcats** make their dens at the mouths of the canyons of Red Rock and spend time hunting for small mammals in this community. Although **bighorn sheep** don't venture far from rocky, craggy terrain, they forage on the shrubs found here.

### • At Red Rock Canyon
This community can be found along the drainages inside each canyon in the Red Rock Escarpment. The Calico Hills feature spots of mixed chaparral hidden in well-watered, gravelly areas among the colorful sandstone formations.

*Great havens for wildlife, mixed chaparral is characterized by dense thickets of shrubs that grow along canyon washes.*

# ► Blackbrush Scrub

This community thrives in steep or rolling hills between 4,000' and 6,000'. Soils are generally rocky or gravelly and shallow (2" to 20"). Plant density is dependent on precipitation. With sufficient watering, some areas support plants growing adjacent to one another.

A rich variety of plant life can be found in this community, from succulent cacti and spring flowers to woody shrubs, such as **blackbrush**, which comes to life during rain showers. While blackbrush typically is the predominant shrub, in certain areas **spiny menodora** is more common, and **Mojave yucca** may be the most conspicuous plant with its head of large spear-shaped leaves.

At higher elevations, Mojave yuccas live alongside the lighter-green **banana yuccas**. In rocky areas, **Utah agave** form beautiful rosettes of short, toothed leaves. Cacti include: **strawberry hedgehog, California barrel cactus, desert spinystar,** and **buckhorn cholla**. The latter forms a spine-covered fruit that is transported by animals that are poked by the spines. · The **desert woodrat** uses these spine clusters to protect its nest from snakes, such as the **red racer** and **Southwestern speckled rattlesnake**, and from carnivorous mammals such as the **coyote, gray fox**, and **kit fox**. **Cactus wrens** also use the spines of the **buckhorn cholla** to impede predators by constructing their nests in the cactus.

Because this plant community covers most of Red Rock Canyon, many of the plant species described in the following pages are found here. Flowers in this community are a diverse group and include: white-flowering **buckwheat**, square-stemmed, purple-flowering **chia**, succulent **desert four o'clock** with its purple trumpet-shaped flowers, deep red **desert paintbrush**, invasive **filaree**, rash-causing **notch-leaf phacelia**, early blooming **Frémont's phacelia**, elegant **desert larkspur**, and **winding mariposa lily**, which is unable to hold itself up and favors the branches of the blackbrush for support. A number of flowers do well in burned and disturbed areas, notably yellow **desert marigold**, **wild rhubarb**, prolific orange-flowered **desert globemallow**, and uniquely-shaped **desert trumpet**.

Shrubs such as **Mojave sage**, **range ratany, indigo bush, cliffrose, Mormon**

*A nearly pure stand of blackbrush grows east of Mount Wilson. During the day, cottontails and jackrabbits are commonly seen. At night, lesser nighthawks and kangaroo rats can be found.*

**tea, yerba santa**, and **desert almond** provide cover for **black-tailed jackrabbits, desert cottontails, deer mice,** and the conspicuous **white-tailed antelope squirrel**. Male **desert tarantulas** also benefit from the shrub cover in the fall when looking for mates.

During winter, when succulent material is hard to find, **bighorn sheep** and **mule deer**, who typically inhabit higher communities, favor **blackbrush** for foraging.

## • At Red Rock Canyon

This community is prevalent at Red Rock and found throughout the conservation area, from the northern reaches of the La Madre Mountains, in and around the Calico Hills, and along the Red Rock Escarpment south to Mount Potosi.

## ► Pinyon-Juniper Woodland

These open, forested woodlands are found between 5,500' and 7,500' in areas that receive 12" to 20" of precipitation annually. Soils tend to be sandy or loamy and vary in depth.

Pinyon pine and Utah juniper are relatively short (less than 25') trees. The blue, robin-sized **pinyon jays** and **Western scrub jays** cache the seeds of the **pinyon pine** for use throughout the year. Although they remember most of their caches, the ones they forget may sprout to form the next generation of trees. **Utah juniper** can be recognized by its scale-like, yellow-green leaves and fragrant blue-green fruit produced in the spring. Fruit-eating birds, such as the **Western bluebird** and **Townsend's solitaire**, consume the juniper berries and carry the seeds to new areas.

When tree density is low, understory forms of **big sagebrush**, **yerba santa**, and **needle grass**. Notable flowers include **Utah penstemon**, **bluedicks**, **desert princesplume**, and **milkvetch**. Cacti include the red-flowering **Mojave kingcup cactus**, and, occasionally, **Plains** and **pancake pricklypears**.

The **black-tailed jackrabbit** is better suited to the cooler environment of this community, and is more often seen than the **desert cottontail**. **Mule deer** use the cover provided by this woodland and forage on the trees and understory. **Bighorn sheep** range here, but never far from craggy terrain. Other mammals, such as **ringtails** and **bobcats**, are rarely seen. Cliffs in this community are home to **peregrine falcons** that prey on colonies of **white-throated swifts**.

### • At Red Rock Canyon

This community is often found on the north-facing hillsides where the density of trees is typically low. Willow Springs, and along the Rocky Gap Road are great places to visit pinyon-juniper woodlands.

*The pinyon-juniper woodland found west of the White Rock Hills is nearly a forest by Red Rock Canyon standards.*

## ► Riparian and Wash

These two communities are found throughout Red Rock Canyon near springs and along drainages.

While riparian areas have a source of water throughout the entire year, wash communities are subject to seasonal flooding. More than 80% of desert animals use riparian areas, and some seldom venture far from the lush surroundings. Most **bats** are drawn to riparian communities for water, as well as for invertebrate prey. The most common amphibian in southern Nevada, the **red-spotted toad**, is frequently seen near springs along the Red Rock Escarpment. **Frémont cottonwoods**, which can reach 90' tall, grow only where the water table is near the surface. Other riparian trees include **velvet ash** and **singleleaf ash**.

Flowering trees and shrubs, such as **catclaw**, **California redbud**, **desert willow**, and **honey mesquite**, typically are found along dry wash beds where flooding helps to decompose their seed pods and spread their seeds. **Mistletoe**, a parasitic plant found predominantly on catclaw and mesquite trees, draws all its water from the host plant. Mistletoe berries make up nearly the entire diet of the red-eyed **phainopepla**.

### • At Red Rock Canyon

There are some 53 springs and numerous washes at Red Rock where unique species thrive and desert dwellers come for water. Some springs, such as in Willow Springs, are host to endemic species of snails found nowhere else in the world. Others, such as La Madre Spring, Ash Creek Spring, Red Spring, and Calico Spring, are lush oases where plants, such as **common reed**, **watercress**, **cattail**, **ferns** and **algae**, can be found. The soil near Red Spring is slightly alkaline, which the rare **alkali mariposa lily** favors. This flower grows only in a few arid locations in southern Nevada and California.

Pine Creek Canyon and Spring Mountain Ranch, popular with visitors, are riparian areas that support a diverse array of wildlife uncommon elsewhere at Red Rock. These areas are good for bird watching and hundreds of species have been recorded. Pine Creek also provides habitat for **Northern Pacific treefrogs** that feed on invertebrates caught with their long, sticky tongues.

By far, the largest assemblage of wetland species at Red Rock exists at Spring Mountain Ranch, where the man-made Lake Harriet draws **mallards**, **American coots**, numerous **owls**, **egrets**, **badgers**, and **skunks**. The lake is home to the only

*Frémont cottonwoods tap into the water table below a dry wash.*

fish at Red Rock: the endangered **Pahrump poolfish**. A small (2" to 3"), guppy-like fish, it was introduced to the lake in 1983 after destruction of its habitat in the Pahrump Valley.

Naturally occurring water tanks also host species uncommonly seen in the Mojave Desert, such as **fairy**, **tadpole**, and **clam shrimp**. One of the largest tanks in southern Nevada is along a popular hiking trail, aptly named the Calico Tanks Trail, described on page 166.

When visiting Red Rock, even if only for an afternoon, a riparian area, such as Red Spring or Willow Springs, is a definite must-see.

*Bird's foot ferns grow in water-saturated rock and soil as velvet ash trees lose their leaves in preparation for winter at First Creek Spring.*

# Mammals
### *of Red Rock Canyon*

All mammals at Red Rock Canyon are physiologically and behaviorally adapted to cope with the intense summer heat, freezing winter temperatures, and general lack of water. Most tend to be nocturnal, avoiding much of the direct heat, and are less-often seen than sun-dwelling desert denizens.

Described here are the most conspicuous and dramatic species one is likely to encounter. Additional resources are listed on page 198.

## Mule Deer..........................................................*Odocoileus hemionus*

These are the only deer in southern Nevada. Bucks have branching antlers that are shed each winter and are regrown before the fall rut. While growing, the antlers are covered with velvet that dries up and is rubbed off when mature. Both sexes have black-tipped tails, cause for their other common name: black-tailed deer.

Mule deer mostly inhabit forested or wooded areas and forage on a variety of plant material, preferring the new growth that is less fibrous and more nutritious. Acorns are a favored food in the fall when deer put fat on for winter.

*A buck mule deer en route to White Rock Spring on an early spring morning. Bucks shed and regrow their antlers each year. Antler size is a rough estimate of age and health.*

They are seasonally migratory, occupying low elevations during the winter and higher elevations during the summer.

Rut occurs in the fall, and males form hierarchies with dominant bucks guarding fertile does. After breeding, bucks take no part in the care of fawns. One or two are born in early summer and lose their spots after four months.

Mule deer are sometimes seen in the winter; even then, they are less commonly seen than bighorn sheep. Spring Mountain Ranch, especially around dawn and dusk, offers the best opportunity to see these creatures. The higher elevations of the Spring Mountains, especially near Mount Charleston, support a larger population than Red Rock Canyon.

## Bighorn Sheep........................................................*Ovis canadensis*

Magnificent and admired, bighorn sheep play a leading role in the image many people have of the region. In fact, they are the state animal of Nevada.

Their preferred habitat is rocky, craggy terrain in which they maneuver with amazing ease. Their specialized hooves serve the animals well as they leap, drop, and climb up cliffs and over rocks. In fact, sheep can land drops of more than 20'. This craggy habitat reduces predation by coyotes and mountain lions, although golden eagles still pose a threat to young lambs.

For most of the year, ewes and their young roam separately from adult males, foraging on various plants. Bighorn sheep are exclusively herbivores: they eat scrub oak, a large variety of spring-flowering plants, yucca fruit, and the flesh of barrel cactus. In addition to the water gained from forage material, sheep drink large amounts of water and are rarely found more than two miles from a water source.

Bighorn sheep migrate from low elevations in the winter to higher elevations in the summer. Prior to breeding, which occurs in late summer and early fall, rams make ritualized displays and engage in posturing to determine the strongest members. It is during this time that they rear up on their hind legs, charge at each other and clash horns. The horns are made of a material similar to human fingernails, which grows outward around a bone protruding from the skull. The horns are not shed and continue growing for the life of the animal. At full maturity, rams have horns that curl around and may form a full circle when viewed from the side (see photo, back cover). Ewes have horns that are slimmer and straighter, but still curve.

Multiple rams are known to mate with one ewe, but ewes mostly mate with the dominant rams. Gestation lasts about six months, with birth usually occurring in the spring.

Most bighorn sheep become mature at two-and-a-half years of age. In the desert, males weigh about 160 to 200 pounds, while females weigh 110 to 150 pounds. The average lifespan of a bighorn sheep is about 11 years.

*Right:* A group of ewes and young ascend a craggy band of Chinle Sandstone in Pine Creek Canyon.

### Local Tip: Seeing a Bighorn Sheep

At Red Rock, bighorn sheep are a fairly common sight if you know where to look. Sheep habituated to humans often approach roads and built-up areas: look for them where crags and rocky outcrops are near water, such as near Willow Springs. When cold weather moves in, sheep typically descend to lower elevations and forage on sunny hillsides, making them more visible.

## Feral Burro ........................................................................*Equus asinus*

Slightly smaller than horses, burros have large ears and black stripes on their shoulders. The hair on their hides is black, gray, or brown in color.

Native to Africa, they were first brought to the Americas by the Spanish in the late 1400s as work animals and to breed with horses to form mules. In the early

1800s, traders on the Old Spanish Trail used burros as pack animals and drove them through southern Nevada. Later in the 1800s, miners used burros to transport equipment and ore. From escape, abandonment, and release, these and later burros became feral.

Well-adapted to the climate, burros have prospered at Red Rock Canyon and present numerous problems for the native ecosystem. Their foraging patterns displace mule deer and bighorn sheep, cause erosion, and are particularly harmful to biological soil crusts (see page 135). Further, burros help spread the invasive and prolific red brome grass, a major factor in the propagation of wildfires.

Despite their faults, burros are popular with visitors to the conservation area and are often seen near roads and built-up areas, such as the village of Blue Diamond. See page 12 for tips on viewing burros.

## Feral Horse ...................................................................*Equus caballus*

Like the burros, the first feral horses descended from horses brought to the Americas by the Spanish in the 1500s. Horses belonging to explorers, traders, and settlers escaped in the 1800s and added new genes to the feral population.

However, most of the horses roaming today trace their ancestry to horses released or abandoned in the 1900s by ranchers.

Feral horses usually travel and congregate in small bands of five to eight animals, but groups can be as large as 35. Each band has a dominant mare that leads the herd to forage and water.

During the day, horses graze roughly 80% of the time; at night they split their time 50/50 between grazing and resting. In addition to communication through facial expressions, a number of vocalizations are used for danger, distress, courtship, and aggression.

In the conservation area, feral horses are sometimes found south of SR-160 in Cottonwood Valley and on the east flanks of Mount Charleston.

# Management of Horses and Burros

*While often criticized, the BLM works within the law to maintain herd populations at environmentally sustainable levels.*

After the early and mid 19th century, when ranchers, hunters, and 'mustangers' had aggressively thinned the stocks of feral horses, the U.S. Congress passed the *Wild Free-Roaming Horses and Burros Act of 1971* in an effort to protect, manage, and control feral horses and burros. The act declared that these animals are "living symbols of the historic and pioneer spirit of the West" while recognizing that impacts from these animals overtax vegetation and negatively affect native species such as bighorn sheep and mule deer.

The legislation authorizes the Bureau of Land Management (BLM), in partnership with the U.S. Forest Service, to conduct population surveys and environmental assessments to determine the number of feral horses and burros that each area can sustain while ensuring a thriving, natural, ecological balance.

The area of Red Rock Canyon south of the La Madre Mountains, including much of Mount Potosi and the Cottonwood Valley, can support as many as 27 horses and 49 burros. A population survey, performed during the spring of 2011, estimated 58 horses and 65 burros in this area. The excess animals are a strain on the ecosystem, especially considering that feral horse populations often grow at rates of 18% to 25% per year because they are not kept in check by natural predators.

The primary means of removing excess animals has been periodic 'gathers.' In the early 1970s, gathers were performed using saddled horses to round up the unshod feral animals into traps, putting considerable stress on them. Since the mid 1970s, helicopters have been used extensively and are touted as a humane method that allows the horses to be chased at a speed that does not overtax them. Once captured, animals that are five years of age or younger are offered for public adoption; older animals are offered for sale to good homes. Animals that are not adopted or sold are maintained in long-term pasture facilities for the remainder of their natural lives.

Outside of the Spring Mountains, the BLM has come under criticism for the methods they use to capture, hold, and offer the animals for adoption and sale. Wild-horse and burro advocates suggest that adoption is not keeping pace with the number of animals gathered, resulting in increased holding costs and concern that animals may end up in a slaughterhouse, an assertion that the BLM adamantly denies. The animal advocates also assert that the helicopter gather techniques are too stressful for the animals, as evidenced by a gather in northern Nevada where of the some 2400 horses gathered, 34 died due to the roundup or were euthanized due to pre-existing conditions. While many organizations, such as The Wildlife Society, Sierra Club, and Friends of Nevada Wilderness support the BLM and their purpose in curtailing feral horse and burro populations, animal advocates continue to speak out against BLM actions, evoking emotional, romantic notions of the Wild West and the free-running mustang.

# Coyote ................................................................................*Canis latrans*

Coyotes at Red Rock are pale reddish-brown to gray, roughly 3½' long head to tail, and live about seven years. They are remarkably adaptable and intelligent.

Their diet consists primarily of small mammals, carrion, seeds, and berries; leafy plant material is also consumed occasionally. It is uncommon for coyotes to take down live mule deer or bighorn sheep. Such large-scale hunting is done in packs that form when environmental considerations, like plentiful food resources, are favorable, which is not the case at Red Rock where coyotes travel alone or paired.

They are seasonally monogamous. Mating occurs in early spring. Each female delivers, on average, six pups that suckle from her in their den.

Coyotes communicate in a number of ways, including urine marking, touch, facial and body language, and through growls, whines, yips, barks, and howls. Often heard after sundown, the quintessential howl is thought to announce location, establish territory, or to express joy.

# Gray Fox ............................................................*Urocyon cinereoargenteus*

The secretive gray fox is sometimes seen trotting across shrub-filled slopes and rocky hillsides near pinyon-juniper woodlands. Roughly the size of a small dog, they can be identified by their bushy tails, which are nearly the same length as their torsos. Their tails have a black stripe

on top, and their bodies are blackish-gray above, and red-becoming-white below.

Primarily nocturnal, they hunt cottontails, mice, and woodrats. Insects, cacti fruit, and berries, when available, also make up a good part of their diet.

Generally solitary, they mate in mid-to-late winter. Two months later, each female gives birth to as many as five pups. The pups mature in the den, and at four months begin to forage on their own.

# Kit Fox ................................................................*Vulpes macrotis*

Kit foxes can be distinguished from gray foxes by their small size (which is roughly that of a large house cat), large ears, and black-tipped tails. They are well-adapted to the desert environment and use good eyesight and hearing to hunt in the cooler hours of dusk and dawn during the summer.

They prey mainly on rodents, desert cottontails, and black-tailed jackrabbits. Their water needs are gained primarily from their prey.

Kit foxes rotate their use of multiple, elaborate dens. This may inhibit parasite infestations as well as provide extra places to hunt for rodents.

After successful winter mating, each female gives birth to, on average, four pups in early spring.

# Mountain Lion..................................................................*Puma concolor*

The rarest of all large mammals to see at Red Rock, mountain lions can be identified by their uniform, light-brown fur and very long tails, which are held close to the ground.

These stealthy predators usually inhabit higher-elevation areas of the Spring Mountains, where mule deer are more common, but will follow deer into Red Rock Canyon during the winter. Chiefly active after dusk, they slowly stalk their

prey for hours, then quickly and efficiently chase, pounce, and kill the prey.

Each lion typically takes one mule deer per week. After eating its full, a lion will often hide the carcass with dirt and loose material so that it can come back for another meal or two. Mule deer make up three-quarters of their diet, but bighorn sheep, coyote, bobcat, ringtail, jackrabbit, rodents, and even insects are eaten as well.

Each lion has its own loosely defined territory and is strongly solitary, rarely bedding in the same location. The only time they are not alone is a short period (no more than a week) when males and females come together to mate. After mating, the cats reassume their solitary ways, and males play no part in raising cubs.

# Bobcat.........................................................................*Lynx rufus*

Bobcats are reddish-brown in color with dappled patches of black, tan, and white. Slightly larger than domestic cats, they can be distinguished by their short tails and tufts of black hair on top of their ears.

Mostly active around dawn and dusk, they prowl rocky areas near the mouths of canyons in search of desert cottontails, black-tailed jackrabbits, small rodents, ground-nesting birds, and occasionally reptiles. They also eat some plant materials to aid in digestion.

Although capable of fast speeds, bobcats typically use a lie-in-wait method of hunting, ambushing their prey from short distances. Using this approach they move swiftly and forcefully, striking prey with sharp claws.

More commonly heard than seen, the bobcat's loud cries are sometimes noticed in late winter when in search of a mate. Bobcats are solitary animals, alone except for breeding in the winter. Females carry the young for just over two months, then give birth to, on average, three cubs in the spring. Cubs learn to hunt with their mothers, but leave on their own before winter.

## Ringtail.............................................................. *Bassariscus astutus*

These shy animals are a bit smaller than house cats and have long, distinctive, white-and-black-ringed tails.

Active mainly at night, ringtails nimbly prowl the craggy areas of Red Rock's

canyons for rodents and birds. When prey is found, a ringtail pounces on it like a cat. They also eat insects, fruit, and acorns.

Despite their other common name: 'ring-tailed cat,' the animal is more-closely related to raccoons. Nevertheless, these adept predators were domesticated by miners of the West in the late 1800s, who used the 'cats' to control rodents in their cabins and mines.

## Black-tailed Jackrabbit...................................... *Lepus californicus*

Jackrabbits have huge ears, long hind legs, large feet, and grow to 2' tall. Always on the lookout, the positioning of their eyes affords a nearly 360° view of

approaching predators.

Unlike cottontails, which rely on cover and stealth, jackrabbits run in large bounds, up to 40 miles per hour, when pursued. Hawks, owls, and snakes pose a threat to their young.

Generally diurnal, jackrabbits have a similar diet to cottontails, with the addition of some non-succulent shrubs, such as creosote bush.

At Red Rock, jackrabbits can breed throughout the year, and each female can produce as many as 15 offspring annually. Newborn jackrabbits are mobile within minutes of being born and before long are taking care of themselves.

## Desert Cottontail ............................................ *Sylvilagus audubonii*

These small 'bunnies' typically are 1' tall and may flash their cotton-ball-like tails when running to avoid predators.

Commonly found on shrubby slopes at low-and-mid-elevations, cottontails voraciously eat plant material, including grasses, succulent shrubs, and

*juvenile*

occasionally cacti and acorns when in season. From these plants they can draw all of their water needs. During the summer, they are most active in the cooler dawn and evening hours, resting in the shade of dense brush during the heat of the day.

When a threat is sensed, a cottontail typically remains motionless in hopes that it will blend into the surroundings, then at the last minute, it bobbles behind a bush for cover. Without predators, such as coyotes, gray foxes, kit foxes, snakes, owls, roadrunners, and hawks, the population of cottontails would explode, devastating the plant life.

## Rock Squirrel ...............................................*Spermophilus variegatus*

These rodents look much like tree squirrels found in urban parks. They have long, bushy tails and grayish-brown fur with grey speckling.

Rock squirrels are adept climbers of trees and rocks. They make shallow burrows under rocks, trees, and other cover. During the day, they forage for a variety of plant material, as well as for invertebrates and meat. When available, pinyon pine nuts and scrub oak acorns compose a large portion of their diets. They hibernate in the winter and restrict their activity in the summer to the cooler parts of the day.

At Red Rock Canyon, rock squirrels are occasionally found in rocky areas near the mouths of the canyons in the Red Rock Escarpment. They are typically seen atop boulders and shrubs surveying the surrounding terrain for predators.

## White-tailed Antelope Squirrel
### *Ammospermophilus leucurus*

The most common and conspicuous rodent at Red Rock Canyon, this ground squirrel, about the size of an avocado, can be distinguished by the white underside of its tail, which when erect (a common posture), gives the animal an appearance like an antelope. They are found in rocky and gravelly areas with well-developed shrub growth.

Their chief source of food is green plant material, but they also eat seeds, insects, and small vertebrates.

They are fast movers and are often seen darting about in search of shelter or food, even at mid-day during the summer. They are well-adapted to the desert heat and can be seen sprawling on the ground, pressing their bellies against the cool dirt to remove excess body heat.

## Desert Woodrat ..........................................*Neotoma lepida*

These relatively large rodents (up to 15" long including their tails) have large ears and big black eyes. They can be distinguished by their tail, which is distinctly dark on top and white below. Although common, they are hard to see because they rarely come out during the day.

Unlike many desert dwellers, woodrats require large amounts of water, most of which they get from a vegetarian diet. To limit water loss, they rest in their nests during the day.

Their nests typically are located under boulders or in crevices and appear to be haphazard jumbles of sticks, cholla spines, and debris. The old nests, which include a collection of various local plants, are used by scientists to study past ecosystems and how the climate has changed.

*juvenile*

## Merriam's Kangaroo Rat.............................*Dipodomys merriami*

This rodent is about 10" in length, 6" or 7" of which is its tail. It has large hind legs and moves by hopping like a kangaroo; thus the name.

When foraging nocturnally, kangaroo rats range hundreds of yards in search of seeds and leaves, which they store in pouches located on the outside of their cheeks. Solitary animals, they construct humid burrows, which are expansive labyrinths of tunnels, store rooms, and nest chambers.

These rats are highly adapted to desert life. Their kidneys reduce water loss by greatly concentrating their urine, their nasal cavities are elongated to condense and capture moisture from their breath, and they are able to metabolize water from the dry seeds they eat, never needing water by itself.

When pursued, kangaroo rats hop away with leaps as long as 10' to escape.

## Pocket Mice ......................................................family: *Heteromyidae*

Pocket mice appear much like typical house mice but have long, tufted tails, and some species are very small (about the size of a man's thumb).

They share certain traits with kangaroo rats: nocturnal activity, extensive

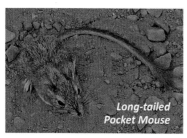

*Long-tailed Pocket Mouse*

burrow construction, nesting habits, and external pouches on their cheeks. Pocket mice, however, do not hop like kangaroo rats; they scurry.

Pocket mice receive most of their water needs from the food they eat. Their diet consists primarily of seeds, green vegetation, and insects.

Of the several species of pocket mice that inhabit Red Rock, the most commonly seen (at night darting across roadways) is the **long-tailed pocket mouse** (*Chaetodipus formosus*).

## Deer Mice ........................................................................*Peromyscus* spp.

Physiologically and behaviorally, deer mice are quite different from pocket mice. Although found in nearly the same desert habitats and plant communities, they are less adapted to the arid environment.

*Cactus Mouse*

These mice typically make nests above ground in small spaces around boulders or dense shrubs, forfeiting the humid water gains of a sealed burrow. They remain active in the winter months. Their diet is largely the same as pocket mice, with seeds being a staple. Seasonally, they eat acorns, berries, and green plant material as they forage, usually at night.

Mice have a lifespan of one-to-three years. Most species reach maturity and are able to breed after two months. Prolific when conditions are favorable, populations fluctuate greatly depending on food resources and the number of predators.

The five deer-mice species at Red Rock are so similar in appearance that DNA analysis is sometimes required for identification. The five species are: **brush mouse** (*Peromyscus boylii*), **canyon mouse** (*Peromyscus crinitus*), **cactus mouse** (*Peromyscus eremicus*), **deer mouse** (*Peromyscus maniculatus*), and **pinyon mouse** (*Peromyscus truei*).

# Bats ............................................................................. order: *Chiroptera*

The only mammals to truly fly, bats are warm blooded, covered with hair, and are primarily nocturnal. Most species are active at dawn and dusk.

The dozen or so species of bats at Red Rock Canyon are insectivorous. All forage while in flight and most capture insects from the air, but some pick their prey from the ground or foliage. Many species, such as the **Western pipistrelle bat** (*Pipistrellus hesperus*), use the flap of skin between their legs to catch prey.

Bats use a system of echolocation where ultrasonic sounds (usually not audible to humans) are emitted, bounce off objects, and are received to create a 'picture' of the environment around them. The system is so efficient that many bats can differentiate between moths, mosquitoes, beetles, and so forth, from long distances.

*Western Pipistrelle Bat*

About the size of a small songbird, a bat's body typically is 3" to 4" long. Whereas bird wings are supported by the bones of the upper and lower arm with hand bones severely reduced, bat wings are supported, in large part, by highly elongated hand bones.

*Long-legged Myotis*

Most bats are not able to take off from the ground and will quickly scamper to a suitable perch. Therefore, they often roost in a hanging position, typically in caves, but also in cracks on cliffs and in trees.

Bats are long-lived and typically give birth (upside down) to one or two offspring per year. Like all mammals, mothers produce milk. Males play no part in raising the young. During winter, bats either migrate south or hibernate, which allows them to survive all but the coldest conditions. The most common bats at Red Rock Canyon are the **Western pipistrelle bat**, the **long-legged myotis** (*Myotis volans*), and the **big brown bat** (*Eptesicus fuscus*).

*Big Brown Bat*

The tiny (wingspan to 8", 3 to 6 grams) **Western pipistrelle bat** is recognized by its small size, tan fur, and black-colored bandit mask. It is the bat most likely to be seen flying during daylight, but typically flies at dusk and dawn when feeding on insects near canyon drainages and in low-elevation, craggy areas. It is generally a solitary animal, and rarely roosts in groups.

The **long-legged myotis** is a large-sized bat (wingspan to 12") with dark-brown-to-reddish fur on its back. It lives in woodland areas. Just after sunset, these bats feed on a variety of soft-bodied insects but favor moths caught in flight. They can operate at lower temperatures than many others, allowing them to be active well into the fall before they hibernate.

Large in size (wingspan to 12"), **big brown bats** have glossy, yellow-brown to dark-brown fur on their backs. They forage aerially for insects at dusk and prefer flying beetles, which they catch with the flap of skin between their legs. While flying, these bats may produce a clicking or chirping sound audible to humans. Big brown bats migrate short distances in winter and hibernate alone or in small groups.

# Birds
### *of Red Rock Canyon*

A wide array of birds with strikingly different shapes, diets, and habits live at, or migrate through, Red Rock Canyon. Many are active during the day and easy to spot, others are elusive and shy away from humans.

Of the roughly 200 species found at Red Rock Canyon, the following descriptions focus on those most likely to be encountered. See page 198 for further resources and page 157 for tips on bird watching spots.

## Golden Eagle
*Aquila chrysaetos*

Active during daylight, golden eagles are very large, dark-brown raptors with a 7' wingspan. Adults have a golden hue on the back of their necks.

Eagles hunt on the wing and swoop down to capture ground squirrels and other medium-sized mammals, occasionally taking birds, reptiles, and carrion. After killing prey, they use sharp talons and their curve-tipped beaks to tear apart the flesh.

They are territorial and build nests of sticks, usually on cliffs. At Red Rock Canyon, look for these majestic birds along the Red Rock Escarpment and mountain ridges.

## Red-tailed Hawk
*Buteo jamaicensis*

These large, stocky, soaring birds have variable plumage, but all adults have the characteristic red tail. Like many soaring birds, red-tails have narrow feathers at the tips of their wings that separate into 'fingers.'

They build nests in tall trees and on cliff faces with good views of the surrounding terrain. Their diet is mainly small mammals, but also includes birds and reptiles. Red-tails have excellent vision with adaptations that allow the colors of their prey to stand out against the desert landscape.

At Red Rock Canyon, red-tailed hawks are the most commonly seen hawk. If you see a hawk, chances are that it is this species. They are found throughout the Calico Hills, along the Red Rock Escarpment, as well as in the creosote bush scrub plant community.

# Turkey Vulture
## *Cathartes aura*

Vultures are large, blackish, bald-headed soaring birds that search for rotting flesh in flight and identify it by sight and smell. They make use of their curve-tipped beaks for tearing rotting meat from carcasses.

The bare skin of their heads is easier to clean after feeding than a head of feathers. In courtship, it is common for pairs to engage in flight displays closely following one another through the air. Turkey vultures typically nest in a scrape on a rocky ledge or use nests built by other birds.

# Falcons.................................................................family: *Falconiformes*

These fast-flying birds of prey can be distinguished from the hawk family by the notches in their beaks, which are used to break the necks of their prey. Further,

*Peregrine Falcon*        *American Kestrel*

their wings are more narrow and pointed at the tips, allowing a greater degree of maneuverability at high speeds.

From a distance, the **peregrine falcon** (*Falco peregrinus*) is dark brown above and has a white underbody with light-brown barring and spotting. It primarily preys on birds, mostly the size of doves and songbirds, as well as bats. The prey is caught after a dive as fast as 180 miles per hour. Its nose has a baffle-like structure that aids in breathing while flying at such speeds.

Peregrines are typically found along the Red Rock Escarpment and mountain ridges, although they are frequently spotted in Blue Diamond village as well.

The small, colorful **American kestrel** (*Falco sparverius*) typically inhabits open country. Its diet focuses on invertebrates (mostly grasshoppers) but also includes small mammals and other birds.

# Greater Roadrunner...................*Geococcyx californianus*

Roadrunners are pheasant-sized birds who prefer bipedal travel over flying. They have two toes forward and two toes back, making their footprint X-shaped.

They are omnivorous, with a diet primarily of reptiles and large invertebrates, and occasionally plant material. They forage at a slow pace among shrubs, then pounce on prey with great speed (up to 18 mph). They even attack rattlesnakes, sometimes acting in pairs where one fans its tail feathers as a diversion while the other grabs the snake from behind.

At Red Rock Canyon, look for roadrunners near the visitor center and at Spring Mountain Ranch State Park.

## Ravens and Jays..............................................family: *Corvidae*

Birds in this family have strong bills, feet, and legs. They are bold and gregarious, and some species are able to learn and adapt to new behaviors. Certain species have a large vocal repertoire, including loud, harsh predator alarms, softer close quarters sounds for bird-to-bird communication, rattling noises, and clear, bell-like tones.

*Common Raven*

Omnivorous, the **common raven** (*Corvus corax*) and some jays eat insects, nuts, seeds, and carrion; and sometimes cache extra food. Populations of ravens are increasing around Las Vegas due to opportunities presented by discarded foods and the increased availability of water.

At Red Rock Canyon, the large, black raven is commonly seen. The black-crested **Steller's jay** (*Cyanocitta stelleri*) and the **Western scrub jay** (*Aphelocoma californica*) are often seen perched or hopping about at Willow Springs. The **pinyon jay** (*Gymnorhinus cyanocephalus*) lives in areas of pines where it eats and caches pine nuts, some of which are forgotten and sprout new generations of trees.

*Steller's Jay*

*Western Scrub Jay*

*Pinyon Jay*

## Owls..............................................................family: *Strigidae*

Owls have large, round heads, big eyes, and asymmetrical ears (one ear is higher than the other) that help in locating sounds. They use a combination of sight

*Great-horned Owl*

*Burrowing Owl*

and hearing to detect prey, bobbing their heads to estimate distance by sight.

Mostly nocturnal, owls catch prey from flight with their feet, which have strong toes: two in front, and two in back. Together, the two feet look like back-to-back Ks from below, forming a web to grasp prey. Typically, prey consists of small mammals. The **great-horned owl** (*Bubo virginianus*) is a large (up to 2' long), strong bird. Each adult can capture and carry prey heavier than itself. Smaller prey is gulped whole, sometimes after removing the head. The indigestible bones and fur are regurgitated as pellets at a rate of one or two per day. At Red Rock Canyon, great-horned owls inhabit craggy areas in the canyons, Calico Hills, Kraft Mountain, and Blue Diamond Hill.

**Burrowing owls** (*Athene cunicularia*) are quail-sized birds that inhabit abandoned tortoise or mammal burrows in dry, open areas with low vegetation. They feed on large invertebrates (especially beetles) and mice.

## Chukar ...........................................................................*Alectoris chukar*

Native to Eurasia, these stocky, partridge-sized ground dwellers have gray breasts, red beaks, zebra-striped sides, and a black band over their eyes. Often, they can be identified by their call, which increases in intensity: *chuck-chucka-chuckKA-chucKAR*.

These birds forage by scratching the ground for seeds, nuts, and occasionally invertebrates.

Typically, flocks of these non-migratory birds are found in rocky areas near the canyons of Red Rock where they nest in scrapes on the ground lined with leaves and feathers. When disturbed, the birds explode into flight then glide to a safe area.

Since they were first introduced to the Great Basin in 1935 for hunting, they have multiplied rapidly and expanded into much of the region.

## Gambel's Quail ................................................ *Callipepla gambelii*

These ground dwellers are a bit smaller than chukars and have ornate plumage, including a distinctive black plume (called a top knot) extending from their foreheads. The male has a black face and a red cap, but the female's head is a comparatively plain gray.

Female (left) and Male Gambel's Quail

Gambel's quail use similar food resources as chukars but inhabit less-rocky areas, such as Calico Basin and Pine Creek Canyon, which have plenty of shrub cover. When disturbed, these birds make a loud entry into flight to startle predators. Non-migratory, they are gregarious and form small social groups. Breeding occurs after spring rains, which bring the promise of plentiful seed.

## Mourning Dove
### *Zenaida macroura*

These medium-sized, gray-brown birds have long, pointed tails, and black, beady eyes that are outlined in pale blue during the breeding season.

Exclusively vegetarian, mourning doves focus on seeds and grains, foods not well suited for young chicks that need mostly protein and fat. To overcome this, adults feed chicks a regurgitated, curd-like substance from a compartment in their digestive system that contains special cells shed from the lining of their throats.

Although well-adapted to urban environments, these birds are commonly found in shrubby areas at Red Rock Canyon. They also inhabit the village of Blue Diamond.

## Lesser Nighthawk
*Chordeiles acutipennis*

These medium-sized birds have stubby heads, small beaks, and a white bar on the underside of each wing.

Active from dusk to dawn, they fly buoyantly among the shrubs and feed on flying insects.

During the day, they roost on the ground where drab plumage provides camouflage. Their preferred habitat is shrubby lowlands near sources of water, such as near Red Spring and the village of Blue Diamond.

## Woodpeckers ................................................................ family: *Picidae*

Most of these small to medium-sized birds find invertebrate prey by sound and forage by hammering their beaks into bark, plant stalks, and wood. They have a number of specialized adaptations to do this: a shock-absorbing system that protects the brain, a long tongue (up to 5") that retracts and wraps around the skull, and a tail that can be used like a third leg when hopping up a tree.

The most commonly seen species at lower elevations at Red Rock is the **ladder-backed woodpecker** (*Picoides scalaris*). This small (to 7" long) woodpecker has a black-and-white striped back and is found in Joshua tree woodlands as well as in lower elevation areas with trees. Males have red crowns while females do not. The **northern flicker** (*Colaptes auratus*) inhabits open woodlands and desert areas with trees, where it often forages on the ground for ants. Flickers are large (to 12" long) and have grayish-brown plumage with black spots on the white breast and belly. Males have a red patch on each cheek.

*Male Ladder-backed Woodpecker*

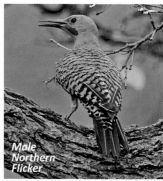

*Male Northern Flicker*

## White-throated Swift
*Aeronautes saxatalis*

These small (to 6") birds have large, stocky heads, sickle-shaped wings, white throats and a white stripe down their breasts.

They are highly maneuverable, aerial foragers that spend the day aloft, often in flocks, eating insects. At home in the air, they bathe, drink, defecate, and copulate in flight. The latter occurs as two birds appear to free-fall entangled together. Swifts use cracks in cliff faces for nest colonies, which can include hundreds of birds.

The rattling *tse-te-te-te-te* screeches of white-throated swift flocks are often heard near the canyons of Red Rock.

# Hummingbirds
family: *Trochilidae*

Male Broad-tailed Hummingbird

Hummingbirds are small and light. At Red Rock, each weighs 3 to 4 grams and has a body length of 3.5" to 4".

Using a unique, figure-eight motion of its wings, a hummingbird hovers and feeds on sugar-rich nectar with an exceptionally long, retractable tongue. Its protein needs are supplied by insects.

During flight, a hummingbird's heart rate is approximately 1250 beats per minute, and its body temperature is about 107°F, but when cold, or food resources are unavailable, it can enter a state of inactivity where its heart rate decreases to 50 beats per minute, and its body temperature drops as low as 55°F.

Male Anna's Hummingbird

At Red Rock Canyon, look for hummingbirds along washes, especially when spring flowers are in bloom. Males have bright, iridescent feathers and flashy courtship displays. Most species migrate and winter south of the U.S.-Mexico border.

Species seen at Red Rock include the **broad-tailed hummingbird** (*Selasphorus platycercus*), **Anna's hummingbird** (*Calypte anna*), and **Costa's hummingbird** (*Calypte costae*). Females are hard to identify, but males are easier because of their iridescent plumage. Broad-tails have green foreheads and red throats, Anna's have red foreheads and throats, and Costa's have purple foreheads and throats.

Male Costa's Hummingbird

# Tyrant Flycatchers..............................................family: *Tyrannidae*

These small-to-medium-sized birds typically have moderately sized, flattened beaks, dark upper parts, and lighter under parts.

As their name implies, they primarily feed on flying insects, which are caught in flight. Some species, however, gorge on fruits and berries when available.

Flycatchers inhabit a variety of habitats. Most species migrate south in the winter.

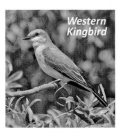

Western Kingbird

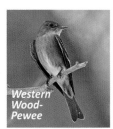

Western Wood-Pewee

The **Western kingbird** (*Tyrannus verticalis*) has a yellow belly and is occasionally spotted near the grassy areas of Spring Mountain Ranch. The **Western wood-pewee** (*Contopus sordidulus*) has white wing-bars and inhabits washes and riparian areas. The **ash-throated flycatcher** (*Myiarchus cinerascens*) has reddish-brown primary feathers and prefers open woodlands. **Say's phoebe** (*Sayornis saya*) has a salmon-colored belly and is found in the creosote bush scrub plant community.

Ash-Throated Flycatcher

Say's Phoebe

Violet-green Swallow

Northern Rough-winged Swallow

Cliff Swallow

## Swallows ................................................................family: *Hirundinidae*

These small (less than 6" long) birds have short, broad bills, and a wide gape that aids in catching insects in flight. Nimble flyers, they feed in an aerial fashion similar to swifts and common nighthawks. They can be distinguished from swifts by wider tails and wings with straighter, sometimes rounded, trailing edges. In winter, when insect populations are low, they migrate south.

The most commonly seen species at Red Rock is the **violet-green swallow** (*Tachycineta thalassina*) that inhabits cliff areas but also forages over grassy areas, such as near Red Spring and Spring Mountain Ranch. They have iridescent, greenish backs and bright-white under parts. **Cliff swallows** (*Petrochelidon pyrrhonota*), found in similar areas, make nests of mud on cliffs and man-made structures. They have white breasts and bellies and reddish-brown throats. The **northern rough-winged swallow** (*Stelgidopteryx serripennis*) inhabits sites similar to those of the violet-green swallow but nests in cavities, including burrows. It has dark-brown upper parts and lighter, whitish-tan under parts.

## Mountain Chickadee
### *Poecile gambeli*
These small (less than 5½" long), perching songbirds have black caps, eye-bands, and throats. Omnivorous, they mainly eat insects, larvae, seeds, and berries. They prefer conifer woodlands at higher elevations, but in winter descend to Willow Springs and the canyons of Red Rock. Their calls are not limited to *chicka-dee-dee*, and include: *fee-fee-fee*, *tseedle-deet*, and *chebe-chebe-chay*.

## Loggerhead Shrike
### *Lanius ludovicianus*
These robin-sized birds use a scan-and-pounce, 'perch-hunting' method to capture large insects and small vertebrates. When food is plentiful, they sometimes hang extra food on cacti for later. Like owls, these birds regurgitate pellets of indigestible material. They inhabit open shrublands and the outskirts of pinyon-juniper woodlands where plant density is low.

Gray Vireo

## Vireos
### family: *Vireonidae*
These small (4" to 6"), perching birds have plump bodies and thick bills. They primarily eat insects but supplement their diet with fruits and berries. They prefer thickets and wooded areas. Species commonly seen at Red Rock Canyon include the **gray vireo** (*Vireo vicinior*), **plumbeous vireo** (*Vireo plumbeus*), and **warbling vireo** (*Vireo gilvus*).

## Verdin
*Auriparus flaviceps*
The gray plumage and yellow faces of these very small (to 4½" long), nimble birds are more pronounced on adult males. Verdins eat insects, plant matter, and berries. In their preferred habitat of mixed chaparral, they build spherical, enclosed nests of twigs that are often well camouflaged.

Male Verdin

## Juniper Titmouse
*Baeolophus ridgwayi*
These small (to 5" long), social birds have uniform, gray plumage and retractable crests. They move about with a fluttery, bouncy flight in search of insects, grubs, berries, and seeds. They inhabit pinyon-juniper woodlands and wooded, riparian areas, such as Spring Mountain Ranch.

## Bushtit
*Auriparus flaviceps*
These very small (to 4½" and less than 6 grams), social birds are typically found in flocks of up to 40 birds. They have long tails, short necks, and gray plumage. Their diet consists mainly of insects and spiders. Look for bushtits in mixed open and brushy woodlands near the canyons of Red Rock.

## Wrens................................................................ family: *Troglodytidae*
These small to medium-sized songbirds have roundish bodies, down-turned bills, and often hold their tails upright. Primarily insectivorous, they sometimes eat fruits and berries. Known for complex songs, wrens sing loudly and frequently.

**Cactus wrens** (*Campylorhynchus brunneicapillus*), the largest (to 9" long) wrens in North America, they have speckled plumage, reddish caps, and white eyebrows. At Red Rock, look for these gregarious birds in areas of buckhorn cholla near the canyons and visitor center. They make nests in these cacti for protection against predators and are often seen standing on the spines. Another commonly seen species is the medium-sized **rock wren** (*Salpinctes obsoletus*), which has grayish-brown upper parts and a pale breast and belly. Rock wrens inhabit rocky areas throughout Red Rock. The medium-sized **canyon wren** (*Catherpes mexicanus*) is reddish-brown, has a white throat and upper breast, and inhabits the canyons of Red Rock. The medium-sized **Bewick's Wren** (*Thryomanes bewickii*) has drab plumage, a bold, white eyebrow, and frequents shrubby areas.

Cactus Wren

Rock Wren

Canyon Wren

Bewick's Wren

# Ruby-crowned Kinglet
*Regulus calendula*
These small (to 4¼" long) songbirds have plain-looking faces, buff-colored under parts, and black and white wing bars. Males have distinct, red crown-patches that usually are concealed. They are constantly in motion, continually flicking their wings and fluttering from perch to perch. In the winter, look for these birds in higher-elevation, shrubby areas and coniferous woodlands.

## Gnatcatchers ....................................................... family: *Polioptilidae*
These chickadee-sized birds have long tails, white eye-rings, and small, thin bills used to catch insects. In the spring and summer, look for the small (4½" long) **blue-gray gnatcatcher** (*Polioptila caerulea*) in Willow Springs and Pine Creek Canyon. Sometimes seen near Red Spring, the **black-tailed gnatcatcher** (*Polioptila melanura*) is a permanent resident. They have black tails, dark-gray upper parts, pale-gray under parts, and in the summer, black caps, which nearly cover their eyes; in the winter their heads are gray.

Blue-gray Gnatcatcher

Black-tailed Gnatcatcher

## Thrushes ........................................................ family: *Turdidae*
These medium-sized songbirds have stout bills, long torsos, and are known for their rich, melodious songs. Primarily insectivorous during summer, they eat fruit and berries when available. They are birds of cooler, forested areas, but often come down to the canyons of Red Rock during winter. The least-colorful, **Townsend's solitaire** (*Myadestes townsendi*), is uniformly gray, has darker wings, and a bright-white eye-ring. Male **Western bluebirds** (*Sialia mexicana*) have dark-blue upper parts and heads, and vibrant, reddish-brown breasts; females are similar, but drab. Male **mountain bluebirds** (*Sialia currucoides*) have sky-blue upper parts and lighter-blue bellies; females are similar, but drab.

Townsend's Solitaire

Western Bluebird

Mountain Bluebird

# Thrashers ..........................................................................family: *Mimidae*

These large songbirds have long tails, long legs, and sturdy beaks. Those with down-turned beaks use them to scrape away leaves and dig in the soil for insects and small reptiles.

Somewhat elusive, these shy birds are more often heard than seen and have a complex repertoire of songs. Loud calls are used for defending territory, attracting mates, and possibly guarding mates. Singing peaks at the onset of breeding season in mid-January.

The brownish **crissal thrasher**

Crissal Thrasher

(*Toxostoma crissale*) has reddish under-tail plumage and inhabits riparian and mixed-chaparral areas. **Le Conte's thrasher** (*Toxostoma lecontei*) is more uniformly light gray, has black eyes, and inhabits shrubby desert areas at lower elevations. The **Northern mockingbird** (*Mimus polyglottos*) lacks a down-turned beak, has white patches on its wings, and is sometimes spotted in Calico Basin.

# Phainopepla
## *Phainopepla nitens*

Male Phainopepla

These medium-sized songbirds are crested and have red, beady eyes. Males are glossy black with white in the wings; females are similar, but gray. They forage on fruit and insects, especially the berries of mesquite mistletoe. They nest in mistletoe-bearing trees and are known for dispersing the tree's seeds through droppings. Look for these conspicuous birds in Calico Basin and near Wheeler Camp Spring.

# Wood Warblers ..............................................................family: *Parulidae*

This large family of mostly small (less than 5½" long), perching songbirds is represented by no-less-than 10 species at Red Rock Canyon. They are colorful (often yellow), prefer wooded and brushy areas, and have small, thin bills used to pick insects from bark and foliage.

Yellow-rumped Warbler

Common Yellowthroat

Although most species are seen during spring and fall migrations, the **yellow-rumped warbler** (*Setophaga coronata*) can be found at lower elevations in the Spring Mountains year-round. Other species seen at Red Rock include: the **common yellowthroat** (*Geothlypis trichas*), **yellow warbler** (*Setophaga petechia*), **orange-crowned warbler** (*Oreothlypis celata*), **black-throated gray warbler** (*Setophaga nigrescens*), **Lucy's warbler** (*Oreothlypis luciae*), and **Wilson's warbler** (*Cardellina pusilla*).

Yellow Warbler

Orange-crowned Warbler

## Western Tanager
*Piranga ludoviciana*

These medium-sized songbirds have yellow bodies and blackish wings and tails. Males have orange heads while females are more drab. Both exhibit more intense plumage color in spring and summer.

They have stout bills used to eat fruit, berries, and insects. They prefer open, wooded areas, such as Spring Mountain Ranch and Pine Creek Canyon.

*Male Western Tanager*

## Sparrows .................................................................. family: *Emberizidae*

This large family of songbirds includes the towhees, juncos, and sparrows.

Towhees are medium-sized and often scratch at the ground for insects and seeds. Species at Red Rock include the black-hooded, orange-flanked **spotted towhee** (*Pipilo maculatus*), and the plain-brown-colored **Abert's towhee** (*Melozone aberti*).

The **dark-eyed juncos** (*Junco hyemalis*) form small, ground-dwelling flocks and are commonly seen during winter months in shrubby areas. Three subspecies of juncos can be found at Red Rock, each with different plumage, but all have white outer-tail feathers.

Sparrows are a bit smaller in size than towhees (5" to 7" long), often

*Spotted Towhee*

form small flocks, have short, conical bills, are typically brownish with streaked backs, and can be difficult to distinguish from each other. The most common species at Red Rock are: the black-and-white-faced, **black-throated sparrow** (*Amphispiza bilineata*); the gray-headed **sage sparrow** (*Amphispiza belli*); the **savannah sparrow** (*Passerculus sandwichensis*), with its brown-streaked breast; and the yellowish-orange-billed **white-crowned sparrow** (*Zonotrichia leucophrys*).

*Dark-eyed Junco*

*Dark-eyed Junco*

*Abert's Towhee*

*Black-throated Sparrow*

*Sage Sparrow*

*Savannah Sparrow*

*White-crowned Sparrow*

## Blackbirds and Orioles ........................................ family: *Oriolidae*

Birds of this family typically are medium-to-large-sized, have strong, pointed bills, and large feet. Omnivorous, they eat fruit, grains, and insects throughout the year, but focus on insects when breeding in the spring.

Male Scott's Oriole

At Red Rock Canyon, male **Scott's orioles** (*Icterus parisorum*) are boldly colored in black and yellow; females are similar, but drab, with less black. In spring and summer, they can be found in areas with plenty of yucca along the base of the Red Rock Escarpment.

**Great-tailed grackles** (*Quiscalus mexicanus*), **Brewer's blackbirds** (*Euphagus cyanocephalus*), and **brown-headed cowbirds** (*Molothrus ater*) are seen less frequently at Red Rock Canyon. Grackles and Brewer's blackbirds are more often seen in urban areas where they have adapted well.

### Lazuli Bunting
*Passerina amoena*

These small (to 5½" long) songbirds have short, conical bills built for a varied diet of seeds, fruit, and insects. Males have bright blue heads, rust-colored upper breasts, and white bellies. Females are pale brown. At Red Rock, they are seen in the spring and summer. Look or listen for these gregarious birds at higher elevations in Pine Creek Canyon and Willow Springs.

## Finches ................................................................ family: *Fringillidae*

Birds of this family typically are small (less than 6" long) songbirds with short, conical bills used to crack seeds, their chief source of food.

Male **house finches** (*Carpodacus mexicanus*) usually have a reddish cast over their heads and upper breasts. The color, however, is acquired from their diet. Therefore, when they lack certain nutrients their coloration is more yellowish. Females lack the red color. Look for house finches throughout Red Rock Canyon, especially near water. Male **lesser goldfinches** (*Spinus psaltria*) have yellow underparts, black wings, and black caps; female plumage is duller. They inhabit a wide variety of areas, but focus on areas where thistle seeds are plentiful.

Male House Finch

Lesser Goldfinch

# Reptiles and Amphibians
## of Red Rock Canyon

Being cold blooded, the body temperature of a reptile or amphibian fluctuates with the heat from its surroundings. While this allows them to expend much less energy than birds or mammals, it means that in cold temperatures they are rather slow and unable to catch prey. Therefore, most are active from spring to fall, retreating underground during winter.

With relatively impermeable, scaly skin to reduce water loss, reptiles are well-adapted to the climate of Red Rock Canyon.

Amphibians, however, are not. They have soft, moist skin, which loses water fast. Accordingly, their lives are deeply intertwined with the permanent springs and seeps of Red Rock Canyon.

*Despite its fearsome appearance and large size, the chuckwalla is an herbivore and will avoid contact with humans. Here an adult female sunbathes near Red Spring.*

### Chuckwalla
*Sauromalus ater*

These large (to 9" head and body), heavy-bodied lizards range in color from dark to light, changing to dark when they are cold to soak up more heat, and turning light when hot to reflect heat. The young and females have bands on their bodies and tails, which fade as they age.

Chuckwallas are herbivores, occasionally taking insects as they eat plants. To deal with periods of drought, they store water in accessary lymph sacs.

They typically are seen perched on rocks, basking in the sun from February to October. Look for them in rocky, south-facing spots along the base of the Red Rock Escarpment and in the Calico Hills. When threatened, they shuffle noisily into an adjacent crack and inflate their bodies to deter extraction.

Southern Paiutes sometimes used these lizards as a source of food.

## Great Basin Whiptail
*Aspidoscelis tigris tigris*
These lizards have long, whip-like tails and relatively short bodies (to 4½" head and body), which are dark with light lines on their backs and light bars or spots on their sides. The young have blue tails. They are fast-moving and are found in lower, open areas where they eat insects and other lizards from late spring to early fall.

## Side-blotched Lizard
*Uta stansburiana*
By far the most common lizard at Red Rock, these small (to 2½" head and body) lizards vary in color between sexes and seasonally, but usually have black blotches on their sides, just behind their front legs.
Insectivorous and active

year-round at lower elevations, they are often observed darting towards shelter or perched on rocks in nearly all habitats at Red Rock Canyon. Prolific, each female can lay as many as 56 eggs per season.

## Long-nosed Leopard Lizard
*Gambelia wislizenii*
These moderately large (to 6" head and body) lizards have leopard-like spots along their backs and tails. They prefer rocky, open areas where they eat lizards as large as they are, insects, and occasionally plant material. Females develop orange spots and bars during breeding season; at other times they appear like males, but larger.

## Yellow-backed Spiny Lizard ..................... *Sceloporus uniformis*
The thick bodies (to 5½" head and body) of these lizards are yellowish-brown and gray, with rather large, spiny scales. They are stocky rock and tree dwellers that have black, triangular marks on their shoulders. While males are blue on the underside of their necks and chests, females are plain beige.
Omnivorous, they inhabit areas along the base of the Red Rock Escarpment, where they seek shelter in rock crevices and mammal burrows.

## Gila Monster ..................................................... *Heloderma suspectm cinctum*

*Although **venomous**, Gila monsters are shy and pose little danger to humans.*

The bodies and tails of these large (up to 2 pounds and 9" to 14" head and body) lizards are orange with irregular black bands and dots. Their skin on their heads, bodies, and sausage-shaped tails is covered with small, bead-like scales. Black, forked tongues flick from their large, powerful jaws.

A rare sight, the Gila monster (pronounced 'hE la') spends most of its life underground hiding or hibernating. As temperatures warm, Gila monsters emerge from their shelter sites in search of prey. Although any small mammal, bird, lizard, frog, or large insect will do, their primary source of food are the contents of nests, such as the eggs of reptiles and ground-nesting birds, and young mammals. A Gila monster is able to consume up to one-third of its body weight in a single feeding. Three of these big meals can supply the energy needs of a Gila monster for one year. Such sparse eating is made possible by a hormone that triggers a prolonged release of insulin, which allows the consumed food to be turned into fat and not blood sugar. This trait was studied extensively and a synthetic drug for type 2 diabetes, based on a protein in Gila-monster saliva, is now manufactured.

### A Secretive Lizard

Spending more than 95% of their lives underground, Gila monsters are difficult to locate, and population numbers are not well known. Due to this lack of information, these enigmatic creatures were first given legal protection in 1952. It is now illegal to harass, harm, pursue, hunt, shoot, wound, kill, trap, capture, or collect Gila monsters in Nevada.

Mainly active in the morning and afternoon, Gila monsters tend to avoid intense heat. They prefer temperatures between 72°F and 93°F, and cannot tolerate temperatures in excess of 100°F. They inhabit rocky slopes in creosote bush scrub and blackbrush scrub plant communities.

With a good bit of patience and luck, Gila monsters can be seen at low to mid-elevation sites, such as Calico Basin, in the late spring and early summer.

## Desert Horned Lizard
*Phynosoma platyrhinos*

Despite its fierce appearance, with a ring of horns on the back of its head, horned lizards are quite small (to 4" head and body) and not venomous. More docile than their similar-sized counterparts, they tend to bask in the sun amid rocks in gravelly areas, where their color acts well as camouflage.

Their favorite food, harvester ants, has a poison the horned lizard can digest with its specialized enzymes. When in danger, these lizards can puff up and threaten to bite. Unlike some species of horned lizards, this species cannot squirt blood from a vessel behind its eye to surprise an attacker and allow for escape.

## Great Basin Collared Lizard
*Crotaphytus bicinctores*

This moderately large (to 4½" head and body), big-headed lizard has a distinctive black-and-white 'collar' around its neck. In the spring, during breeding season, the female develops bright orange bars on its sides.

Omnivorous, these collard lizards have a diverse diet of insects, fruit, plant matter, small mammals, and other lizards. Often seen perched on rocks, they are able to run on their hind legs to catch prey or escape predators. Look for these lizards in sparsely vegetated, rocky areas within the creosote bush scrub and blackbrush scrub communities and in the lower reaches of the pinyon-juniper woodlands.

## Desert Iguana
*Dipsosaurus dorsalis*

These moderately large (to 5¾" head and body) lizards, have a streamlined shape and dark bands on their long tails.

These lizards primarily are herbivorous, eating flowers, fruits, and leaves of many plants, including creosote bush flowers. They can tolerate hotter temperatures than any other lizard in North America.

Desert iguanas inhabit sandy areas in the creosote bush scrub community and can be found in the shade of a bush, even during the middle of a summer day.

### Northern Mohave Rattlesnake
*Crotalus scutulatus scutulatus*
These thick-bodied, triangular-headed snakes grow to 4' and have diamond-shaped patches on their backs. Although commonly called 'Mojave green,' green and brown shades are known from the same brood. Primarily nocturnal, they feed on ground squirrels, mice, birds, and other reptiles. They inhabit shrubby flats, primarily in the creosote bush scrub plant community.

### Southwestern Speckled Rattlesnake
*Crotalus mitchelli pyrrhus*
Similar to the Northern Mojave in size and shape, these snakes have a generally faded-looking body coloration that varies to match the surroundings. They primarily feed on small mammals. Like all rattlesnakes, they gain a segment of rattle each time they shed their skins. Preferring rocky areas, these are the most frequently seen rattlesnakes at Red Rock.

### Mohave Desert Sidewinder
*Crotalus cerastes cerastes*
Typically less than 18", these snakes are pinkish-tan with dark blotches on their backs and horns above their eyes. They are usually found in sandy soil with sparse vegetation where they can move in a unique sideways fashion, which is especially effective on loose sand. When stalking prey they are known to submerge their bodies under sand to avoid detection.

## Rattlesnake Safety

Although a rattlesnake's venom can be deadly, killing these animals is not necessary. In fact, certain populations have seen alarming declines due to human impacts, such as hunting, habitat loss, and road crossings.

The potential of encountering a rattlesnake should not deter anyone from enjoying Red Rock Canyon, but precautions can be taken: When hiking, stay on the trail. Watch where you place your hands and feet, especially in areas of rocks and shrubs. Wear loose-fitting long pants and sturdy high-top boots that act to shield a strike.

If you see a rattlesnake, count yourself lucky and remember: 1) *Don't play with the snake; when coiled with its rattle in the air it feels threatened and is ready to strike*, and 2) *Keep at least 10' away*.

## California Kingsnake
*Lampropeltis getulus californiae*
These harmless, medium to large-sized (to 7' 1"), small-headed snakes are smooth, shiny, and have distinctive black and white bands. Carnivorous, they prey on small mammals, birds and their eggs, frogs, and other reptiles. They are active in the morning and evening in the spring and fall, and nocturnal in the summer.

## Great Basin Gopher Snake
*Pituophis catenifer deserticola*
These medium to large (to 9' 2") snakes are yellowish-cream with dark blotches along their backs and sides. Sometimes mistaken for rattlesnakes, they have slightly triangular heads and shake their tails when threatened as if having rattles, but are harmless. Found in all but high-elevation habitats, these snakes are fairly common.

## Red Racer
*Coluber flagellum piceus*
These long (to 8' 4"), slender, fast-moving snakes have a light-brown or reddish-pink, banded appearance and dark heads. They feed on lizards, birds and their eggs, small mammals, and insects. Active during the day, they can be found in rocky areas along the base of the Red Rock Escarpment. They are harmless.

## Striped Whipsnake
*Coluber taeniatus*
These harmless, long (to 6'), thin snakes have large eyes and are brownish with yellow-striped sides. Unlike garter snakes, their backs lack a yellow stripe down the center. These snakes inhabit pinyon-juniper woodlands, where their chief food sources, side-blotched lizards and insects, are prevalent.

## Western Patch-nosed Snake
*Salvadora hexalepis*
This harmless, medium-length (to 3' 10") snake is marked with pale gray and tan stripes, and is characterized by a large, patch-like scale on the tip of its nose. During the day, they often search burrows, hunting for small mammals and lizards. Look for these snakes in open, shrubby or rocky areas throughout Red Rock.

## Desert Tortoise ...................................................*Gopherus agassizii*

These are the only members of the turtle family found at Red Rock Canyon. In the wild, mature individuals are 8" to 12" long and have domed shells that resemble the surface of a soccer ball.

They spend most of the summer and winter in a hibernation-like state within their burrows. Summer burrows usually are shallow, but winter burrows can be 30' deep. The burrows may be shared by a few tortoises and used year after year, sometimes inhabited for many generations.

After emerging from their burrows in the spring, these herbivores feed on new-growth foliage with a high water content, such as beavertail cacti, cacti fruit, and succulents; rocks and soil are also ingested, perhaps to aid in digestion. Although their water needs can be met by the foods they consume, desert tortoises are able to drink water in large amounts (up to 45% of their body weight), which is stored for future use. They are, however, subject to dehydration, and when handled will urinate as a defense mechanism. Because this causes a tortoise to lose its critical water stores, they should never be handled.

Desert tortoises inhabit the gravelly slopes outside the canyons of Red Rock within the creosote bush scrub and blackbrush scrub plant communities. From birth to death, a lifespan of up to 80 years, most tortoises remain within two miles of their birth site.

### Mojave Max

A sure-fire way to see a desert tortoise is simply to visit the tortoise habitat at the Red Rock Canyon Visitor Center in the spring or fall. There lives Mojave Max, a tortoise recovered after being poached from the wild. He usually emerges from his burrow in March or April.

This trait makes the desert tortoise especially susceptible to habitat loss. Expanding urban areas and human collection have had serious detrimental effects on populations of desert tortoises in and around the Las Vegas Valley. Additionally, urbanization fosters higher-than-normal populations of ravens, which prey on young tortoises. In response to declining populations, the desert tortoise was listed federally as a threatened species in 1989. Currently, there are a number of organizations dedicated to protecting this venerable species.

## Northern Pacific Treefrog.................................. *Pseudacris regilla*

These small (to 2" long), green or brown frogs have suction cups on their toes. Active night and day, they feed primarily on flying insects caught with their sticky tongues. Despite their name, these treefrogs are typically ground-dwellers who live among the low-growing vegetation in riparian areas. They are commonly encountered in the pools of First Creek, Pine Creek, and La Madre Spring in the spring and late summer. Northern Pacific treefrogs are quite vocal, especially during the evening, and make the quintessential *rib-bit* call as well as a *kreck-ek*.

## Red-spotted Toad............................................. *Anaxyrus punctatus*

These amphibians, the most common at Red Rock, are slightly larger than a silver dollar and have red-tipped warts that pale as they age. They feed on a wide variety of insects, which they catch using their long, sticky tongues. Primarily nocturnal, they can be seen in the daylight during breeding season, which lasts from March to September. Females lay large clutches of eggs (sometimes as many as 5000) in nearly any pool, stream, or puddle. The male's call, which is a prolonged, high-pitched trill, is often heard at dusk near Calico Spring, Ash Creek Spring, Willow Spring and along intermittent streams in the canyons of Black Velvet, First Creek, Pine Creek, and Ice Box.

# Invertebrates
### *of Red Rock Canyon*

This section describes some of the more common and dramatic invertebrates found at Red Rock.

An invertebrate does not have a backbone and has either an exoskeleton, such as spiders, beetles, and snails; or no skeleton at all such as worms and caterpillars. Many of these species are low in the food chain and provide food for other organisms.

*A male tarantula searching for a mate near White Rock Spring.*

### Desert Tarantula ................................................*Aphonopelma iodius*

These strikingly large (to 5" across), hairy spiders use fangs to inject venom into a variety of insects and small vertebrates. The venom dissolves the soft tissues of their prey, allowing tarantulas to suck the carcasses dry.

They are nocturnal and live in silk-lined burrows of their own construction. In late summer, males are often seen during daytime in the washes and canyons of Red Rock in search of mates. After mating, the female sometimes catches and eats the male. Although venomous, tarantulas avoid conflict with humans. The effect of a bite is reportedly similar to that of a bee sting.

### Tarantula Hawk
*Pepsis* spp.

These large (up to 2"), metallic-blue-black wasps have orange wings. A pregnant female paralyzes a tarantula by stinging it, then lays eggs in the tarantula's body where the larvae will feed. Although not aggressive to humans, tarantula hawks will sting when provoked. The sting causes immediate, excruciating pain.

## Giant Hairy Scorpion ................................... *Hadrurus arizonensis*

These are the largest (to 6" long) scorpions in North America. They can be identified by their yellow color, black backs, stinger-tipped tails, and large forearms equipped with pincers.

Scorpions hunt at night using vibrations picked up by body hairs to detect prey, which includes insects and small vertebrates. During the day, they are found in their burrows, under rocks, or in shady crevices. After birth, young scorpions ride on their mothers' backs for a week or more before leaving.

For humans, a sting from this species is painful, but considered relatively mild unless an allergic reaction occurs.

## Desert Recluse Spider
*Loxosceles deserta*

Closely related to the brown recluse, these venomous spiders are about the size of a quarter and uniformly brown in color with a very faint violin shape behind their eyes. They are occasionally encountered when disturbing brush and debris in shady areas. They will not bite unless cornered. If bitten, medical attention is needed ASAP.

## Black Widow Spider
*Latrodectus hesperus*

Identified by a red hourglass on the underside of its bulbous, black abdomen, these spiders can be found in recessed areas during warmer months. Although they produce a powerful venom, deaths are rare because the spider is not aggressive towards humans and injects only a tiny amount of venom.

## Jerusalem Cricket
*Stenopelmatus* spp.

Neither from Jerusalem nor a cricket, these large (to 2½" long), nocturnal creatures have black-banded abdomens and big, tannish-orange heads. They burrow in organic soils and primarily feed on decomposing plant material. These insects bite, but are not venomous.

## Wind Scorpions
order: *Solifugae*

Neither scorpions nor fond of wind, these large (to 3" wide, including legs), nocturnal creatures feed on termites, beetles, spiders, and even small reptiles with their unusually large and powerful, pinching mouthparts. Although non-venomous, wind scorpions can inflict a painful bite if handled. Found at low elevations at night.

## Darkling Beetles
family: *Tenebrionidae*

These black beetles are about 1" long and feed on decaying material. They are commonly seen crossing trails and washes. If disturbed, they assume a defensive pose by standing on their heads and releasing a foul odor, which earns them the name 'stink bug.' At Red Rock, the two most commonly seen types can be distinguished by their wing covers: smooth or grooved.

## Ticks
chiefly *Dermacentor hunteri*

These parasitic members of the arachnid family (they have eight legs) feed on the blood of mammals and occasionally birds and reptiles. Their standard pose, as seen in the photo, is at the end of a shrub or grass, arms stretched ready to attach to a host. They are capable of engorging their bodies to many times their original size. At Red Rock, ticks are occasionally found in the fall and spring, especially around the brushy areas in the canyons. Although these ticks can transmit disease, infection is unlikely if they are removed in a timely fashion.

*Variegated Meadowhawk*

## Dragonflies

These insects have long tails, big eyes, and hold their four wings outstretched at rest. They are fast-flying predators that eat flying insects, such as mosquitoes, flies, and bees. Dragonflies begin life as aquatic nymphs, then metamorphose into adults. There are many species at Red Rock, and colors include red, blue, green, and brown.

*Vivid Dancer*

## Damselflies

These dragonfly relatives can be distinguished by their smaller size and wings that are held *along* their bodies when at rest. Weak fliers, they are most often found near water, whereas strong-flying dragonflies can be found far from water. Their coloration typically is blue or green, and females may be brown.

## White-lined Sphinx Moth
*Hyles lineata*
These large (wingspan 2" to 3"), brown moths have white lines on their wings and bodies. As caterpillars, they are yellow or green and black and feed on plant foliage. Adults feed on flower nectar much in the same fashion as hummingbirds. They can be found in the spring and summer in areas with abundant flowers.

## Yucca Moths
*Tegeticula yuccasella* species complex
These small (less than 1"), moths are crucial for the reproduction of yuccas and Joshua trees, which are unable to self-pollinate. Female yucca moths stuff rolled balls of pollen, laden with their eggs, into a flower (see photo). The larvae eat some of the plant's seeds, but many are left to germinate.

## Western Tent Caterpillar
*Malacosoma californicum*
Each spring, the tent-like nests of these large (1½" long), light-blue-flanked, hairy caterpillars can be found, mostly in desert almond bushes. The caterpillars feed on the leaves of the plant, then metamorphose into moderately large (wingspan to 2"), brown moths. The desert almond bushes are left to regrow their leaves.

## Fairy, Tadpole, and Clam Shrimp
This diverse group of small (½" to 1" long) creatures lives in temporary pools and tanks that fill with rainwater. As the water source dries, eggs are laid that hatch when rains return. Fairy shrimp lack shells, while tadpole shrimp have single shells, and clam shrimp have clamshell-like shells. All are vulnerable to human activity. Do not disturb dry tanks or introduce materials to wet ones.

*Tadpole Shrimp*

## Springsnails
*Pyrgulopsis turbatrix* and *P. deaconi*
Endemic to southern Nevada, these two species of springsnails are found in certain perennial springs at Red Rock Canyon. Both species are tiny (less than ⅛" long), dark brown or black in color, and feed on algae and detritus. They are species of conservation concern and require a steady flow of clean water.

*Southeastern Nevada Springsnail (Pyrgulopsis turbatrix)*

Butterflies begin their lives as eggs that hatch into caterpillars, which feed on the foliage of certain plant hosts, then metamorphose into winged butterflies. Winged butterflies feed mainly on flower nectar and deposit eggs onto host plants for the cycle to continue.

Over 100 species of butterflies have been recorded in the Spring Mountains, which include Red Rock Canyon. Below are some of the more common and conspicuous species that are likely to be encountered. Further resources are listed on page 198.

# Butterflies and Skippers

### Indra Swallowtail
*Papilo indra*
**Wingspan:** 2½" to 3" - moderately large.
**Identification:** Wings and bodies are black with a pale-yellow stripe across the wings. Orange-black 'eyes' are on the hindwings behind the body.
**Plant hosts:** Members of the parsley family.
**Habitat:** Hilly, rocky areas in and just below the pinyon-juniper woodlands.

### Orange Sulphur
*Colias eurytheme*
**Wingspan:** 1⅜" to 2¾" - medium-sized.
**Identification:** Large green eyes. Yellow, sometimes orangish wings with black borders on the upperside. Two dark rings are visible on the underside of each wing.
**Plant hosts:** Chiefly plants of the pea family.
**Habitat:** Many habitats: one of the most common butterflies in North America.

### Gray Hairstreak
*Strymon melinus*
**Wingspan:** ⅞" to 1⅜" - small.
**Identification:** Wings are blue-gray above, gray below, with yellow or orange spots near the tail.
**Plant hosts:** Many, chiefly members of the pea and mallow family.
**Habitat:** Open, non-forested, weedy areas: Spring Mountain Ranch.

### Northern White-skipper
*Heliopetes ericetorum*
**Wingspan:** 1¼" to 1½" - medium-sized.
**Identification:** Orange-tipped antennae. Wings are white-tan with dark chevrons along the upperside trailing edge.
**Plant hosts:** Members of the mallow family.
**Habitat:** Open areas with moderately dense vegetation: canyon mouths along the Red Rock Escarpment and Calico Hills.

## Western Pygmy Blue
*Brephidium exilis*
**Wingspan:** ½" to ¾" - tiny.
**Identification:** Wings are light brown with blue the near body, and have a row of black dots at the edge of the hindwings.
**Plant hosts:** Members of the goosefoot family, such as four-wing saltbush.
**Habitat:** Low areas with disturbed or alkaline soils: Red Spring.

## Queen Butterfly
*Danaus gilippus*
**Wingspan:** 2⅝" to 3⅞" - large.
**Identification:** Underside of wings is bright orange with white spots, black borders and veins. Unlike the monarch butterfly, the upperside of the wings have, at most, pale black veins.
**Plant hosts:** Desert milkweed.
**Habitat:** Low, open areas and gravelly slopes.

## Arizona Sister
*Adelpha eulalia*
**Wingspan:** 3" to 5" - large.
**Identification:** Wings are dark brownish-black above with a white bar across the middle and orange spots at the wingtips. Underside of wings is multi-colored.
**Plant hosts:** Members of the oak family.
**Habitat:** Areas of mixed chaparral with scrub oak, usually near water.

## Sagebrush Checkerspot
*Chlosyne acastus*
**Wingspan:** 1½" to 2" - medium-sized.
**Identification:** Upperside of wings is checkered orange and black or brown. Underside of hindwing has white checkers.
**Plant hosts:** Rabbitbrush and certain other members of the aster family.
**Habitat:** Washes and gravelly areas in pinyon-juniper woodlands.

## Painted Lady
*Vanessa cardui*
**Wingspan:** 2" to 2⅞" - moderately large.
**Identification:** Upperside of wings is orange with patches of brownish-black. Wing tips are black with white patches.
**Plant hosts:** Many, especially members of the thistle, mallow, and pea families.
**Habitat:** Many habitats: the most widely distributed butterfly in the world.

# Fossils
### of Red Rock Canyon

With a trained eye, fossils are surprisingly easy to find. However, complete, well-preserved specimens are rare.

The limestones and dolomites at Red Rock Canyon hold a diverse and fascinating collection of fossils from sea-dwelling animals who lived millions of years ago during the Paleozoic.

Later, during the age of dinosaurs, the landscape was not as conducive to fossil forming but some trace fossils do remain.

Trace fossils are usually marks made by an animal, such as footprint tracks. They can reveal clues about their makers behavior and the environment they lived in. Body fossils, alternatively, are body parts that have been replaced with minerals or, less commonly, remain in their natural state.

More information on the rock formations mentioned below can be found on pages 15 and 23.

*Actinocoelia sp.*
Kaibab Fm.

## Sponges...............Phylum: *Porifera*

Sponges are colonies of specialized cells that catch food from passing water. Found in nearly all carbonate rocks of the Spring Mountains, their fossilized remains take many forms, such as the honeycomb at left; collections of radially extending hair-like skeletons, as in the genus *Chaetetes*; dark brown or black rounded nodules; and stromatoporoids, described below.

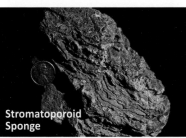
Stromatoporoid Sponge

## Stromatoporoids
### Class: *Stromatoporata*

This class of sponges were dominant reef builders in Paleozoic oceans. The living tissue of the sponge existed on the surface of the skeleton where it fed by filtering food particles from the water. Small bumps, called mamelons, on the surface served to convey water out of the sponge and can be found on well-preserved specimens. As it grew, the sponge secreted calcium-rich minerals into layers, which serve to characterize the fossils. However, not all layered mineral formations in carbonate rocks of the region are stromatoporoids. In the Bird Spring and Mountain Springs Formations at Red Rock Canyon, the fossils are typically dome or mat-shaped and can be many feet wide. The stick-shaped *Amphipora* are found only in the Sultan Formation of the Devonian Period.

*Amphipora* sp.

## Trilobites ................Class: *Trilobita*

After flourishing during the Cambrian, populations of these marine arthropods declined steadily until extinction at the end of the Permian. While some had legs and scavenged the sea floor, others were filter feeders able to swim. At Red Rock, trilobites occur in the Bird Spring and Bonanza King Formations as well as the Dunderberg Shale of the Nopah Formation.

## Forams ........Phylum: *Foraminifera*

Inhabiting nearly all zones in the ocean, animals in this diverse group are about the size of a grain of rice or smaller and have a shell. *Foraminifera* commonly make up plankton in the oceans today. Well-preserved specimens display elaborate structures inside the shell. At Red Rock, they are best known from the Bird Spring Formation.

Bird Spring Formation

## Snails ..................Class: *Gastropoda*

Characterized by their coiled shells, which come in many shapes, snails were abundant in the Paleozoic seas of this region. However, their fragile shells typically broke apart before fossilization could occur. At Red Rock, they are found in the Virgin Limestone and Bird Spring Formation, and occasionally in the Monte Cristo and Sultan Formations.

*Maclurites* sp.

## Sea Lilies ..............Class: *Crinoidea*

Connected to the sea floor by a stem, sea lilies have a crown-like cluster of 'arms' that sway with the ocean's current and catch food particles. Their stems usually break into small disks before being fossilized and are more commonly found than the entire animal. They are found in the Kaibab, Toroweap, Bird Spring, and Monte Cristo Formations at Red Rock.

Stem Fragment Kaibab Formation

## Moss Animals  Phylum: *Bryozoa*

*Bryozoa* are tiny, soft-bodied, filter feeders that mostly live in large colonies. Individuals within the colony have specialized roles and cannot survive alone. Some colonies built lacy, fan-like skeletons that have been fossilized. At Red Rock, these fossilized skeletons are usually less than a few inches wide. They can be found in most post-Cambrian limestones.

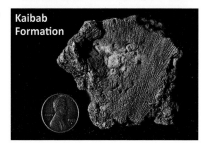

Kaibab Formation

*Caninia* sp.

*Lithostrotionella* sp.

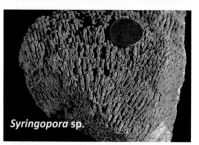
*Syringopora* sp.

Productid Brachiopod Kaibab Formation

*Spirifer* sp. Bird Spring Formation

## Rugose Corals ...... Order: *Rugosa*

This extinct group of corals lived attached to the sea floor. Their skeletons, which we see fossilized today, have radial partitions that look like spokes in a wheel. The soft parts of the animal, called polyps, lived between the spokes. Each polyp trapped food with tentacle-like arms. Simple digestive organs processed the food.

Solitary rugose corals are also known as horn corals because of their horn-like shape, which is often hard to distinguish in poorly preserved specimens. Colonial rugose corals, such as *Lithostrotionella* spp. from the Spring Mountains, are tube-shaped and usually found in large clusters. Some unusually long (up to 10") solitary rugose coral specimens are found in the Monte Cristo Formation at Mount Potosi. Both types are found in the Bird Spring Formation and the Sultan Limestone.

## Tabulate Corals Order: *Tabulata*

This extinct group lived on the sea floor and fed in a similar fashion as the rugose corals. Their skeletons, however, are dense clusters of long, slender tubes with horizontal platforms where the polyps lived. At Red Rock Canyon, these fossilized corals can be found in the Bird Spring and Monte Cristo Formations and the Sultan Limestone.

## Seashells or Brachiopods

Phylum: *Brachiopoda*

These animals have two shells that open to feed and close for protection. Most brachiopods attach themselves to the sea floor with a soft-tissue stalk. Unlike clams, oysters, and mussels (Class: *Bivalvia*), the upper and lower shells of brachiopods are not symmetrical. The left and right sides of each shell, however, are symmetrical.

During the Paleozoic, brachiopods were abundant in warm, shallow seas and a dominant life form in reef environments. After the Permian extinction, brachiopods were out-competed by bivalves and a less-diverse group of species exists today.

At Red Rock, fossilized brachiopod shells are found in the Virgin and Sultan Limestones and in the Kaibab, Toroweap, Bird Springs, Monte Cristo, and Nopah Formations.

## Petrified Wood
In the Upper Triassic at Red Rock, trees from a coniferous forest were quickly buried by gravels and sand carried by a torrential flow of water. The cells of the wood were replaced by silica minerals from groundwater to become stone. Trace minerals often give petrified wood fantastic colors. The specimens at Red Rock are typically shades of brown and beige.

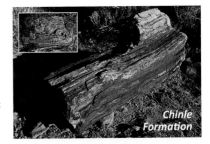
Chinle Formation

## Grallator
*Grallator* (a name given specifically to the tracks, not any one species) tracks were made by a large-dog-sized, carnivorous dinosaur that walked on two legs, such as those depicted on page 19. *Grallator* tracks were first discovered at Red Rock in 2011. The presence of such an animal indicates there was a thriving ecosystem in the vast sand dunes of the Early Jurassic.

Aztec Sandstone

## Octopodichnus
These track fossils were made by an eight-legged arthropod, likely an extinct ancestor to scorpions or spiders of today. The tracks, made in Aztec Sandstone, would have been laid down when the sand was wet, probably during seasonal monsoons like those found in central Africa today. *Octopodichnus* tracks are arranged in alternating left-right groups of four.

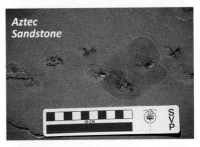
Aztec Sandstone

## Brasilichnium
These track fossils, found in Aztec Sandstone, were made by squirrel-sized, mammal-like reptiles of the synapsid clade. The animals were communal at times, but little is known of their appearance. They may have had fur, as portrayed on page 19, but just as likely had scales like lizards of today. Well-preserved tracks are about ½" wide and show four toes.

Aztec Sandstone

## Dendrites
These pseudofossils are mineral deposits that often take on a tree-like form. They form when minerals, such as manganese, precipitate out of water, usually in small cracks in the surrounding rock. At Red Rock, black-colored manganese dendrites are commonly found in limestones and Aztec Sandstone. Red-colored hematite dendrites are also found in Aztec Sandstone.

Manganese Dendrite

# Yuccas and Agave
## *of Red Rock Canyon*

Native to the Americas, yuccas and agaves are known for their rosettes of tough, dagger-shaped leaves and large clusters of cream-colored flowers. The channeled leaves direct rainfall towards the roots and are pointed to guard water reserves. Some species have chemicals on their leaf tips, which can cause allergic reactions in humans.

To reproduce, all species have a symbiotic relationship with yucca moths (see page 101) that pollinate flowers and lay eggs, which hatch in the fruit to eat some, but not all, of the seeds.

### Joshua Tree .............................................................. *Yucca brevifolia*

Joshua trees have clusters of dagger-like leaves at the ends of their upright branches. The trees can grow to about 30' tall. They bloom in early spring if the winter was cold enough. The cream-colored rosettes of flowers, which form at the tips of the branches, are pollinated exclusively by yucca moths (see page 101). The pickle-shaped seed pods mature in early summer and eventually fall to the ground.

Endemic to the Mojave Desert, Joshua trees, once classified under the lily family, are members of the agave family. They are common at lower elevations at Red Rock Canyon (3500' to 4300'), especially on the flats and rolling hills below the Red Rock Escarpment.

The stiff, pointed leaves were once fed upon by now-extinct giant sloths (see page 25). Today the flowers and fruits feed small mammals that help spread the seeds. Ladder-backed woodpeckers are often seen probing the trunk and old fruits for grubs. The Southern Paiutes ate the fruits after boiling or pit roasting, and the seeds after drying and grinding them into meal. The name of the plant was given by Mormon settlers in the mid 1800s who thought the tree looked like the biblical character Joshua holding his arms to the sky in prayer.

## Mojave Yucca
*Yucca schidigera*

Mojave yucca is an upright, tree-like species that typically grows 6' to 8' tall. A few specimens, however, reach heights of 30' and are thought to be over 100 years old. The leaves of this species are bright yellow-green and grow to about 3' long. A large cluster of cream-colored flowers is produced in the spring, followed by hard, pickle-shaped fruits. Mojave yucca is found throughout the lower elevations of Red Rock on hillsides to about 4500'. The Southern Paiutes used this plant in a number of ways: leaf fibers for baskets and sandals, roots for making soap and shampoo, and the sweet-tasting flowers for food.

## Banana Yucca
*Yucca baccata*

Banana yucca is a low-growing, shrub-like species that typically grows no higher than the 3' leaves can reach. The leaves of this species are dull green with a hint of blue. A large cluster of cream-colored flowers is produced in the spring. These flowers become firm, banana-shaped fruits, hence the name of the plant. Banana yucca inhabits higher elevations, such as near the High Point Overlook on the Scenic Drive and higher up into the mountains. The Southern Paiutes used this plant as they did the Mojave yucca, although the dried fruit of this species was preferred, like dried apples of today.

## Utah Agave...................................................................................... *Agave utahensis*

Found above 4000' in rocky areas, this hardy species has a thick, basal rosette of short, toothed leaves. The plant grows for 7 to 10 years, then in late April, it rapidly shoots a stiff, tall stalk that draws all of the nutrients from the plant to produce flowers and seeds. So many nutrients go into the flowers and seeds that the plant dies after the seeds are ripe.

Native peoples harvested the hearts of Utah agave in early spring when sugars were concentrated in the plant. After roasting in earthen pits, the hearts were eaten in the manner artichokes are eaten today, but their though fibers were also chewed then spit out.

flowering stalk

after flowering (left), with stalk (right)

# Cacti
## *of Red Rock Canyon*

To deal with infrequent, and sometimes brief, heavy rainstorms, cacti have widespread, shallow root systems to better capture rainfall, a sponge-like interior for storing water, and in some species, a corrugated exterior, which allows expansion of the to accommodate water reserves, and shrink when dry.

Without leaves, cacti conduct photosynthesis on the surface of their stems. To reduce the amount of water lost through evaporation in hot temperatures, they switch to a method of photosynthesis whereby they can store carbon dioxide during the day and use it to photosynthesize during the night when temperatures are lower.

To protect their stored water from animals, cacti are covered with spines and infuse the water with oxalic acid, which makes it toxic or unpalatable to most mammals. Spines also serve to shade the plant and dissipate heat.

### California Barrel Cactus ........................ *Ferocactus cylindraceus*

Barrel-shaped and typically growing singly, this species is densely covered with stout spines that are sometimes hooked and vary in color from stunning magenta

to yellow, gray, and black. Their yellow flowers bloom in late spring in a ring at the top of the plant and are followed by dry seed pods.

Exceptionally slow growing, after four years these cacti are only 3" to 4" tall, at maturity they are typically 3' to 4' tall. The largest specimens, which occasionally reach 9', are over 100 years old. They are commonly found on rocky, south-facing slopes at middle elevations throughout Red Rock Canyon.

California barrel cacti are infrequently eaten by mule deer and bighorn sheep, which are able to knock the spines away with their hooves to get at the moist, spongy interior. Although moist, the interior is unlikely to please thirsty humans since it contains bitter alkaloid compounds.

### Cottontop Cactus
*Echinocactus polycephalus*

This species appears similar to the California barrel cactus, but it grows in clumps, is rarely over 18" tall, and the spines are less colorful. After yellow flowers bloom in the spring, a fluffy, cotton-like tuft forms containing seeds. Although not abundant at Red Rock, this cactus can be found at lower and middle elevations on rocky hillsides.

## Strawberry Hedgehog
*Echinocereus engelmannii*
This cactus grows as a low (less than 18") clump of several upright stems. The spines are straight and colorful—yellow, pink, white, brown, gray, and occasionally black—hence the alternate name: calico cactus.

Its magnificent funnel-shaped fuchsia flowers form in late April and early May. The sugar-rich fruits that follow are an important food item for birds, squirrels, and other rodents. This cactus is found in rocky and gravelly soils up to 5000' throughout Red Rock.

The strawberry-tasting fruits were collected and eaten fresh by Southern Paiutes in the summer. Even today, many report that they are the best tasting fruits of any cactus species in the region.

*Right: The big, beautiful flowers of the strawberry hedgehog delight visitors in April and May. Look for them in Calico Basin and below the canyons.*

## Mojave Kingcup Cactus
*Echinocereus mojavensis*
This cactus has many short, upright stems that grow in mound-shaped clumps with interlocking, gray and white spines. Brilliant red flowers, produced in the spring, are followed by juicy, edible fruit. One of the less common cacti at Red Rock Canyon, this cactus prefers higher elevations with rocky terrain, such as the White Rock Hills.

## Desert Spinystar
*Escobaria vivipara* var. *deserti*
This small (less than 8" tall), barrel-shaped cactus is covered in small, straight, white spines with reddish-brown tips. While inconspicuous, they can be seen emerging from the ground in rocky and gravelly areas above 3300'. In late spring, straw-colored flowers bloom, but each flower opens for only about two hours.

## Pricklypear Cacti................................................................ *Opuntia* spp.

There are four species, plus several varieties, of pricklypear cacti that grow at Red Rock Canyon. Pricklypear cacti are recognized by their roundish, flat pads. While distinctions between some species and their varieties are technical, the casual observer will easily recognize three types: those with spines and large pads (up to 8" wide), those with spines and small pads (less than 4" wide), and those without spines.

Pancake Pricklypear

Tulip Pricklypear

Grizzlybear Pricklypear

Beavertail Cactus

At Red Rock, pricklypears with large pads and spines are uncommon, but include the **pancake pricklypear** (*Opuntia chlorotica*) and the **tulip pricklypear** (*Opuntia phaeacantha*). **Pancake pricklypear** is easily recognized by its stout trunk; in contrast, **tulip pricklypear** grows in a sprawling manner. **Pancake pricklypear** inhabits steep, south-facing, rocky areas throughout the Calico Hills and rocky outcrops along the Red Rock Escarpment. The trunkless **tulip pricklypear** grows in well-drained soils, chiefly in the area around Willow Springs, and forms plump, pale blueish-green pads.

At Red Rock, pricklypears with small pads are fairly common, and include at least two varieties of **Plains pricklypear** (*Opuntia polyacantha*) that can be distinguished by the length of their spines: **Hairspine pricklypear** (*Opuntia polyacantha* var. *polyacantha*) has spines that look 'normal' for a cactus, while **grizzlybear pricklypear** (*Opuntia polyacantha* var. *erinacea*) has spines that can grow to 6" in length and sometimes look like long, gray hair hanging off the pads. Both varieties are shrub-like and can grow to about 3' high. In late spring, attractive yellow or peach-colored flowers bloom, followed by dry, spine-covered seed pods. This species can reduce the water content in its sap to tolerate higher elevations and colder temperatures than other cacti.

The only pricklypear without spines at Red Rock is the **beavertail cactus** (*Opuntia basilaris*). The plant is protected by clusters of short, sharp bristles (called glochids) that are irritating to the skin and hard to remove. This pricklypear is low growing (to 2' tall) and has medium-sized, flat pads. From March to early June, before other cacti species bloom, beautiful, magenta flowers are produced. The fruit that follows is hard and dry when ripe.

The Southern Paiutes ate the pads and fruit of all pricklypear species. They also rubbed the short bristles (glochids) into warts to remove the growths.

# Buckhorn Cholla
*Cylindropuntia acanthocarpa*

This upright cactus grows from a central stalk and has long, slender, branching stems that may reach a height of 5' to 6'. The yellow or orange flowers bloom in late May with a purple to reddish-brown tint that increases as the flower ages. Interestingly, if the stamen filaments within the flower are touched, they move.

The flowers produce a dry seed pod that is covered with spines. When seed pods or stem segments fall to the ground, desert woodrats pile them up for nest protection. Sometimes, animals and humans accidentally transport the seed pods, bringing seeds to new locations.

Although not common throughout the Mojave Desert, buckhorn cholla is a prevalent species below the Red Rock Escarpment and in the Calico Hills.

# Silver Cholla
*Cylindropuntia echinocarpa*

This species appears similar to the buckhorn cholla, but its branches are more densely clumped together. Between March and early May, yellow flowers bloom with tinges of red at the edges. Like the buckhorn cholla, its seed pods are covered in spines. Silver cholla can be found in the Calico Hills and along SR-159.

# Blue Diamond Cholla
*Cylindropuntia multigeniculata*

This species is a local specialty originally known only from the south end of Blue Diamond Hill. The cactus is similar in size to the silver cholla, but has spineless fruit and very short, compact branches that can nearly obscure the stems from view. It grows on well-drained, rocky slopes at a certain few locations in the region.

# Branched Pencil Cholla
*Cylindropuntia ramosissima*

Typically less than 4' tall, the branches of this cactus are thin (¼" to ⅜"), like a pencil, with long spines. Quarter-sized, yellow flowers are produced in the spring. When this species loses water in response to dry or cold conditions, the stems turn purple. The pencil cholla grows on gravelly, middle-elevation slopes at Red Rock.

# Trees and Shrubs
## *of Red Rock Canyon*

Although much of the Mojave Desert is too hot to support trees, the higher elevations at Red Rock provide a more moderate climate that allows a number of trees and shrubs to take root. Usually, trees form a single trunk, whereas shrubs have many branches originating at the ground. Both are perennial, meaning they normally live for more than one year, although some become seasonally dormant.

### Ponderosa Pine ........................................................*Pinus ponderosa*

A majestic tree that can grow over 200' tall and live more than 450 years, the ponderosa pine has three long (5" to 10") needles per follicle and a stout, relatively straight trunk. The bark has a delightful aroma, described by some as vanilla, others as butterscotch. Ponderosa pines can be found in the cool, moist canyons of the Red Rock Escarpment. These trees are thought to be descendants of a Pleistocene forest that was contiguous with those of Mount Charleston.

### Pinyon Pine ..............................................................*Pinus monophylla*

The pinyon pine has only one 2" needle growing from each follicle. It grows as tall as 25' and has a wide, spreading crown. Pinyon pines are found near the mouths of the canyons, at Willow Springs, and atop the Red Rock Escarpment where they can be beautifully sculpted by the wind. Pinyons produce cones filled with pine nuts every year, but only once every two to three years is a heavy crop put forth. In years of plentiful nuts, Southern Paiutes gathered multiple family groups together to harvest the crop as well as perform songs, dances, and storytelling in accordance with their concept of *puha* (see page 35). They also used the pine pitch for waterproofing baskets, adhesives, mortar, sealants, and chewing gum.

# Utah Juniper.................................................. *Juniperus osteosperma*

Utah juniper grows to 20' in areas above 4500' and has a broad, rounded crown. The tree can live for 650 years. At Red Rock Canyon, it is the predominant conifer with scale-like, yellow-green leaves and a reddish-brown, fibrous bark. In the spring, juniper berries are produced, important fodder for many species. The Southern Paiutes used the bark fibers for sandals, skirts, rope, and slow-burning matches. They also boiled the twigs and berries to make a cold remedy.

# Frémont Cottonwood.......................................... *Populus fremontii*

Frémont cottonwoods are tall (to 100'), deciduous trees with heavily-furrowed gray bark and broad, heart-shaped leaves. They grow only near water or where their deep roots tap into underground moisture. In the spring, mature trees produce white, cotton-like seeds that float in the wind. Deciduous, the leaves drop after a burst of yellow in the fall. The wood is soft and weak, requiring the trunk and load-bearing branches to be of a large diameter to support the weight of the tree. Notable places to find cottonwoods are Willow Springs and near Blue Diamond, which was previously named Cottonwood Ranch due to the abundance of this tree.

# Singleleaf Ash........................................................ *Fraxinus anomala*
# Velvet Ash ................................................................ *Fraxinus velutina*

Velvet ash is a tree that may reach 40' and has leaves that are compound with three to nine leaflets. Singleleaf ash is more shrubby, grows only to about 25', and has simple leaves. In the spring, both species produce maple-like, winged seed packets. Both ash species occur in riparian areas, but singleleaf ash can also be found in wash plant communities. Because of its strength and straight grain, the wood of the velvet ash was used by Southern Paiutes for making tools.

*Velvet Ash*    *Singleleaf Ash*

### Scrub Oak
*Quercus turbinella*
Growing less than 8', this evergreen shrub has stiff, holly-like, spine-tipped leaves and small acorns. It forms thick brush, occupying every bit of sunlit space wherever it is found, primarily along washes and in the mixed chaparral. **Canyon live oak** (*Q. chrysolepis*) is a taller, more tree-like oak that inhabits mid-elevations.

### Honey Mesquite
*Prosopis glandulosa*
This tree grows to 20' and has long, white thorns and compound leaves with narrow leaflets. It is found below 5200' in sunny areas where groundwater or rainwater is available. Seeds and pods were a staple in Southern Paiute diets: Fresh, they were eaten raw; and mature, they were dried, ground into meal, and stored for later use.

### Catclaw
*Acacia greggii*
Growing to 10' tall, this tree has small, compound leaves that do well to hide the many claw-like thorns that line its younger branches. Sharp enough to draw blood, the thorns often catch clothing. In late spring, pale yellow, cylindrical flower clusters bloom. These are followed by flat, pea-like pods that contain nutritious seeds.

### Utah Serviceberry
*Amelanchier utahensis*
This deciduous shrub, which usually grows to 5', has smooth, gray bark. Its leaves are serrated and can be smooth or fuzzy. In early spring, five-petaled, white flowers bloom. These are followed by currant-like, blueish berries that ripen in the fall. The berries were eaten by Southern Paiutes. Deer and sheep browse on the leaves.

### Coffeeberry
*Frangula californica*
This fast-growing evergreen shrub usually grows to 6' but can reach 20'. Its leaves are oval, 1" to 3" long, and smooth. This shrub produces tiny flowers in the spring that mature to black, pea-sized berries, which look like coffee beans. It is found in gravelly or rocky areas along the base of the Red Rock Escarpment.

## California Redbud
*Cercis orbiculata*

California redbud is a many-branched, deciduous shrub that grows to about 20'. Before the simple leaves appear in early spring, small, purplish, pea-like flowers cover the plant, making this wash-dwelling species unmistakable when Willow Springs and the canyons of Red Rock are splashed with color.

## Desert Willow
*Chilopsis linearis*

This deciduous shrub usually grows to 15'. Its slender leaves are 4" to 6" long and somewhat curved. Large, fragrant, pink flowers bloom in late spring and early summer, followed by pencil-shaped seed pods that can be 14" long. This species is found along washes, such as those leaving Calico Basin and Willow Springs. Although the leaves are willow-like, the plant belongs to the bignonia family, which includes many tropical trees with large flowers. Like willows, the plant creates deep (up to 50') root systems to draw water. Its hard, rot-resistant wood is used for fence posts.

## Ashy Silktassel
*Garrya flavescens*

This fast-growing, evergreen shrub grows to 10'. Its leaves are oval, grayish-green, and sometimes pointed at the tip. Spring-blooming flowers, formed in drab-colored, hanging clusters, are followed by pea-sized fruit. This shrub is found in all of the canyons of Red Rock and provides forage for mule deer and bighorn sheep.

## Skunkbush Sumac
*Rhus trilobata*

This deciduous shrub typically grows to about 6' at middle elevations in washes and on rocky hillsides. The leaves are three-lobed and glossy-green. In the spring, clusters of small, yellow flowers form into red berries. The Southern Paiutes highly valued its branches for basket making and were known to cultivate it for that purpose.

## Desert Almond
*Prunus fasciculata*

Desert almond is a many-branched, deciduous shrub that does not have shiny leaves like those of the similarly shaped creosote bush. In early spring, fragrant ¼" white flowers line the branches and become small, inedible, almond-like fruits. Western tent caterpillars often weave silken nests in the plant (see page 101).

## Creosote Bush ........................................................*Larrea tridentata*

This many-branched shrub grows to 12'. Its nickle-sized, five-petaled, yellow flowers bloom in April and May, then form into white, fuzzy seed-balls. The shiny leaves, indigestible for mammals, have resinous coatings that reduce moisture loss. At Red Rock, it occurs mostly in low areas at the south end of the Red Rock Escarpment and east of the Calico Hills. The plant was used extensively by Southern Paiutes for tools, shelter materials, firewood, and glue for arrowheads. They also made preparations from the plant to cure chicken pox, cramps, venereal diseases, and to sooth burns.

## Manzanita ......................................................*Arctostaphylos pungens*

Manzanita grows to 10' and has exquisite red bark that is smooth to the touch. Its violet-pink to white flowers form in clusters of ¼" bells in late winter and early spring. The name (little apple in Spanish) comes from the fruit, which looks like tiny apples. It is found in all the canyons, the Calico Hills, and atop the Red Rock Escarpment, where it is shorter, gnarled, and spreading.

## Indigo Bush
*Psorothamnus fremontii*
In late spring, deep-purple, pea-like flowers cover the smooth white-gray branches of this 2' to 6' deciduous shrub, making it stand out against the desert backdrop. It is found in flat, rocky slopes outside of the canyons. The plant's binomial name refers to John C. Frémont, who traveled through Red Rock in 1844 (see pages 38 and 40).

## Cliffrose
*Purshia stansburiana*
Growing to 10', this shrub has shaggy, brown bark and small (½" long) leaves. In the spring, five-petaled, rose-like, white flowers cover the plant. Each flower is followed by a small number of yellowish, fuzzy seed-plumes. The Southern Paiutes used the fibrous bark for rope, shirts, sandals, blankets, diapers, and mats.

## Apache Plume
*Fallugia paradoxa*
This 2' to 6'-tall shrub has shaggy, brown bark. It appears similar to cliffrose, but each of its large-petaled flowers produces many pinkish seed plumes. It is found on dry, gravelly slopes and alongside the Red Rock Canyon Scenic Drive. Apache plume and cliffrose are heavily browsed by small mammals and mule deer.

## Four-wing Saltbush
*Atriplex canescens*
This evergreen shrub is densely branched and has small, gray-green leaves. On female plants, inconspicuous green flowers turn into four-winged seed pods. The Southern Paiutes ate the seeds of this plant and used its wood for arrowheads and shafts. At Red Rock, it can be found in areas with alkaline soil, such as near Red Spring.

## White Bursage
*Ambrosia dumosa*
This low (1' to 2') shrub is drought-deciduous and has gray-green leaves. It produces male and female flowers on the same plant. When pollination occurs, a ¼" spherical bur is produced, which contains seeds. Common in the Mojave Desert, this plant inhabits gravelly slopes at lower elevations at Red Rock Canyon.

### Big Sagebrush
*Artemisia tridentata*
Aromatic and growing to 6', sagebrush have fuzzy, gray-green leaves. In the summer, tiny flowers grow along the stems of its upright branches. It's the quintessential Great Basin shrub and the state flower of Nevada. At Red Rock, the plant is not common, but it can be found at higher elevations, such as near Willow Springs.

### Mojave Sage
*Salvia mohavensis*
A low (to 3') shrub with foliage the same color as sagebrush, Mojave sage produces clusters of purple-blue flowers in late spring. It inhabits gravelly areas below the pinyon-juniper woodlands. Southern Paiutes smoked the dried leaves for medicinal purposes and made tea with fresh leaves for sore throats and colds.

### Range Ratany
*Krameria erecta*
This low (to 3'), spreading shrub has grayish-green leaves and produces magenta flowers in the spring. A barb-covered seed pod (inset) follows that acts like Velcro and is occasionally found stuck to clothing. The plant is found in rocky soils below 4000'. Southern Paiutes gathered its tiny seeds for food and made a dye from the roots.

### Paperbag Bush
*Salazaria mexicana*
This low (to 3'), deciduous shrub has branches that grow at right angles. In late spring, each small, purple flower is engulfed by a pinkish sac that grows from the base of the flower. The sac, filled with air and seeds, is transported by the wind. The plant can be found on gravelly or rocky slopes at mid-elevations at Red Rock.

### Spiny Menodora
*Menodora spinescens*
As the name implies, the green branches of this low (to 3') shrub form spines at their tips. While not as sharp or stiff as those of a cactus, the spines are apparent when touched. Small (¼"), white flowers bloom in April and May, followed by two-lobed, pea-sized fruit. The plant is found in gravelly soil throughout Red Rock at mid-elevations.

Mormon Tea

Nevada Jointfir

## Mormon Tea.................................................................. *Ephedra viridis*
## Nevada Jointfir .................................................... *Ephedra nevadensis*

Of the five species of *Ephedra* found at Red Rock, Mormon tea and Nevada jointfir are the two most commonly encountered. These non-flowering plants form erect, broom-like clusters of green, jointed stems that grow to 5' tall. In late spring, male plants produce pollen cones, and female plants produce seed cones. Mormon tea is more yellow-green than Nevada jointfir, which has more angular branches. Mormon tea is common in and near the canyons of Red Rock, and Nevada jointfir is typically found on gravelly slopes below the canyons.

## Turpentinebroom
*Thamnosma montana*

A low (to 3'), branching, green-stemmed plant, turpentine broom has a strong odor. In the spring, bean-sized, deep-purple flowers are followed by two-lobed fruit. The Southern Paiutes made a tea with the plant to treat internal disorders, but in large quantities, the tea would make one 'crazy like coyotes' for a short time.

## Yerba Santa
*Eriodictyon angustifolium*

An evergreen, yerba santa grows to waist-height and has long, slender, dark green leaves. In late spring and summer, clusters of dime-sized, white flowers form at the tips of its upright branches. It inhabits dry, rocky hillsides above 3000'. A tea made from the leaves of the plant is an effective decongestant and allergy reliever.

## Winterfat
*Krascheninnikovia lanata*

This low (to 3½'), evergreen shrub has whitish-green leaves and produces dense tufts of white 'hair,' which follow the small, inconspicuous, spring-blooming flowers. It can be found throughout Red Rock Canyon at mid-elevations, such as in Calico Basin. The name derives from its forage value for livestock during the winter.

Blackbrush

## Blackbrush...................................................... *Coleogyne ramosissima*

This common shrub grows to 5' and is typically less than 3'. For most of the year it is drab-colored, and during the summer, the plant sheds some of its ½" green-gray leaves to reduce moisture lost through evaporation. When wet, its branches transform from dull gray to a rich black, giving the plant its common name. Its dime-sized, yellow flowers bloom in April, May, or June.

Because blackbrush does not recover well after wildfires, but is widespread and of great value to wildlife, the plant has been studied extensively. Research reveals that it takes many thousands of years for a nearly pure stand to form. At Red Rock, such a stand is found east of Mount Wilson (see photo, page 65).

## Cottonthorn
### *Tetradymia axillaris*
Armed with sharp spines, this rounded shrub grows to 5' and produces small (⅜"), petal-less, yellow flowers in May. The flower heads become fuzzy, white seedpods, which resemble cotton balls. This plant can be found on dry, gravelly slopes at mid-elevations along the base of the Red Rock Escarpment.

## Mojave Rabbitbrush
### *Ericameria paniculata*
Growing to waist-height, this densely-branched, broom-shaped shrub blooms in late summer with an explosion of yellow, petal-less flowers. Because its resinous sap contains a small amount of rubber, the plant was considered for economic use during World War II. It is found in washes and sandy canyon bottoms at Red Rock.

## Nevada Goldenrod
### *Solidago spectabilis*
Growing to about 3½', this perennial has an erect, green stem with long, slender, green leaves. In the summer and fall, clusters of many small (⅛"), yellow flowers bloom on small branches atop the stem. The plant, uncommon in the Mojave, is found in moist meadows and stream environs, such as in Pine Creek Cyn. and near La Madre Spring.

## Matchweed
*Gutierrezia sarothrae*
Growing to 18", this evergreen shrub has green (green-gray in winter), resinous leaves. The plant is rather inconspicuous until late summer and fall when numerous clusters of small, yellow flowers form at the tips of its branches. It is common along roadsides and in burned or disturbed gravelly areas.

## Narrowleaf Goldenbush
*Ericameria linearifolia*
This round, mound-shaped shrub grows to 5' and has resinous, green stems that grow from woody branches. In May, daisy-like yellow flowers bloom profusely, nearly covering the plant. Narrowleaf goldenbush inhabits dry, gravelly hillsides and slopes below 6000', such as near the Sandstone Quarry and around the White Rock Hills.

## Whitestem Paperflower
*Psilostrophe cooperi*
This dome-shaped low (to 2') shrub produces large-petaled, yellow flowers in the spring. The five-petaled flowers persist on the plant until they are brown in the fall. With sufficient summer rain, a second blooming occurs in the fall. The plant can be found in gravelly areas below 5000' at Red Rock Canyon.

## Virgin River Brittlebush
*Encelia virginensis*
This 3'-tall shrub produces daisy-like yellow flowers from March to June. It is distinguished by long, unbranched, slender stems, which extend about 1' above a leafy, green dome of foliage below. The plant inhabits rocky slopes, open areas, and roadsides below 4500' throughout Red Rock Canyon.

## Nevada Goldeneye
*Heliomeris multiflora*
This perennial shrub grows in small, bushy clumps. In the spring, yellow, daisy-like flowers bloom at the end of its stems. The plant can be distinguished by its long, slender leaves that grow on opposite sides of the brownish stem. It is found on gravelly soil and roadsides at middle and higher elevations at Red Rock Canyon.

# Flowers
## *of Red Rock Canyon*

This section describes those plants best-known for their flowers; many are non-woody plants that sprout, grow, flower, create seed and die within the span of a year (annuals) or two (biennials). Flowers are arranged by color: white, pink, red, orange, yellow, then shades of purple.

### California Evening Primrose
*Oenothera californica*
This night-blooming plant has large (to 3"), white flowers, and a basal rosette of leaves. In the spring, the sandy areas that the plant inhabits are littered with the fragrant, floppy flowers. Of the eight species of *Oenothera* found at Red Rock Canyon, this species has the widest range and is the most commonly encountered.

### Forget-me-not
*Cryptantha* spp.
Of the many *Cryptantha* species found at Red Rock Canyon, all are less than 18" tall and have tiny (¹⁄₁₆" to ¼"), five-petaled, white flowers and hairy stems. After the flowers bloom (February to May), hairy seed-pods form giving the plant a fluffy appearance. Seed analysis is often necessary to distinguish species.

California Buckwheat

### Buckwheat
*Eriogonum* spp.
There are roughly 21 species of buckwheat that inhabit Red Rock Canyon. All are low (to 3') growing shrubs with dense clusters of whitish-pink flowers that persist from April to November. The plants can be found in rocky soil near the canyons and in the Calico Hills. Buckwheat flowers are a popular source of nectar for bees.

### Jimson Weed
*Datura wrightii*
This perennial plant appears out of place in the desert. In the summer it has large (to 8"), deep-green leaves and produces big, trumpet-shaped, white flowers. A hallucinogenic drink made from this plant was *rarely* used by Southern Paiutes to cure sickness, visit dead relatives, find lost objects, or see the past and future.

## Winding Mariposa Lily
*Calochortus flexuosus*
This delicate and beautiful flower is 1½"
wide, three-petaled, white or light purple
in color, and yellow below the stamens.
Unable to support itself, this fragile
perennial is usually found growing within a
blackbrush or other shrub, which it braces
against. It blooms in the spring and can be
found at mid-elevations at Red Rock.

## Yerba Mansa
*Anemopsis californica*
This creeping perennial has hairy stems and
large (to 6"), basal leaves. In the spring and
summer, its cone of white flowers blooms
above large, white bracts. It grows near
certain springs, such as Red Spring. The
Southern Paiutes used its roots and leaves
in preparations to treat colds, swelling,
muscle pains, and to inhibit infections.

## Rattlesnake Weed
*Chamaesyce albomarginata*
This sprawling perennial has small (¼"),
green leaves that blanket the ground. In
April the plant is covered with flowers. Each
'flower' is actually 15-30 very small flowers
surrounded by white and red bracts. The
plant is found on dry, gravelly slopes.
Southern Paiutes applied the crushed plant
to rattlesnake bites; hence its name.

## Desert Wishbone-bush
*Mirabilis laevis*
This knee-high, spreading perennial has
branches that fork like a wishbone and
hairy, dark-green leaves. Its attractive,
dime-sized, white flowers have long
stamens and bloom in the spring. The plant
can be found in gravelly soils along the
base of the Red Rock Escarpment and in
Calico Basin.

## Foothill Death Camas
*Zigadenus paniculatus*
This perennial grows to 2' from a bulb in
a fashion similar to onions. The bulbs of
this plant, however, are toxic, and human
poisoning has been documented. It is
found at higher elevations, such as in the
vicinity of Willow Springs, in April and May
when a dense cluster of cream colored, ¼"
diameter flowers bloom atop its stalk.

### Desert Pepperweed
*Lepidium fremontii*
Growing to 2', this intricately branched
perennial is an inconspicuous green-drab
color until spring when many clusters
of small, white flowers bloom. The
foliage smells of cabbage or broccoli
when crushed. The plant is a common
component of the creosote bush scrub
plant community.

### Bastard Toadflax
*Comandra umbellata*
This perennial grows to 18" and has slender
leaves along its upright stem. Multiple
plants are often found growing together
in sandy and rocky terrain along washes
and hillsides. In the spring, a cluster of four
or five-petaled, white flowers bloom atop
each stalk. As the flowers age, they become
hues of pink and brown.

### Desert Tobacco
*Nicotiana obtusifolia*
This perennial grows to 3' and has sticky,
dark green leaves, which get smaller along
the stem. In the spring, whitish-green
tubular flowers dot the plant. It is found
in rocky areas below 4000'. The Southern
Paiutes, who believed this plant had large
amounts of *puha,* smoked it and a related
species for health, ceremony, and pleasure.

### Transmontane Sand Verbena
*Abronia turbinata*
This small (less than 10"), spreading
perennial has pinkish stems and oval,
fleshy, green leaves covered in fine hairs. In
the spring, it produces heads of fragrant,
¼"-wide, white flowers. As the name
suggests, the plant favors sandy, well-
drained areas, such as parts of Calico Basin,
and the Wheeler Camp Spring area.

### Flatbud Prickly-poppy
*Argemone munita*
This erect perennial grows to 4' and
has thistle-like leaves along its stalk. In
late spring and early summer, the plant
produces floppy, white flowers. It is
common in dry washes and disturbed areas
along SR-157, but is seldom found along
the escarpment. Southern Paiutes used the
seeds to induce vomiting or as a laxative.

## Desert Milkweed
*Asclepias erosa*
This tall (to 3') perennial has leathery, opposite leaves that ooze a white 'milk' when broken. In late spring and summer, one or more nearly-spherical clusters of small (¼"), greenish-cream flowers bloom atop each stem. Milkweed was an important fiber source used by native peoples for nets, textiles, and mats.

## Canyon Grape
*Vitis arizonica*
This sprawling vine has three-lobed leaves. In April, inconspicuous greenish-white flowers bloom and become edible grapes that ripen in the summer. The plant is found near water, such as in Pine Creek Canyon and near Lost Creek Spring. Both Southern Paiutes and Euro-Americans tended the plant for its fruit.

## New Mexico Thistle
*Cirsium neomexicanum*
This robust, spiny-leaved biennial grows to 8' and has a single stem that branches near the top. From late spring until fall, the plant puts forth showy, pom-pom-like, white or pinkish flowers at the ends of its stems. The plant can be found in gravelly or rocky areas. Before the spines formed, Southern Paiutes ate the young shoots of this plant.

## Scarlet Gaura
*Gaura coccinea*
Growing to 2', this attractive perennial has clusters of unbranched stems and opposite, lance-shaped leaves. Its many flower buds bloom sequentially up to the top of the stem. Each white flower has spoon-shaped petals, long stamens, and becomes reddish with age. The plant can be found in dry areas with rocky or gravelly soil.

## Palmer's Penstemon
*Penstemon palmeri*
This perennial forms clusters of tall (to 5'), erect stems with thick, lance-shaped leaves. In the spring, elegant and fragrant pink flowers line its stems. Each chambered flower has a tuft of yellow hair at its entrance to facilitate pollination by bumble bees. The plant is found on dry, gravelly slopes and along the Scenic Drive.

### Stream Orchid
*Epipactis gigantea*
This upright, large-leaved perennial grows to 3' and blooms quarter-sized, pinkish-green flowers with purple veins in the spring. The plant is found only near permanent sources of water, such as deep in the canyons of Red Rock and near Red Spring. It is quite rare in the Mojave Desert and should not be disturbed.

### Wild Rhubarb
*Rumex hymenosepalus*
This succulent, knee-high perennial can be identified by large, romaine-lettuce-shaped leaves and a tube-like stalk. In early spring, a large head of flowers appears and turns from green to red atop the stalk. The plant can be found in gravelly and sandy areas, such as the dry slopes below the canyons of Red Rock.

### Cardinalflower
*Lobelia cardinalis*
This perennial has an upright stem that grows to about 3'. In late summer, many, vibrantly red, five-lobed flowers bloom at the end of the stem. The flowers are pollinated by hummingbirds. This plant is found only in riparian areas with a year-round flow of water, such as below La Madre Spring and in Pine Creek Canyon.

### Desert Paintbrush
*Castilleja angustifolia*
This unique perennial has a cluster of stems that reach 18". In the early spring, it draws attention with its bright, almost iridescent, red color. While the flowers are tipped red, it is actually the leaves just under the flowers that produce the show. The plant is parasitic, and its roots tap into neighboring plant species for nutrients.

### Utah Penstemon
*Penstemon utahensis*
The tall (to 2'), slender stems of this erect perennial hold many tubular, red flowers, which have striped lobes that fold backwards. It is found in rocky soil along the base of the Red Rock Escarpment. This species and **firecracker penstemon**, which is similar in appearance and habitat, restrict pollen access to hummingbirds.

## Desert Globemallow
*Sphaeralcea ambigua*
This perennial forms clumps of many upright, fuzzy stems that grow to 3'. Its quarter-sized, cupped, orange flowers are some of the first to bloom, beginning in March, and remain blooming until June. Abundant at Red Rock, this plant is often found in gravelly soils, where it does well after fire or along roadsides.

## Desert Poppy
*Eschscholzia glyptosperma*
Growing to 10", this annual has a basal rosette of blueish-green leaves and one or more leafless stems. In the spring, a large (to 2"), showy, four-petaled, yellow-to-orange flower blooms atop each stem. The plant grows in gravelly flats and sandy washes, often associated with the creosote bush scrub plant community.

## Lavenderleaf Sundrops
*Calylophus lavandulifolius*
A low (to 1') perennial that grows in a mound shape, this plant produces large (to 2½"), fragile-looking yellow flowers beginning in April. Blooms occasionally recur at four to five week intervals. Typically found at higher elevations, lavenderleaf sundrops are also found on dry, rocky or gravelly slopes in Calico Basin.

## Desert Marigold
*Baileya multiradiata*
Usually about 18" in height, this short-lived perennial has woolly, white-green stems and basal leaves. Its long-blooming, daisy-like flower is rich yellow in color and first seen in early spring. Common and widespread, this plant inhabits sandy or gravelly flats and hillsides below 5000' throughout Red Rock Canyon.

## Wallace's Wooly Daisy
*Eriophyllum wallacei*
This tiny (typically 2" tall) annual has hairy, whitish-green foliage and emerges in late March. Its flowers, which bloom throughout the spring, are ¼" wide and golden yellow. Commonly found in sandy soils, this diminutive plant can be found in Calico Basin and dry, sunny spots outside of the canyons of Red Rock.

### Desert Dandelion
*Malacothrix glabrata*
This annual grows to 16" and has a basal rosette of hairless, green leaves, which wither by the time its yellow or pale-yellow flowers open. Each showy flower is up to 2" wide and produces a pom-pom of seeds, which are transported by wind. The plant is occasionally found in sandy flats, along roadsides, and other disturbed areas.

### Desert Princesplume
*Stanleya pinnata*
Growing to 5', this perennial has a woody base and prominent stalks, which support plumes of yellow flowers. It can be found in washes and slopes with gravelly soil. Although high in selenium, this plant is nutritionally similar to spinach. It was cultivated by Southern Paiutes who ate the green leaves after repeated boiling.

### Seep Monkeyflower
*Mimulus guttatus*
This small (less than 8") perennial has reddish-green, toothed leaves. In the spring, deep-throated yellow flowers form atop the stem. Each flower has a red dot to attract pollinators. This plant is found at higher-elevation seeps and streams, such as La Madre Spring and deep in the canyons.

### Smoothstem Blazingstar
*Mentzelia laevicaulis*
This erect, branched perennial grows to 3½' and has spear-shaped leaves with wavy or toothed edges. Its large (to 3¼"), five-petaled, yellow flowers bloom in the summer and have very long (to 2¼") stamens. Look for this plant at middle and higher elevations, such as along SR-160 and SR-157, where it thrives in gravelly areas.

### Desert Trumpet
*Eriogonum inflatum*
This knee-high perennial is easily identified by a bizarre, inflated pod in its blueish-green stem. Above the pod, the stem forks and produces tiny yellow flowers in late spring. The unique pod is used to store carbon dioxide so the plant can photosynthesize during the night, losing less water than in the daytime.

## Filaree
*Erodium cicutarium*

This European native is commonly found matting the ground when it blooms from February to May. It has small (¼" wide), five-petaled, lavender-pink flowers and unique seed pods that have long (to 1½"), spike-like protrusions. A common plant at Red Rock Canyon, it can be found in dry, open areas below 6000'.

## Frémont's Phacelia
*Phacelia fremontii*

This low growing (to 8") annual is one of the first to bloom in March. Its bell-shaped, ½"-wide, light-purple flowers have yellow centers. Commonly found in gravelly soil, this plant grows in groups and often covers large patches of ground. Unlike the notch-leaved phacelia of the same genus, this flower does not cause a rash.

## Chia
*Salvia columbariae*

Growing to 18", this annual has a leafless, square stem, which supports up to three round clusters of lavender-colored flowers with purple bracts. A member of the mint family, the plant often grows in groups on sunny, rocky hillsides near the canyons of Red Rock. Southern Paiutes made a mush from the roasted, ground seeds.

## Prairie Clover
*Dalea searlsiae*

This perennial has a long (to 1½'), slender stem, which supports a spike of small (¼" wide), purple flowers with yellow stamens that bloom in late spring, sequentially from bottom to top. The plant can be found in areas of well-drained, sandy or gravelly soil at mid-elevations, chiefly in the blackbrush scrub plant community.

## Notch-leaf Phacelia
*Phacelia crenulata*

**Upon contact with this plant some people experience a poison-ivy-like rash.**
Typically about 12" tall, this spring-blooming annual has glandular hairs on its stems and leaves. Attractive, ⅜"-wide, purple flowers bloom from coiled flower stalks. The plant inhabits sandy or rocky soil and is prolific near Kraft Mountain.

### Blue Eyed Grass
*Sisyrinchium radicatum*
Not actually a grass, this perennial has long, slender stalks that grow to about knee height. From late spring until mid-summer, blueish-purple, six-petaled flowers bloom atop the stalks. This plant, which is of conservation concern, occurs in moist, slightly alkaline meadows and riparian areas, such as those found in Calico Basin.

### Milkvetch
*Astragalus* spp.
Of the 20 species of milkvetch at Red Rock, **freckled milkvetch** (*A. lentiginosus*) is the most common. Most are low-growing (to 18") plants with multiple stems, compound leaves, and many small, pea-shaped, purple flowers that line the stems. They are found in gravelly soils and disturbed areas throughout the conservation area.

### Mojave Woodyaster
*Xylorhiza tortifolia*
This low-growing (to 2') perennial has hairy, elliptical, light-green leaves. Many large (to 2½" wide), pale-purple, yellow-centered, daisy-like flowers bloom above the foliage in the spring, and, with sufficient rainfall, sometimes in the fall. The plant grows in rocky or gravelly soils at mid-elevations at Red Rock Canyon.

### Hoary Tansyaster
*Machaeranthera canescens*
This knee-high, woolly-haired plant has many branching stems and small leaves. Multiple ¾" wide, daisy-like, purple-petaled flowers with yellow centers line the plant in the spring. The plant is found at mid-elevations along roadsides and areas of gravelly soil throughout Red Rock Canyon.

### Darkthroat Shooting Star
*Dodecatheon pulchellum*
This perennial grows to 14" and has erect stems, each of which supports multiple flowers in the spring. Its distinctive, down-turned flowers have purple petals and a yellow center. While not especially common in southern Nevada, this attractive flower can be seen near certain, slightly saline springs at Red Rock Canyon.

## Colorado Four O'clock
*Mirabilis multiflora*
The big (to 2½" wide), beautiful, trumpet-shaped, purple flowers of this sprawling perennial bloom from April to August. The plant has opposite, heart-shaped leaves that lose their fine hairs as they age. The Colorado four o'clock inhabits gravelly terrain, such as dry washes, at mid-elevations throughout Red Rock Canyon.

## Desert Larkspur
*Delphinium parishii*
This tall (to 36"), single-stemmed, erect perennial has triangular, basal leaves. Its distinct, spring-blooming, purplish-blue flowers form along the stem and have tube-like spurs where nectar forms. Although beautiful, this plant is poisonous to humans. It can be found at mid-elevations throughout Red Rock Canyon.

## Bluedicks
*Dichelostemma capitatum*
The long (1' to 2'), slender stems of this perennial grow from an underground bulb and are usually supported by neighboring plants. Each stem is topped with clusters of 2 to 15, ⅜"-wide, lavender-blue flowers. The plant is found along the base of the Red Rock Escarpment. Southern Paiutes ate the bulbs, fresh and dried.

## Woolly Bluestar
*Amsonia tomentosa*
This spring-blooming perennial has a cluster of five-petaled, light blueish-purple flowers atop each of its 10" stems; bean-pod-like seed pods follow. Two varieties exist at Red Rock: those with a hairy, whitish-green stem and leaves, and those with hairless, green foliage. The plant grows in groups in sandy areas.

whitish-green variety

## Alkali Mariposa Lily
*Calochortus striatus*
This low-growing (to 16") perennial has grass-like leaves, which grow from a bulb. Medium-sized, tulip-shaped, whitish-violet flowers with purple veins bloom in the spring. A fairly rare species, this delicate flower prefers alkaline soils and is now flourishing at Red Spring after extensive renovations to the area in the mid-2000s.

# Other Plants and Organisms
## of Red Rock Canyon

This section describes some of the more conspicuous plants and organisms that do not fit well with other sections. Although not especially showy, some of these species play a large role in the ecosystem and support many other forms of life.

## Red Brome
### Bromus rubens
This European-native annual grows to 8" with a head of paintbrush-like seeds. When dry, plant and seeds persist and present a major fire hazard to Mojave Desert ecosystems. Indeed, the number and extent of fires that have plagued Red Rock Canyon in recent times are directly related to this prolific species.

## Desert Needlegrass
### Achnatherum speciosum
This perennial grass grows in clumps 1' to 2' tall. Its basal sheaths are hairy, and the tips of the stems have soft, almost fluffy tufts. It is named because the blades of grass are stiff, pointed, and needle-like when broken. This hardy grass prefers rocky or gravelly areas throughout Red Rock Canyon.

## Indian Ricegrass
### Achnatherum hymenoides
Growing to 2', this perennial grass grows in bunches in dry, sandy soils. Atop its upright stems are masses of thread-like branchlets that support a crown of seeds. Its small, rice-like, black seeds were an important food for Southern Paiute groups. The seeds were gleaned by threshing, then winnowed in baskets, roasted, and ground into flour.

## Common Reed
### Phragmites australis
Growing to 12', this erect, perennial grass forms dense stands in riparian areas. It can be identified by round, hollow stems and long (to 1.5'), ¾" wide leaves. In the fall and winter, fluffy plumes of hairy seeds mature atop the stems. This plant is found only in areas with permanent water sources, such as below La Madre Spring.

## Ferns
### Phylum: *Pteridophyta*
Ferns are non-flowering and require moist conditions to reproduce. However, at Red Rock there are a number of ferns that live in dry, rocky areas where rainfall runoff is concentrated into cracks. Additionally, there are many species that can be found near springs, especially in the cooler, shaded areas deep in the canyons of Red Rock.

Giant Chain Fern
Pine Creek

## Watercress
### *Nasturtium officinale*
This floating perennial has hollow stems and spreads its compound leaves with round leaflets across the surface of water. In the spring and early summer, small, four-petaled, white flowers bloom. This edible plant can be found near permanent water sources, such as White Rock, Wheeler Camp, and Red Springs.

## Mistletoe
### *Phoradendron* spp.
These parasitic plants are found on mesquite, catclaw, Utah juniper, and scrub oak. They look like brown clumps or nest-like clusters and grow roots into the host tree to draw nutrients and water. In February or March, tiny green flowers form and give off a pleasant odor. The flowers turn into pinkish-red, round berries.

## Lichen
Lichen is the product of a symbiotic relationship between algae, which gather nutrients through photosynthesis; and fungi, which provide support and structure. Lichens can become dormant during periods of drought. At Red Rock, lichen is often found on rock surfaces. Generally, each color represents a different species, of which there are thousands.

## Biological Soil Crusts
In arid regions, these complex associations of cyanobacteria, algae, lichens, mosses, fungi, and bacteria grow in the top few inches of soil. They play a vital role in stabilizing the soil from wind and water erosion while adding nutrients for other plants and animals. The crusts form very slowly, approximately ¼" per 100 years and should not be disturbed by human traffic.

½" wide 'bloom'

# Red Rock Canyon Visitor Center
*Administered by the Bureau of Land Management*

N o matter how much time is available or what kind of activities are desired, the visitor center can stimulate ideas and provide assistance.

## ► A Great First-stop

The facilities at the visitor center are designed to enhance the Red Rock Canyon experience. Indeed, most people take away a deeper appreciation of the land, its history, and the plants and animals that call it home.

The facilities include numerous exhibits and displays, many of which are hands on; a desert tortoise habitat; a book shop; and a theatre with a short video about Red Rock Canyon. Knowledgeable volunteers staff an information desk to answer questions and provide brochures about the area, including a free Junior Ranger Discovery Book for kids.

## ► Exhibits and Displays

Inside, visitors will discover professionally-mounted animals, samples of local rocks and fossils, actual petroglyphs created on Aztec Sandstone, beautiful images of the conservation area, and a lizard habitat where a chuckwalla and a desert iguana live. One of the main attractions is an 80'-wide panoramic window that beautifully frames the Calico Hills.

Outside, with a backdrop of colorful sandstone, the Discovery Plaza has nearly 23,000 square feet of interpretive exhibits. The exhibits are set amid nicely-done modern architecture in a setting that makes for a pleasant stroll. Handsome, bronze sculptures of local wildlife dot Discovery Plaza alongside native-plant landscaping. Exhibits use the themes of earth, wind, fire, and water to help describe the plants, animals, desert climate, local history, and geology of the region.

*Discovery Plaza, located at the visitor center, is an ideal place to stretch out the legs and learn. Modern architecture is combined with playground-like gadgets for the kids and numerous exhibits that are thoughtfully designed to provide information for an entertaining and meaningful experience.*

### ▶ Desert Tortoise Habitat

The Discovery Plaza has a desert tortoise habitat that is home to several female tortoises and one male tortoise, Mojave Max. These tortoises were recovered after being illegally taken from the wild. They spend most of their lives in burrows but come out during the spring and fall, primarily to feed on green vegetation.

An education program, aimed at grade-school kids, has been developed around Mojave Max. The program promotes better understanding and stewardship, not only of tortoises, but of the entire Mojave Desert. Visit www.mojavemax.com for more information.

### ▶ LEED-certified Building

Completed in the spring of 2010, the visitor center is LEED gold certified. This means that the building meets criteria set by the Leadership in Energy and Environmental Design (LEED) Green Building Rating System, developed by the U.S. Green Building Council, a nonprofit organization that promotes environmentally responsible building design.

To save energy, the facility uses solar lighting instead of conventional lights, solar water heating, specialized mechanical systems, a rainwater collection system to provide water for exhibits and landscaping, and a 60-kilowatt photovoltaic array that can supply up to 20% of the building's power needs.

The construction costs of the new 16,650 square-foot facility were funded, in part, by the Southern Nevada Public Lands Management Act (see page 54). The old visitor center, located next door, now serves as administrative offices for the BLM.

### ▶ Bookstore and Gift Shop

One of the few places within the conservation area to get books, souvenirs, jewelry, maps, clothing and other Red-Rock-themed items is Elements, a bookstore and gift shop located within the visitor center. The proceeds of the shop go to the Red Rock Canyon Interpretive Association (RRCIA).

*An 80'-wide panoramic window is a showcase feature of the visitor center. It frames the Calico Hills so well that visitors feel like they can reach out and touch them.*

The RRCIA provides a wide variety of programs and services, such as free guided hikes, school field trips, maintenance of certain facilities, and other activities beneficial to the health of the conservation area. See page 12 for more information.

### ▶ Directions

From the junction of the Clark County 215 Beltway (CC-215) and W. Charleston Blvd., follow W. Charleston Blvd. (which becomes State Route 159) west for 5.2 miles and turn right into the entrance for the visitor center and Scenic Drive. A fee is required (page 11). Follow signs to the visitor center.

The junction of W. Charleston Blvd. and the CC-215 is accessible from many points in Las Vegas. If traveling from Las Vegas Blvd. (The Strip), take I-15 north and exit onto the US-95 northbound. After 5.0 miles, take exit 81A onto Summerlin Parkway, and follow it for 6.4 miles to its junction with the CC-215. Head south on the CC-215, take exit 26 and turn right onto W. Charleston Blvd. Then follow the directions described above.

# Spring Mountain Ranch
*Administered by Nevada State Parks*

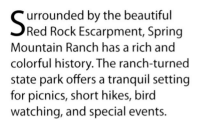

Surrounded by the beautiful Red Rock Escarpment, Spring Mountain Ranch has a rich and colorful history. The ranch-turned state park offers a tranquil setting for picnics, short hikes, bird watching, and special events.

### ► Plants and Animals

With six naturally occurring springs, Spring Mountain Ranch is located on some of the best-watered land in the Spring Mountains. The abundance of water and a higher elevation attracts a diverse group of animals to the area. It also allows a number of plant species to take root that do not normally occur in the arid Mojave Desert.

*Surrounded by acres of grassy pastures, the Ranch House was built by Chet Lauck in 1948. Today, visitors can tour the house and view possessions from some of the famous people who have owned the ranch.*

Especially nice during spring blooms, the flowers at the ranch include yerba mansa, Searls' praire clover, pricklypear, and watercress. In addition to the native species, a number of foreign species have been planted, such as apple, fig, pear, apricot, and Western sycamore trees; as well as Scotch broom. While mule deer are a surprisingly common sight, other mammals, such as foxes, badgers, and skunks, are a treat to see.

Lake Harriet, first stocked with fish for sport, is now populated exclusively by the Pahrump poolfish (*Empetrichthys latos*). These small (about 2" long) fish are native only to the Manse Spring, which dried up in 1975 due to excessive groundwater pumping in the Pahrump Valley. In an attempt to save these guppy-like fish from extinction, some were placed here as well as in two other springs in Nevada. However, the species is still considered endangered.

### ► Bird Watching

Spring Mountain Ranch is arguably the best place to go bird watching at Red Rock Canyon. In addition to the grassy pastures where flycatchers, kingbirds, and meadowlarks are found, Lake Harriet draws aquatic species, such as mallards and American coots, typically seen nowhere else at Red Rock. Birds more common in the Mojave, such as roadrunners, cactus wren, and Gambel's quail, can also be seen. A complete checklist of birds sighted at the ranch is available at the Ranch House.

### ► Picnicking

With over 30 picnic tables and grill stands, a verdant lawn, and plenty of shade trees, Spring Mountain Ranch was chosen in 2009 by the staff of the Las Vegas Review-Journal as the best picnic spot in the Las Vegas area. Indeed, the spot is quite popular, especially in the spring and fall, but never feels crowded because of the large, grassy meadow.

### ► Short Hikes

There are three self-guided hikes at the ranch: the Ash Grove Loop, Overlook Trail, and Plant Trail.

The **Ash Grove Loop** begins immediately east of the Ranch House. This relatively flat hike is 0.75 miles long and takes visitors through a picturesque wooded glade populated by velvet ash trees. From the trailhead, walk along a white fence down the hill and rock-hop across a small creek. After the creek, the trail forks to form a loop, which can be strolled in either direction.

The **Overlook Trail**, marked by a sign, begins on the west side of the parking area and climbs a small hill to a rocky outcrop of Shinarump Conglomerate (see page 15). The overlook provides views of the entire ranch as well as the stunning Red Rock Escarpment. From the overlook, it is possible to return to the parking area or continue southwest, past the Wilson Cemetery, to Lake Harriet and the Plant Trail.

The **Plant Trail** begins adjacent to the calving shed (east of the Ranger Station) and winds its way up a pleasant, wooded hill past the old reservoir. At the top of the hill, the trail comes to a T-intersection. Head left and visit Lake Harriet or right to link into the Overlook Trail.

### ▶ Ranch History

Before the arrival of Euro-Americans, the multiple springs surrounding the ranch supported a meadow area substantially larger than present-day Red Spring. Water flowed far into Cottonwood Valley (a name used in the 1800s and early 1900s to describe the valley east of the Red Rock Escarpment). It is generally accepted that this fertile enclave would have been frequented by the **Desert Archaic people, people with ties to the Anasazi**, as well as the **Southern Paiute**. Southern Paiutes were known to use fertile areas such as this for seasonal gardening in early historic times. The relative wealth of resources here would have allowed them numerous opportunities for gathering, hunting, and large garden plots where beans, sunflowers, corn, melons, and squash may have been grown.

The first Euro-American credited with using the site is **Old Bill Williams**, who explored southern Nevada as early as 1835. A famous fur trapper and renowned mountain man, Old Bill was fluent in several Native-American languages and lived with a number of native groups. Today, there are several places named after him throughout America, including the town of Williams in Arizona. In the

1840s, while the Southwest still belonged to Mexico, Old Bill and his associates made a number of raiding trips to steal horses from the ranches and missions in southern California. After driving a herd through the dry, harsh Mojave Desert, the crew stopped

*Initially constructed for irrigation, Lake Harriet is fed by springs at Spring Mountain Ranch and supports a diverse array of wildlife not usually seen elsewhere at Red Rock. The prominent peak is Mount Wilson, highest in the Red Rock Escarpment, named after James B. Wilson, who established the ranch in 1876.*

at the springs here to rest (see page 39). Although it is unclear if Old Bill and his crew constructed any buildings, later maps indicate the spot as 'Bill Williams Ranch.'

About this time, travelers and merchants scouted better variations of the **Old Spanish Trail**. The route through Cottonwood Valley was one alternative likely preferred by those driving horses and cattle, because the valley helped to

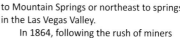

*The endangered Pahrump poolfish lives in Lake Harriet.*

confine the animals, and the numerous springs provided water and forage material. The travelers and merchants would have stopped at the springs here to water and graze their livestock before heading southwest to Mountain Springs or northeast to springs in the Las Vegas Valley.

In 1864, following the rush of miners who flocked to the silver mine on Mount Potosi, some resourceful **prospectors** established a temporary camp here. They began planting crops and raising cattle to

*James B. Wilson and his adopted sons, Jim Jr. and Tweed, pose for a photo in front of the Sandstone Cabin, circa 1900. The Wilsons had a thriving business providing fresh beef and vegetables to nearby mining camps and way stations. Willard George, who later owned the ranch is seated behind James B. Wilson.*

to partner with **George Anderson** and file for 320 acres at 'Sand Mountain,' which became known as Sandstone Ranch in 1876.

Anderson met and married a Southern Paiute woman, Annie, who had one son named Jim Jr., and probably lived with her family near present-day Bonnie Springs. Not long after Annie gave birth to her second son, Tweed, George and Annie left the ranch in the 1880s. James B. Wilson adopted Jim Jr. and Tweed and raised them as his own.

Using the 'Flying 5' brand, Wilson and his boys raised a healthy herd of cattle that grazed throughout Cottonwood Valley from Calico Basin and Willow Springs down to the slopes of Mount Potosi. They also planted numerous fruit trees, as well as some vegetables and grains, to supply miners at Potosi, Ivanpah, and Eldorado Canyon. When James B. Wilson passed away in 1906 he deeded the ranch to **Jim Jr. and Tweed Wilson**.

The winter of 1909 saw 10,000 head of sheep belonging to **Charles Kaiser** come to graze the Spring Mountain Range. The wealthy rancher purchased the ranch to use as a base of operations, then sold it back to the Wilson brothers after he found that the range provided inadequate fodder for the sheep.

By the 1910s, the San Pedro, Los Angeles & Salt Lake Railroad was making frequent trips between Los Angeles and Salt Lake City, which allowed cattle from

supply the mining camps. The remains of a fig tree planted by these miners can still be seen near the blacksmith shop today.

**James B. Wilson**, who served in the Army at Fort Mohave during the Civil War, was drawn west after the 1849 gold rush that brought many hopeful prospectors to California. After his stint in the military, Wilson came to Las Vegas in 1869 and began working for fellow Ohioan, O.D. Gass. Gass had moved into the old Mormon Fort four years prior and created a blossoming ranch and farm. But he was rather cunning with his business, sometimes underhandedly so. For example, after Wilson disclosed that he wanted a property adjacent to his, Gass immediately filed on the water rights for the property. Wilson later found that he could file for property rights to the land but had no access to water. This incident led Wilson

*Brands used at the ranch through time, from left to right: The Flying 5 used from 1876 to 1929 by the Wilson Family, the K Bar 2 used from 1929 to 1948 by Willard George, the Bar Nothing used by Chet Lauck from 1948 to 1955, the Diamond Vee used by Vera Krupp from 1955 to 1967, and the Hughes Tool Company Brand used while the ranch was owned by Howard Hughes from 1967 to 1974.*

the ranch to reach lucrative markets. With this added income, the ranch was doing well. Mining was a booming industry in nearby Goodsprings, so Jim Jr. and Tweed invested in specialized horse-drawn carts, used for hauling ore from the mines to the railroad. The timing of their investment, however, was unlucky: World War I was ending, and the need for lead and zinc from the mines fell drastically. Compounding the problem, tractors and trucks were beginning to haul the ore. The horse-drawn carts were being phased out and Jim Jr. and Tweed were losing money. To pay the outstanding loan, they resorted to mortgaging the ranch in 1919.

Ten years later, **Willard George**, a childhood friend of the Wilsons, paid off the loan and acquired the ranch. He made arrangements for the brothers to live on the property for as long as they wished. After acquiring the Sandstone Ranch, he left its operation to the Wilson brothers for over a decade, only occasionally visiting. In 1941, however, he brought his family to live at the ranch. George was known as 'furrier to the stars' in Hollywood and built a shed on the ranch to house his hundreds of small, furry chinchillas. At the ranch, he developed an exotic breed of the South American rodents named 'Blue Mist.'

In 1944, George leased the ranch to **Chet Lauck**, who purchased the property in 1948. Lauck had become well-known for his Lum and Abner radio show, which aired from 1931 to 1954. The radio show was adapted into seven motion pictures and led to Lauck's inauguration into the National Association of Broadcasters Hall of Fame. The ranch was a vacation retreat for Lauck, who changed the name to 'Bar Nothing Ranch' after the brand of the same style. He made significant improvements to the property, such as constructing the Ranch House (today's visitor center) using stones gathered from an abandoned building at the Sandstone Quarry. And later, he excavated Lake Harriet to encompass three acres at a depth of 15' to 20'. The lake was stocked with bill gill and largemouth bass to provide fishing for a boys camp that Lauck opened on the property. For his own amusement, Lauck raised race horses and cattle. The latter were stolen at alarming rates, because he spent so much time away

from the ranch, leaving only his hired hands on the lookout.

In 1955, **Vera Krupp** purchased the property from Lauck and renamed it 'Spring Mountain Ranch.' Vera was born in Germany in 1909 to a middle-class family. She acted in a number of German films in the 1930s and looked forward to a promising career. After divorcing her first husband, she immigrated to

*Although the comedy of Lum and Abner is often overlooked by the current generation, during the 30s and 40s their radio show was immensely popular and led to seven movies. Chet Lauck, who played Lum, owned the ranch from 1948 to 1955.*

Hollywood in 1938 where she married a movie producer and sought to become a movie star. However, the U.S. was involved in World War II, and Hollywood was not eager to cast Germans. So, Vera worked at a department store, and then a dentist's office where she met her 3rd husband; the dentist for whom she worked. Soon after the wedding, she divorced the dentist and was described as "one of the charter members of the jet set," spending time in Las Vegas, dining with actors, mobsters, and wealthy magnates.

In 1953, she married her 4th husband, Alfried Krupp, who had been convicted of using slave labor to build arms for the Nazis and could not enter the U.S. By 1956, Vera was publicly listing reasons for a divorce and asked to settle for $5 million plus $250,000 in alimony per year. An ensuing scandal was averted by Alfried, who settled out of court.

Aside from her romantic issues and

despite her great wealth, Vera Krupp enjoyed ranching at Red Rock and raised a large herd of hybrid Hereford-Brahman cows. Like those before her, Vera ranged her cattle throughout Cottonwood Valley and attended to the herd on horseback (see photo, page 47).

*The last live-in owner, Vera Krupp enjoyed sporting a ring, shown here on her left ring finger, with the enormous diamond that bears her name. The ring was stolen from Vera's hand in a dramatic episode that occurred at the Ranch House in 1959.*

Vera Krupp is perhaps best-known for being the namesake of the Krupp Diamond, which was given to her by Alfried. The massive stone, weighing 33.19 carats, was stolen from her finger in a dramatic episode that occurred at the Ranch House:

Vera was finishing dinner with her foreman when three men arrived at the door offering to blacktop the driveway. Within seconds the men forced their way in, ripped the ring off Vera's finger and tied the pair blindfolded back-to-back with an electric cord. Vera and her foreman eventually got free and called the authorities. The FBI got involved and found one of the thieves in Louisiana, and the other two, with the diamond, in New Jersey.

After nearly 10 years of living on the ranch, Vera left in 1964 due to health reasons related to diabetes. She moved to Bel Aire and passed away in 1967. Before her death, she attempting to sell the property to Clark County Parks, who

refused, then sold the ranch to Hughes Tool Company, owned by **Howard Hughes** in 1967. The next year, the Krupp Diamond was bought at auction for $305,000 by Richard Burton, who presented it to his wife, Elizabeth Taylor.

By 1967, Howard Hughes was already a famous business tycoon, aviator, and film producer. He was living on the top floor of the Desert Inn in Las Vegas and is reported to have visited Bonnie Springs but it cannot be said for certain that he ever stepped foot on Spring Mountain Ranch. He purchased it as a home for his wife, Jean Peters. She, however, never moved to the ranch or Las Vegas and Hughes sold the ranch for a good profit to **Fletcher Jones and William Murphy** in 1972.

The duo proposed that Clark County rezone the property so they could build an 'equestrian-oriented' townhouse and condominium community for roughly 5000 residents. When an overwhelming public outcry against the project arose, the **State of Nevada** stepped in and purchased the 520-acre ranch for $3.25 million in 1974.

► **Guided Tours and Activities**

Led by a staff of friendly volunteers, tours visit the historic landmarks and buildings on the ranch. Tours are given daily at noon, 1:00 pm, and 2:00 pm; and on weekends, at 3:00 pm.

Throughout the year, full-moon hikes are guided by park staff. These social events stroll the Ash Grove Loop or hike into Sandstone Canyon. Reservations are required and dates vary depending on moon phases. Call (702) 875-4141 for details.

Every Thursday in the summer, the ranch organizes a 'Summer Hands-On Craft Ranger' program for kids. Parents accompany their little ones and help them make necklaces, birdhouses, and other items. A nominal fee is required; call (702) 875-4141 for details.

► **Special Events**

Each summer, for over 30 years, the **Super Summer Theatre** has produced a handful of plays at Spring Mountain Ranch. The plays are selected to appeal to both children and adults and typically run from June until September. Performances are in the evening when temperatures are cooler.

Many spectators bring blankets or chairs for sitting in the open pasture. Tickets are reasonably priced and can be purchased in advance. They may also be available at the door if the show is not sold out. For shows, dates, and tickets visit www.supersummertheatre.com or call (702) 594-7529.

In the spring and fall, the ranch presents **Living History Programs**, which give visitors an opportunity to view life at the ranch as it might have been and interact with characters from the past. Some of these events include:

**Ranch Day** in early May: A barbecue with games for adults and children, stick-horse racing, cow-pie-throwing contests, cow roping, sack races, tug-of-war, and wheelbarrow racing.

**Pioneer Day** in late September: Old pioneer skills and crafts, Dutch oven cooking, spinning and weaving, black powder shooting, needlework, and candle making. Old-time fiddlers play music.

**Civil War Reenactment** in late October.

**Mountain Man Rendezvous** in mid-November: A large demonstration event with primitive camps, tomahawk, knife, and lance throwing, archery, black-powder rifle shooting, blacksmithing, atlatl demonstrations, and vendor booths

The ranch also hosts the **Red Rock Rendezvous** annually in March, a clinic-oriented rock climber gathering.

Holiday programs geared for kids occur in late October, with the Halloween Spooktacular, and in mid-December with Ranch Christmas.

Call (702) 875-4141 or email smr-interp@parks.nv.gov for exact dates and more information.

Occasionally, the Las Vegas Astronomical Society sets up telescopes at the ranch for stargazing and special astronomical events. Visit their website: www.lvastronomy.com for more info.

## ► Fees, Hours, and Directions

Spring Mountain Ranch State Park requires a fee separate from the Red Rock Canyon National Conservation Area. The fee is $9.00 per vehicle with a $2.00 discount for Nevada residents. Walk-ins and bicycles are $1.00 each. Annual passes are also available.

The park and picnic area are open daily from 8:00 am until dusk. The Ranch House is open daily from 10:00 am until 4:00 pm.

**To get to Spring Mountain Ranch:** Follow SR-159 (the extension of West Charleston Boulevard) for 3.2 miles past the exit of the Red Rock Canyon Scenic Drive (see map, inside back cover). Turn right, passing under the ranch-style sign that says 'Spring Mountain Ranch State Park.' After 0.3 miles, the gate-house is reached; the park lies 0.7 miles further down the road.

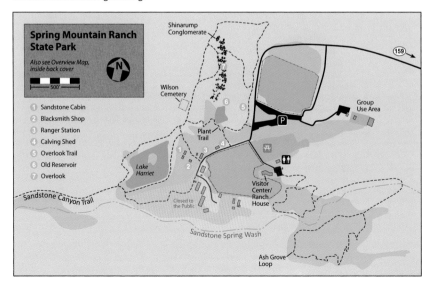

**Spring Mountain Ranch State Park**

*Also see Overview Map, inside back cover*

500'

1 Sandstone Cabin
2 Blacksmith Shop
3 Ranger Station
4 Calving Shed
5 Overlook Trail
6 Old Reservoir
7 Overlook

Shinarump Conglomerate

Wilson Cemetery

Plant Trail

Sandstone Canyon Trail

Lake Harriet

Closed to the Public

Group Use Area

Visitor Center/ Ranch House

Sandstone Spring Wash

Ash Grove Loop

159

# Bonnie Springs
*A private ranch at Red Rock Canyon*

Offering a number of attractions, including horseback riding, a petting zoo, and a Wild West theme park, Bonnie Springs is an appealing spot for families or even a romantic getaway.

### ► Old Nevada

Spanning the length of a city block, Old Nevada is a re-creation of an 1880s mining town. Strolling the main street, visitors can interact with friendly 19th-century characters and pop into a number of authentic-looking buildings.

Some of the rustic establishments, of which there are 45, include a blacksmith shop, a working stamp mill, bank, opera house, schoolhouse, shooting gallery, sheriff's office, and chapel. There are also a number of old-fashioned general stores selling tourist-oriented wares. A museum has a diverse collection of antiques from Nevada and staff take portraits with an old-style camera of visitors dressed up in vintage 19th-century costumes. A wax museum, not as ambitious as Madame Tussauds', is charming nonetheless.

The saloon, located at the top of the street, is a handy place to stop for a drink. At frequent intervals, entertainingly cheesy melodramas are staged here, and kids have a good time.

Following the melodrama, the Old West actors put on the hanging show. The plot follows law-men pursuing a bank robber and bringing him to justice. Without a strict adherence to historical accuracy, the enthusiastic actors are free to keep the performances engaging and lively. Audience participation is encouraged, especially when a visitor is selected to preside over the hearing of a bank robber sentenced to hang.

While some might find Old Nevada too hokey, most take it for what it is and have a good time with the amusing and outgoing Old West characters.

*Gettin' ready for a hangin'. Performing three-times daily, the cast of the dramatic 'hanging' show at Old Nevada entertains young and old with witty dialogue and comical scenes of classic Western scenarios.*

### ► Petting Zoo

A small petting zoo and aviary are operated at Bonnie Springs. Kids delight in petting and feeding the docile deer, sheep, pigs, and rabbits, while more exotic animals, such as wolves, Canadian lynx, coatimundi, emus, and llamas, can be viewed in their pens. Although the wire-mesh cages can be disheartening, the staff is caring and attends to the needs of the animals. Keep an eye out for the free-roaming peacocks that occasionally spread their tails for a photo op.

*At the petting zoo, visitors can get up close and personal with an eclectic mix of animals, from deer and goats, pictured here, to more exotic species such as llamas, Canadian lynx, emus, and coatamundi.*

Admission to the petting zoo is a nominal fee, and the aviary is free; both are affiliated with a non-profit organization.

### ► Horseback Riding

A great way to see the stunning scenery surrounding Bonnie Springs is on horseback. The stables offer guided, hour-long trail rides throughout the day. Cost is $60.00 per person.

There are also breakfast, lunch, and dinner rides, which cost from $118.00 to $134.00 per person. Horse boarding and self-guided use are also available. Although the minimum age for horseback rides is six, pony rides provide an enjoyable activity for younger kids. For more information, call (702) 875-4191.

### ► Stay and Dine

In addition to the bar-style options available at Old Nevada, the Bonnie Springs Ranch Restaurant & Bar serves breakfast, lunch, and dinner seven days a week. Popular with locals and tourists, the fare is simple, good, and reasonably priced. The bison burgers and slow-cooked ribs are local favorites. On Saturday evenings, entertainment is provided at the restaurant, usually by a lively country-music band.

The motel, open year-round, offers various room-style options from basic to deluxe suites with Jacuzzis, kitchens, and themed decor choices, including Old West, Spanish, Chinese, and Native American.

The location makes for a great base camp from which to explore Red Rock Canyon. Prices range from $85.00 to $165.00 per night. Reservations are recommended; call (702) 875-4400.

### ► History of Bonnie Springs

Many generations of Native Americans used the springs and surrounding terrain near Bonnie Springs for seasonal wild plant

*The most popular horseback rides at Bonnie Springs are the hour-long tours. Reservations are recommend, but last-minute bookings are sometimes available.*

*Bonnie (kneeling) nails the final stake in the track of Old Nevada's replica train, circa 1974. The Wild West theme park, dreamed up by Bonnie's husband, established Bonnie Springs as a bona fide tourist destination and led to its inclusion in a number of movies (see page 56).*

harvesting and animal hunts.

When merchants and travelers first explored Red Rock in the early 1800s, they encountered friendly Southern Paiutes who managed gardens with a wide array of crops, including mesquite and squash, near springs in the Las Vegas Valley. One of the best recorded explorations was undertaken by John C. Frémont and his party. They traversed the Spring Mountains near Mountain Springs in May of 1844. From there, it can be argued that they followed the springs along the base of the Red Rock Escarpment, possibly stopping at Bonnie Springs.

In the late 1800s and early 1900s, James B. Wilson and his adopted sons grazed cattle throughout the valley east of the Red Rock Escarpment and would surely have watered them at Bonnie Springs. In fact, the Wilsons used a road that traversed the property to travel south towards Goodsprings, where they sold fresh beef to miners. As the ranching presence increased, some Southern Paiutes intermarried with Euro-Americans. Others

*Male peacocks make showy displays on the grounds.*

moved to newly established reservations, but many remained on their traditional lands, which were seasonally occupied.

In the 1940s, the Chambers family lived in a small house on the property. When they left, the property changed hands to Dr. Fortier, who had a caretaker that failed to properly look after the place. By the time Bonnie McGaugh came around in the early 1950s, the property was a rural junk yard and not seen as a valuable piece of real estate.

Raised around the southern California entertainment industry, Bonnie had a gift for dancing. She worked as a showgirl with Folies Bergère when it was a traveling show in the early 1940s and toured the country with ice skating shows in her early 20s. Her first experience with Vegas came in 1942 when she performed in an ice skating show at the Last Frontier.

About 10 years later, she visited Red Rock and immediately fell in love with the beautiful mountains, fresh air, and ranching lifestyle. She gave Dr. Fortier a down payment on the ranch and commenced to spruce it up and open a bar.

Al Levinson heard that Bonnie was working on the ranch and began visiting frequently. The couple were married shortly thereafter and worked to expand the ranch. At first, with a couple of horses, only a few facilities, and no electricity, Bonnie's showgirl friends came out to the ranch on weekends. Buster Wilson, James B. Wilson's grandson from the neighboring Spring Mountain Ranch, came often to help with work around the ranch and showed Bonnie how to use native plants for shampoo and herbal remedies.

Despite the Spartan accommodations, the

ranch was a hit, and the Levinsons decided to build a stable and small restaurant to entertain their guests. The ranch proved to be a popular spot, and amenities were continually added. Al's interest in history led to the construction of Old Nevada, which began in the early 1970s.

As the resort took shape, more and more people have come to enjoy it. Today, it is estimated that over 12 million people have visited.

### ► Special Events

Bonnie Springs is set up to accommodate conventions, weddings and wedding receptions, birthday parties, and other group events. They host a number of special events throughout the year.

On weekends in October, Old Nevada is transformed into a spooky ghost town, complete with haunted houses, ghouls, magic shows, and goody bags for the kids.

A similar seasonally-themed makeover is usually done for Christmas.

For more information on special events, call (702) 875-4191 or email: events@bonniesprings.com.

### Paranormal Activity

Bonnie Springs was featured in an episode of the Travel Channel's Ghost Adventures show, which aired in January 2011. The cast spends a night at Old Nevada in hopes of finding spirits of old gunslingers and Native Americans.

### ► Fees, Hours, and Directions

The petting zoo is $7.00 per child and $10.00 per adult. It is open from 10:00 am to 6:00 pm in the summer and 10:30 am to 5:00 pm in the winter.

Admission to Old Nevada is $5.00 per person on weekdays and $7.00 per person on weekends; it is closed on Mondays and Tuesdays. Hours are generally 10:30 am until 5:00 pm or 6:00 pm depending on the season. The melodrama and hanging shows are performed three times daily. The posse show is performed twice daily on weekends. Call (702) 875-4191 for more information.

On weekends, a free, miniature train takes visitors on a ride from the parking lot to Old Nevada and is popular with kids.

**To get to Bonnie Springs:** Follow SR-159 (the extension of W. Charleston Blvd.) for 3.4 miles past the exit of the Scenic Dr. (see map, inside back cover). Turn right, passing under the 'Bonnie Springs Ranch' sign. After driving 1.1 miles from SR-159, Bonnie Springs is reached. From the other direction, Bonnie Springs Rd. is located 5.0 miles from SR-160.

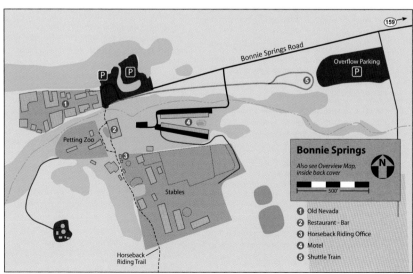

Bonnie Springs

Also see Overview Map, inside back cover

500'

1 Old Nevada
2 Restaurant - Bar
3 Horseback Riding Office
4 Motel
5 Shuttle Train

# Sightseeing
*at Red Rock Canyon*

Even if visiting for only a few hours, there are plenty of safe and accessible ways to get out and enjoy the outdoors at Red Rock Canyon.

### ► Landscape and Wildlife

Red Rock Canyon, less than 20 miles from the Las Vegas Strip, is a magnificent, natural retreat with stunning vistas and remarkable places to explore.

One of the focal points of the scenery is the Red Rock Escarpment, a 13-mile-long buttress of sandstone cliffs colored red, white, pink, and even purple. Situated in the middle of the escarpment is Mount Wilson at 7070', the highest sandstone peak at Red Rock Canyon.

North of the Red Rock Escarpment, the brightly colored Calico Hills seem to rise from the relatively drab-colored surrounding desert. These sandstone monoliths have been carved into ornate shapes by millions of years of rain and weathering and are one of the key stops for visitors.

Considering its proximity to the sprawling city of Las Vegas, the diversity of plants and animals at Red Rock is astounding. Some of the best-known are bighorn sheep, mountain lions, bobcats, coyotes, foxes, ringtails, golden eagles, peregrine falcons, desert tortoises, and Gila monsters. Both auto tours, described on pages 150 and 153, offer the chance of seeing local wildlife, especially if a short walk is added along the way.

### ► To See and Do

Red Rock Canyon provides a wide variety of activities: world-class rock climbing, scenic horseback riding and mountain biking, and numerous exceptional hiking trails. There are a number of less physical and less time

*Red Rock Canyon was voted "Best Picnic Spot" eight years in a row by readers of the Las Vegas Review-Journal.*

consuming ways to see the conservation area, which are described below.

### ► Picnicking

One laid-back way to get out and enjoy Red Rock is to pack a picnic. For those well stocked up, nearly any spot can prove enjoyable. Many locals take a stroll into the Calico Hills and find a flat rock from which to dine and gaze at the gorgeous scenery. If a meal calls for more formal furnishings, there are four developed picnic areas: Red Spring, the visitor center, Willow Springs, and the Red Rock Overlook, as well as the facilities at Spring Mountain Ranch. While Red Spring and Willow Springs have barbecue stands and picnic tables, the visitor center and Red Rock Overlook have only picnic tables. See maps, pages 151 and 155.

### ► Auto Touring

The easiest thing to do is take an auto tour. Described on pages 150 and 153 are two of the most popular routes. The auto tours describe some of the more dramatic things to see, such as the distinct color separations in the rocks, the plant communities and animals that live in them, and notes on the history of Native Americans and Euro-Americans at Red Rock.

**Auto Tour 1** makes a loop of the Scenic Drive, a one-way road that was literally built for sightseeing. Along the way, stop at a number of points to admire the marvelous views, take a short hike, or have a picnic.

**Auto Tour 2** is equally captivating; it passes a remarkable natural spring near the Calico Hills, then takes State Route 159 south along the Red Rock Escarpment with stops at historic sites such as Spring Mountain Ranch and Wheeler Camp Spring. Visitors can stop over at 'Old

Nevada,' a Wild West themed park at Bonnie Springs, to see entertaining shows and attractions, and grab a bite to eat.

### ► Guided Auto Tours

With rave reviews, the **Scoot City Red Rock Tour** is a relatively new and unique way to see Red Rock Canyon. The two-seat, three-wheeled scooters look like something from an amusement park. Visitors hop in the brightly-colored contraptions and line up like a string of M&Ms. Guides point out interesting geological, historical, and ecological details as the tour scoots around the Scenic Drive. The tours begin in Las Vegas, last about five hours, and make a few stops along the way, usually at the visitor center, Calico I, and the High Point Overlook. Tours run from March through November, and prices start at $125.00. Water is provided. For more information visit www.scootcitytours.com, email info@scootcitytours.com, or call (702) 699-5700.

The **Pink Jeep Tours**, a visitor favorite, have been providing auto tours for over 50 years. Passengers ride in plush, specially-modified, ten-person 4x4s while tour guides describe the surrounding terrain and tell interesting stories of the area's history. The tour stops at certain locations along the Scenic Drive for viewing special features and points of interest. About halfway through the Scenic Drive, the tour takes the lesser-known Rocky Gap Road up into a picturesque valley filled with juniper and pinyon pine trees. On the way back down, passengers can examine rock art (see page 30) estimated to be some 1000 years old. Tours are given year-round and last about four hours. Hotel pick-up and drop-off is provided from most locations. Cost is $97.00 per person. For more information, visit www.pinkjeep.com, email lvreservations@pinkjeep.com, or call (888) 900-4480.

**Las Vegas Hummer Tours** specializes in giving guests an authentic off-the-beaten-path journey through some lesser-known parts of the conservation area. Guests ride in Hummer H2s while tour guides spin yarns about the olden days on the Old Spanish Trail, comment on the stunning geology, and point out wildlife that may be

sighted. Tours are offered at 8:00 am and 1:30 pm daily. Duration is about 4 hours. Cost is $139.00 per person, including hotel pick-up and drop-off. For more information visit www.lasvegasoffroadtours.com, or call (866) 627-4014.

*The Scoot City Tours are a fun way to cruise the loop, feel the breeze in your hair, and learn a bit about the area.*

### ► Be Prepared

The amazing backdrop of Red Rock Canyon is great for picture taking, so don't forget the camera. Clothing needed varies with the season. In summer, most people wear thin, light-colored clothes that protect the skin from the sun and allow air movement. Water and sunscreen are necessary. On some days in the spring and fall, a sweater and hat are good to have, but other days require shorts and a T-shirt. In the winter, wear pants, a sweater, and maybe even a warm hat.

### ► Directions

There are two ways to access the visitor center and Scenic Drive:

From the north end of Las Vegas, travel west on W. Charleston Boulevard, which becomes SR-159. Set the odometer at the CC-215 and continue west on SR-159. The landscape transitions from urban to desert, and Joshua trees begin to appear. Turn right, 5.2 miles from the CC-215, into the entrance for the visitor center and Scenic Drive.

From the south side of Las Vegas, travel west on SR-160 (Blue Diamond Road) to its intersection with SR-159. Turn right onto SR-159 and follow it for 10.6 miles, then make a left into the entrance for the visitor center and Scenic Drive.

# AUTO TOUR 1: SCENIC DRIVE

A perennial classic, the Scenic Drive is *THE* auto tour at Red Rock Canyon, giving visitors a little taste of all the place has to offer.

Start the drive at the **Red Rock Canyon Visitor Center ❶**; for directions and info about the visitor center, see page 137. Take time to explore the exhibits, videos, and gift shop. The visitor center is open from 8:00 am to 4:30 pm and closed on holidays.

*The vibrantly colored scenery at Calico I makes for a great photo opportunity.*

From the visitor center, follow signs to the Scenic Drive (a two-lane, one-way loop road). Take the Scenic Drive for 1.0 miles to the **Calico I ❷** pullout. Along the way, the road crosses through a good example of the creosote bush scrub plant community (see page 63). The multi-stemmed creosote bushes are prevalent and grow to about 8' high. Also look for Joshua trees, which have pom-pom-looking, spine-tipped leaves atop their shaggy-looking branches.

At Calico I, vistas encircle the visitor: to the north and east (right) are the Calico Hills, and bordering the valley to the west is the Red Rock Escarpment. Both are composed of Aztec Sandstone, created from sand dunes that existed some 190 million years ago. A short, well-trodden trail leads down from the pullout to the

sandstone itself where visitors can discover colorful, wildly-shaped formations. The area below the pullout is a popular spot, especially for kids, so expect to share the place. From the pullout, rock climbers can often be spotted on cliffs in the Calico Hills.

Continue 1.5 miles along the Scenic Drive to a right turn into the **Sandstone Quarry ❸**. Along the way, the Calico Hills will draw passenger's attention to the right. Surrounding the road, the vegetation is recovering from the Loop Fire of July 2005. In the spring, the roadside is lined with desert marigold and desert globemallow. The Sandstone Quarry is the location of a stone quarry that operated in spurts beginning in 1905 (see page 45 for more info). The main quarry site is located about 170 yards from the parking area. About 0.15 miles further up the trail, visitors can see an ancient roasting pit used by Native Americans (see pages 32 and 166 for more info).

Past the Sandstone Quarry, the Scenic Drive winds and climbs for 1.9 miles to the **High Point Overlook ❹**. As the name implies, this is the highest point along the Scenic Drive at 4780', and the views of the Red Rock Escarpment and Calico Hills are amazing. Notice the prominent peak of Bridge Mountain (see photo, inside front cover), which rises from the depths of Ice Box Canyon. These sandstone monoliths have been carved by nearly 65 million years of erosion and weathering. Underfoot is soil composed of gray Paleozoic-age limestones and dolomites that were eroded from the surrounding La Madre Mountains and cemented into caliche. The limestones and dolomites were brought to rest above the younger sandstone by the Keystone Thrust (see page 22).

Around the High Point Overlook, the

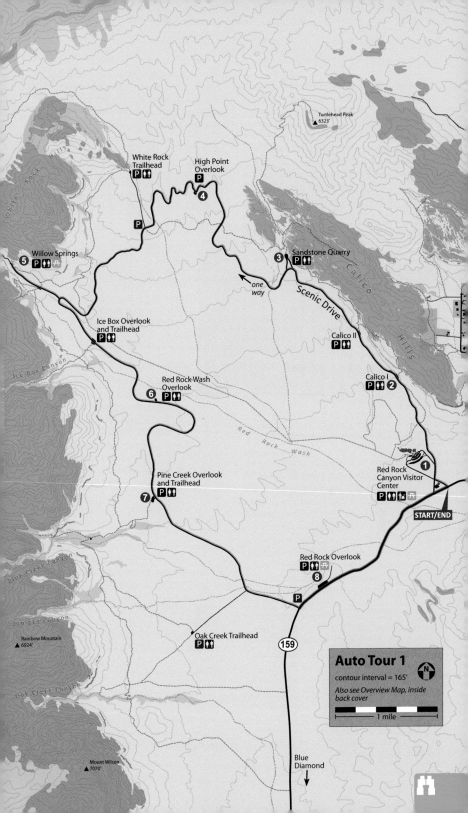

White Rock
Trailhead
P

High Point
Overlook
P

④

P

Willow Springs
⑤ P

Sandstone Quarry
③ P

one way

Scenic Drive

Calico II
P ⑥

Calico I
P ②

Ice Box Overlook
and Trailhead
P

Red Rock Wash
Overlook
⑥ P

Red Rock Wash

Red Rock
Canyon Visitor
Center
P
①

START/END

Pine Creek Overlook
and Trailhead
⑦ P

Red Rock Overlook
P
⑧

P

Oak Creek Trailhead
P

Turtlehead Peak
6323'

Calico Hills

White Rock Hills

Ice Box Canyon

Pine Creek Canyon

Juniper Canyon

Rainbow Mountain
▲ 6924'

Oak Creek Canyon

Mount Wilson
▲ 7070'

159

Blue
Diamond

**Auto Tour 1**

contour interval = 165'

*Also see Overview Map, inside
back cover*

N

1 mile

plant community is a mix of blackbrush scrub and pinyon-juniper woodland, which is found at higher elevations (see pages 65 and 66). Along the roadside, visitors can spot cliffrose, Apache plume, Mojave rabbitbush, and the occasional Utah juniper. Away from the road, banana yucca, blackbrush, and Mormon tea are prevalent. Black-tailed jackrabbits and desert cottontails make their homes in this habitat and are often seen at dawn and dusk running across the road.

High Point Overlook

From the High Point Overlook, the Scenic Drive snakes downhill east of the White Rock Hills for 2.7 miles to a hairpin turn. A right turn within the hairpin leads 0.5 miles to the parking area for **Willow Springs ❺**, where the pavement ends. This must-visit spot has so many things to see and do that pages 174 to 177 are devoted entirely to it. The area is great for kids, bird watching, hiking, learning about Native American lifeways, and experiencing the geology of Red Rock. While opportunities for rock climbing, rappelling, and canyoneering are available here, most choose to keep their feet on the ground with a casual picnic. Often, a number of creatures come out to visit in the shade provided by Frémont cottonwoods near Willow Spring. Stellar's Jays, pinyon Jays, ravens, white-tailed antelope squirrels, even gray foxes have been conditioned to 'gathering' food from willing, and unwilling, picnickers. This practice is strongly frowned upon, because it is not healthy for the animals or the ecosystem they live in. Please let the wildlife be wild and do not feed these creatures.

After taking time to explore Willow Springs, backtrack to the Scenic Drive and follow it for 1.5 miles to the **Red Rock Wash Overlook ❻**. At this pullout, one can see the massive amount of soil and rock that has been eroded from the surrounding mountains and transported by flash floods. As the course of the wash changed through the years, the water cut into older deposits, leaving cliff-like faces along its banks.

Continue along the Scenic Drive for 1.6 miles to the **Pine Creek Overlook and Trailhead ❼** on the right. This parking area offers a great photo opportunity of the stunning, multi-colored Red Rock Escarpment. For those feeling energetic, the Pine Creek Canyon Trail (page 182) leads down to the wash and into the canyon, one of the most beautiful and ecologically diverse at Red Rock.

The Scenic Drive descends from the Pine Creek Overlook and Trailhead and runs along Pine Creek Wash. It can be seen on the right side of the road and offers a good example of a wash plant community, with numerous scrub oak, desert willow, silktassel bush, and the occasional honey mesquite. On the hillside left of the road are a number of beige cones. These cones are plant enclosures used to study how certain plants return to burned areas, such as this area, which burned in the Scenic Fire of September, 2006. After driving 2.0 miles from the Pine Creek Overlook and Trailhead, take a left on SR-159 at the end of the Scenic Drive. SR-159 climbs a slight hill and the **Red Rock Overlook ❽** is found on the left. An interpretive sign about the Old Spanish Trail invites visitors to consider a time when Red Rock was a thoroughfare of commerce and outlaws (see also pages 39 and 40). The overlook has a short, paved trail that leads through Joshua trees to a point of land with excellent views of the Red Rock Escarpment and Calico Hills.

From the Red Rock Overlook, turning left on SR-159 will take you past the visitor center towards Las Vegas, and turning right will lead you past Blue Diamond to SR-160 and the south side of Las Vegas.

# AUTO TOUR 2: STATE ROUTE 159

No less impressive than the Scenic Drive, this auto tour allows for stops at a tranquil state park and lively Wild West themed park.

This drive starts at the **Red Rock Canyon Sign** ❶. To reach the sign, drive west on West Charleston Boulevard, which becomes State Route 159. Pass the Clark County 215 and continue for 2.2 miles. The sign is found on the right, in a roadcut. *Be cautious when pulling off the road. Hazards include an uneven shoulder, as well as bike and auto traffic.* The large, sandstone sign is a popular photo-op and it is possible to compose the Red Rock Escarpment in the background of the photo.

From the Red Rock Canyon Sign, follow SR-159 west, towards Red Rock for 1.5 miles and make a right onto Calico Basin Drive. Follow this road for 1.2 miles and continue straight into the **Red Spring** ❷ parking area. Adjacent to the ample parking area are many picnic tables with grills, and just beyond is a group of tall velvet ash trees that obscure the Red Spring meadow. Take time to stroll the boardwalk (ADA compliant), which makes a loop around the spring-fed meadow and features numerous interpretive signs describing the geology, plants and animals, and Native American and contemporary uses of the area. See page 161 for more info on Red Spring.

After visiting Red Spring, return to SR-159 and follow it west for 1.4 miles, then turn right into the entrance for the visitor center and Scenic Drive. Pass through the gate (a fee is required, see page 11) and follow signs for the **Red Rock Canyon Visitor Center** ❸. Here, visitors can explore exhibits, see videos, and peruse a gift shop, all of which is described on page 136. The visitor center is open from 8:00 am to 4:30 pm and is closed on holidays.

From the visitor center, follow signs back to SR-159 and make a right towards Blue Diamond. Here the road zips through a Joshua tree woodland. To the left is Blue Diamond Hill; notice the gray, fossil-bearing Kaibab Limestone. These formations were deposited on the bottom of a warm, shallow sea that covered most of the Southwest more than 250 million years ago. See page 14 for more info.

*Spring Mountain Ranch State Park was once a thriving cattle ranch. Today, friendly volunteers guide tours of the beautiful property, which has an extensive picnic area.*

After 1.6 miles on SR-159, turn right into the **Red Rock Overlook** ❹. The overlook has a short, paved trail that leads to a point of land, which provides excellent views of the Red Rock Escarpment and Calico Hills. One of the interesting aspects of the sandstone, which composes these dramatic formations, is the multitude of colors they display. A stunning example is Rainbow Mountain (see photo, inside front cover). A detailed description of the reason for these colors and their distinct separations can be found on page 18.

From the overlook it is also possible to

observe the differing plant communities. Within the canyons are dark green, dense thickets of mixed chaparral, which grade into wash plant communities as the dry streambeds enter into the valley. Adjacent to the washes, blackbrush scrub dominates and grades into pinyon-juniper woodlands found along the base of the Red Rock Escarpment.

An Old Spanish Trail interpretive sign at the overlook invites visitors to consider a time when Red Rock was a thoroughfare for commerce and outlaws (see also pages 39 and 40). In the

*Backtracking the route provides equally stunning views of the Red Rock Escarpment.*

1840s, fur traders took to stealing horses from California. They likely used the springs along the Red Rock Escarpment to water their horses and holed up at the next stop on the drive: Spring Mountain Ranch.

From the Red Rock Overlook, take a right onto SR-159. To the right are the canyons and peaks of the Red Rock Escarpment. The broad peak is Mount Wilson (see photo, inside front cover). After 3.1 miles, turn right under a ranch-style sign for **Spring Mountain Ranch** ⑤ and pay a fee (see page 143) at the gate house. The access road heads east towards the Red Rock Escarpment. Along the way, the Joshua tree woodland grades into a blackbrush scrub plant community.

The ranch-turned state park was first homesteaded in 1876 and currently provides a great place to picnic, bird-watch, take a short hike, see the largest lake in the Spring Mountains, and learn about the historical events of Red Rock and the Southwest. The ranch and activities are described in more detail on page 138.

From the state park, return to SR-159 and turn right. After 0.7 miles on SR-159, make a right under the Bonnie Springs Ranch sign onto the access road that leads 1.2 miles to **Bonnie Springs** ⑥. Offering a number of attractions, including horseback riding, a petting zoo, multiple eateries and bars, a hotel, and a Wild West theme park, Bonnie Springs (page 144) is a unique spot for families to get some old-fashioned fun, tourists to get in the Old-West spirit, and couples to wed and honeymoon.

After experiencing Bonnie Springs, return to SR-159 and turn right. After 1.2 miles make a right into a dirt parking lot for **Wheeler Camp Spring** ⑦, a lesser-known spot good for getting a taste of nature. From the parking area, a network of trails leads through wash and riparian plant communities with numerous honey mesquites, yerba mansa, and Frémont cottonwoods. The lush surroundings attract many forms of wildlife and are popular for bird watching. The spring, located in the course of the wash, is named after Lt. George Wheeler, who led a number of survey expeditions in this region during the 1870s.

From Wheeler Camp Spring, continue to the right along SR-159 for 3.8 miles to its junction with SR-160. From this junction, take a left to Las Vegas or a right to Mountain Springs and Pahrump.

## Local Tip: Great Photos

Although the landscape of Red Rock is stunning, many return home to find their photos disappointing. The biggest cause of mediocre photos is poor lighting. To get better shots, try coming earlier: the Red Rock Escarpment receives early morning light that accentuates the vibrant colors and intricate features of the cliffs. In the afternoon, the escarpment is shaded; check out the Calico Hills while the sun is setting.

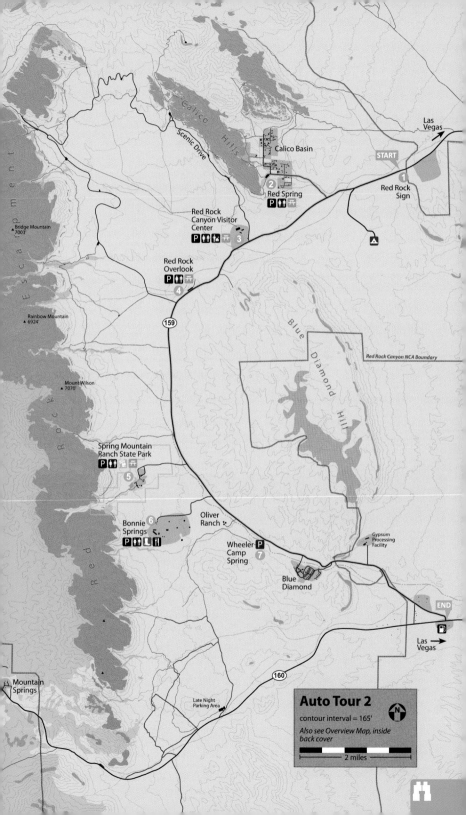

Las Vegas

Calico Hills

Scenic Drive

Calico Basin

START

Red Rock Sign

**1**

**2** Red Spring

Escarpment

Red Rock Canyon Visitor Center

**3**

Red Rock Overlook

**4**

Bridge Mountain
7003'

159

Rainbow Mountain
6924'

Blue Diamond Hill

Red Rock Canyon NCA Boundary

Mount Wilson
7070'

Red Rock Escarpment

Spring Mountain Ranch State Park

**5**

Bonnie Springs **6**

Oliver Ranch

Wheeler Camp Spring **7**

Gypsum Processing Facility

Blue Diamond

END

Las Vegas

Mountain Springs

160

Late Night Parking Area

**Auto Tour 2**

contour interval = 165'

*Also see Overview Map, inside back cover*

N

|——— 2 miles ———|

# Stargazing
### at Red Rock Canyon

With the naked eye or a specialized telescope, the topography at Red Rock Canyon keeps the sky dark and the stars bright.

### ► Escape the City Lights

Since the early 1980s, Red Rock Canyon has been a popular spot for Las Vegans to escape the light pollution of their city and gaze at the heavens. In fact, when Haley's Comet streaked across the night sky in 1986, some 1200 people came out to view the event.

Today, the lights of the city are even brighter, but crowds are rarely encountered on trips to view the night sky. On moonless nights, the swath of stars that fill the Milky Way are visible to the naked eye, and numerous constellations can be recognized.

### ► Where to Go

The best spots to park and watch are along SR-159, east of the Red Rock Escarpment. However, certain parking areas along SR-159 and in Calico Basin are for day-use only, and after-dusk parking is not allowed.

### ► When to Go

The best times to see the stars are clear, moonless nights.

Late summer is usually regarded as the prime meteor-shower season, but shooting stars can be seen year-round.

### ► Special Events and Night Hikes

The Las Vegas Astronomical Society, in coordination with the BLM and Spring Mountain Ranch State Park, periodically hosts 'Astronomy in the Park' events. At these sociable gatherings members of the society give informative presentations and set up high-powered telescopes for viewing the moon and planets in our solar system, as well as distant galaxies, nebulae, and other wonders. The society is made up of amateur astronomers who aim solely to promote the love and enjoyment of astronomy. Visit www.lvastronomy.com for more information.

The Red Rock Canyon Interpretive Association occasionally offers nighttime star hikes at Red Rock Canyon. The details of this organization are found on page 12.

*The Red Rock Escarpment is illuminated by Las Vegas as the earth turns.*

# Bird Watching
### *at Red Rock Canyon*

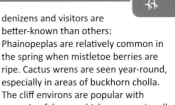

Red Rock is a good place to see our feathered friends, offering a dramatic setting and varied habitats for viewing these captivating creatures.

### ► Places to Go
Generally, the best spots to see birds at Red Rock Canyon are near springs, which draw birds from the surrounding landscape to drink.

**Spring Mountain Ranch State Park** is arguably the best and most active spot for bird watching. With pastures, trees, springs, and a man-made lake, the area appeals to a wide variety of species, including many aquatic birds that are usually not seen elsewhere in the conservation area. The staff is friendly and knowledgeable about when and where to look. They also have a checklist available at the Ranch House. See page 138 for details.

**Pine Creek Canyon** is another good spot with a perennial water supply. Start out at the meadow behind the Horace Wilson homestead and venture into the mixed chaparral along the wash, which provides cover for a number of species, such as spotted towee, Gambel's quail, and chukar. See page 183 for directions.

The picnic area at **Willow Springs** is situated at the edge of a pinyon-juniper woodland and attracts gregarious scavengers. Raptors and various songbirds can be seen in the nearby Lost Creek area. See page 175 for directions.

**Red Spring** offers easy access to a spring-fed meadow where swallows and lesser nighthawks are known to feed. With luck, it's possible to see a great-horned owl or other large raptor in the nearby velvet ash trees. See page 161 for directions.

### ► Species to See
Roughly 200 species have been recorded at Red Rock Canyon (see page 78). Some denizens and visitors are better-known than others: Phainopeplas are relatively common in the spring when mistletoe berries are ripe. Cactus wrens are seen year-round, especially in areas of buckhorn cholla. The cliff environs are popular with peregrine falcons, which are occasionally seen catching white-throated swifts in flight. Red-tailed hawks are common, and American kestrels can be found on the outskirts of urban environments.

The Nevada Department of Wildlife has complied a checklist of species recorded in southern Nevada. It can be found at: www.ndow.org/wild/bird/snvbird.pdf.

*A local resident, Mike Ward, scans Lake Harriet at Spring Mountain Ranch for aquatic species not found elsewhere in the conservation area.*

### ► Guided Tours and Programs
The Red Rock Audubon Society occasionally guides bird-watching trips at Red Rock for its members. The society aims to preserve bird and animal habitat in Nevada by engaging in stewardship, education, and science. Visit their website at www.redrockaudubon.org or call (702) 390-9890 for details.

The Red Rock Canyon Interpretive Association periodically offers programs to learn about the avian fauna of the area. The details of this organization are found on page 12.

# Hiking
## *at Red Rock Canyon*

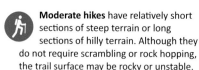

With a beautiful landscape and natural surroundings, Red Rock provides hiking trails that can be enjoyed by all manner of people.

### ▶ A Great Experience

One of the best ways to see and appreciate Red Rock Canyon is to take one of the many hiking trails. The hikes range from casual to strenuous and bring visitors up close and personal with the unique geological, historical, and ecological treasures found here. Even the easiest hikes require some fitness and dexterity. Permits are not required for day hikes but good shoes are helpful, as the trails can be rocky.

### ▶ Difficulty Ratings

Hikes are divided into three categories based on how physically strenuous they are: casual, moderate, and difficult.

 **Casual hikes** are generally flat and have a firm, solid walking surface. The hike distance tends to be shorter.

 **Moderate hikes** have relatively short sections of steep terrain or long sections of hilly terrain. Although they do not require scrambling or rock hopping, the trail surface may be rocky or unstable.

 **Difficult hikes** have extended sections of steep terrain and occasionally require maneuvering around rocks or obstructions.

### ▶ Quality Ratings

Hikes are given up to three stars based on their quality. Although subjective, the quality ratings are determined by the variety of the terrain, points of interest, and appeal of the scenery.

### ▶ Time Ratings

 The time ratings given for each hike are based on a fit adult hiking with a small day pack. Because levels of fitness, ability, and number of stops vary, time ratings can fluctuate wildly from party to party.

### ▶ Icons

Each hike is given a set of icons that describe some of the features and interesting things to see and do along the hike or in the area. A legend is provided on the inside back flap.

### ▶ Special Considerations

Although Red Rock may seem like an untouched wilderness, it is a fragile place that cannot handle irresponsible land use. Below are some things to keep in mind while out and about:

**Stay on the trail:** Desert ecosystems, heavily reliant on organisms living in the crust of the soil, can be devastatingly impacted by foot traffic.

**Pack It In – Pack It Out:** We all share this precious place. Learn the Leave No Trace ethic from page 13 and implement it.

**Hike quietly:** Many come to escape the hustle and bustle of the city. Additionally, human noise can disrupt wildlife.

**Report vandalism:** While the BLM has put forth a number of management policies for the conservation area, they cannot be everywhere at all times to enforce them. If you see vandalism occurring, call (702) 515-5151.

### ▶ Guided and Group Hikes

Guided hikes are a great way to become familiar with the area. A friendly guide can ensure safety and point out interesting details about the landscape.

A valued resource for locals and visitors is the **Red Rock Canyon Interpretive Association** (RRCIA, see page 12), which offers hikes and programs. This group's staff of knowledgeable naturalists provides hiking tours of some of the most popular trails, including the La Madre Spring, Moenkopi Loop, Rock Garden, Calico Tanks, Pine Creek Canyon, and Ice Box Canyon. In addition to the informative hikes, the RRCIA hosts programs where visitors can learn about the geology of Red Rock, search for elusive animals, or try their hand at painting. Hikes and programs are free of charge, but space is limited and reservations are required. The schedule varies, so check www.redrockcanyonlv.org

to see what's available.

A number of local groups get together for hikes at Red Rock Canyon. One of the largest and most active is **VegasHikers**. The friendly group is free to join. A calendar of events and more information can be found at www.meetup.com/VegasHikers.

### ▶ Commercial Tours

Described below are the four companies that are permitted by the BLM to provide guided hiking tours. Reservations are strongly recommended. However, last-minute bookings are sometimes available.

The world's first carbon-neutral outfitter, **Escape Adventures**, operates throughout the American West as well as internationally. At Red Rock Canyon, they offer half-day hiking tours, which last four hours and begin daily at 8:00 am and 1:00 pm. Guests can choose from three of the finest hikes Red Rock has to offer: White Rock Hills Loop, Calico Hills, or Ice Box Canyon. Tours cost $109.00 per person. Transportation and water are provided. Visit www.escapeadventures. com, email info@ escapeadventures.com, or call (800) 596-2953 for more information.

A Las Vegas-based company focused on guiding hikes at Red Rock Canyon, **Hike This!**, caters to groups and individual visitors looking for fresh air and fun in a stunning setting. While they can guide any trail at Red Rock, their specialty is rock scrambling adventures, which are quite popular with fit, active people. Tours are given to each party separately, not in conjunction with others. The morning tours last four to five hours. Transportation, water, and snacks are provided. Prices range from $99.00 to $159.00 per person, depending on group size. Visit www.hikethislasvegas.com, email hikethis@cox.net, or call (702) 393-4453 for more information.

A renowned rock climbing and mountaineering outfit, **Jackson Hole Mountain Guides**, also gives hiking tours at Red Rock Canyon. They guide hikes and scrambles in many of the classic canyons, from half day strolls to full-day journeys. Visit www.jhmg.com, email redrock@jhmg.com, or call (702) 254-0885 for more information.

**Red Rock Canyon Tours** packs a lot into a short time frame. They typically take small groups on the best short hikes and sightseeing at Red Rock Canyon, but can also accommodate families and large groups. Tours last three hours and cost as little as $59.00 per person, depending on tour length and arrangements. Pick-up and drop-off is at the Paris Las Vegas, unless otherwise arranged. Visit www. redrockcanyon-tours.com, email rrcnca@gmail.com, or call (702) 497-5238 for more information.

*Awe-inspiring rock formations are found in the Calico Hills.*

### ▶ Directions – Maps

For each hike described in this guide, directions are given from either the junction of the Clark County 215 Beltway (CC-215) and West Charleston Boulevard or from the fee booth at the beginning of the Scenic Drive. Both West Charleston Boulevard (which becomes SR-159) and the CC-215 are accessible from many points within Las Vegas. The beginning of the Scenic Drive is 5.2 miles west of the CC-215 - West Charleston Boulevard junction.

Nearly all of the described hikes feature a detailed map showing the route of the hike, natural features, and points of interest. Overview maps of the area are found on the inside back cover.

| Hikes and Trails at Red Rock Canyon | Length (miles) | Time (hours) | Style | Difficulty | Quality | Map Location |
|---|---|---|---|---|---|---|
| Red Spring Boardwalk | 0.5 | 1 | Loop | Easy | ☆☆ | 6-D |
| Gateway Canyon | 3.3 | 2.5 | Loop | Difficult | ☆☆ | ❼ |
| Moenkopi Loop | 2.0 | 1.5 | Loop | Easy | ☆☆ | ⓫ |
| Calico Hills Trail | 3.2 | 2.5 | Point to Point | Moderate | ☆☆ | ⓬ |
| Grand Circle Trail | 11.6 | 7 | Loop | Difficult | ☆☆ | ❹ |
| Calico Tanks Trail | 2.3 | 2 | Out and Back | Moderate | ☆☆☆ | ❻ |
| Turtlehead Peak | 4.3 | 4 | Out and Back | Difficult | ☆☆☆ | ❺ |
| White Rock Hills Loop | 6.2 | 3.5 | Loop | Moderate | ☆☆ | ❷ |
| Keystone Thrust | 1.9 | 1.5 | Out and Back | Moderate | ☆☆ | ❸ |
| La Madre Spring Trail | 3.6 | 2.5 | Out and Back | Moderate | ☆☆ | ❶ |
| Willow Springs Loop | 1.5 | 1 | Loop | Easy | ☆☆ | 7-B |
| Children's Discovery Loop | 0.6 | 1 | Loop | Easy | ☆☆ | 7-B |
| SMYC Trail | 1.1* | 1 | Point to Point | Easy | ☆ | 7-B |
| Ice Box Canyon | 2.2 | 2.5 | Out and Back | Moderate | ☆☆ | ❽ |
| Dale's Trail | 2.1* | 1.5 | Point to Point | Moderate | ☆ | ❿ |
| Bridge Mountain | 6.4 | 6 | Out and Back | Difficult | ☆☆ | ❾ |
| Pine Creek Canyon | 2.4 | 2 | Out and Back | Easy to Moderate | ☆☆ | ⓭ |
| Fire Ecology Trail | 0.9 | 1 | Out and Back with a Loop | Easy | ☆ | 6-C |
| Oak Creek Canyon | 2.2 | 1.5 | Out and Back | Easy to Moderate | ☆☆ | ⓯ |
| Arnight Trail | 1.7* | 1.5 | Point to Point | Easy | ☆ | 6-C |
| Knoll Trail | 1.2* | 1.5 | Point to Point | Easy | ☆ | 6-C |
| First Creek Canyon | 3.0 | 2 | Out and Back | Easy to Moderate | ☆☆ | ⓰ |
| Black Velvet Canyon | 1.8 | 1.5 | Out and Back | Moderate | ☆☆ | ⓱ |
| Windy Peak | 4.2 | 4.5 | Out and Back | Difficult | ☆☆ | ⓲ |

*Map location reference is found on the inside back cover.*
*\* Distance measured is length of trail, not including to and from parking areas.*

# RED SPRING AREA

With easy access to a variety of user-friendly facilities and points of interest, Red Spring is a great place to get a taste of Red Rock Canyon.

### ▶ Beautiful Setting
Red Spring and its surrounding spring-fed meadow are nestled below the striking red and white sandstone of the Calico Hills, at the edge of Calico Basin.

### ▶ Casual to Strenuous
There are a number of options available to experience Red Spring and its surroundings. The most casual, and a good option for kids, is a short loop on the boardwalk, which has signs describing the geology, ecosystem, plants, animals, and history of the area. For the more adventurous, several trails begin at the parking area. One popular path leads south up a short hill to an overlook (marked on the map) with nice views back towards Calico Basin. The craggy, sandstone hillside above Red Spring is another well-liked option for those in good physical shape and up for scrambling.

### ▶ Unique Plants and Animals
In addition to a wide variety of birds, Red Spring hosts numerous species only found in riparian areas, such as the alkali mariposa lily and stream orchid. Look for tall velvet ash trees just behind the picnic area and near the spring.

### ▶ Prehistoric and Historic Sites
Thought to be used since Desert Archaic times, Red Spring has a diverse collection of petroglyphs. The area was used for seed processing, suggesting that it may have been a base camp from which people would make foraging and hunting expeditions into the surrounding hills.

In the early 1910s, Miss Ella M. Mason started a small ranch adjacent to the meadow where she likely grazed cattle. The foundation of her home can be seen near the boardwalk (see also page 48).

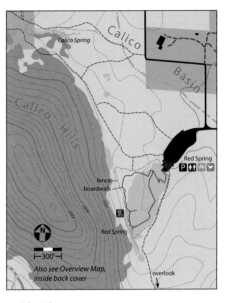

### ▶ Directions
Follow West Charleston Boulevard/SR-159 5.2 miles from its junction with the CC-215, and make a right onto Calico Basin Drive. After 1.2 miles, the Red Spring parking area is found straight ahead.

The entrance to the boardwalk and a number of picnic tables are at the end of the parking area. Popular trails begin adjacent to the toilets located on both sides of the parking area.

*Red Spring feeds a grassy-meadow oasis that has been frequented by people for thousands of years.*

# GATEWAY CANYON

E xceptionally scenic, Gateway Canyon is a relatively secret wildlife enclave guarded by craggy hillsides and a boulder-filled wash.

### ► Impressive Surroundings

A great place to expose kids to Red Rock, the front (south) side of Kraft Mountain is relatively flat and strewn with house-sized boulders that are popular with rock climbers. However, the trail in the canyon itself may prove too difficult for little ones.

In Gateway Canyon, the trail follows a wash surrounded by cliffs and boulders of Aztec Sandstone, some of which have been beautifully sculpted by storm-water runoff for millions of years. In fact, a major storm event occurred in the summer of 2007 that changed the landscape of the wash dramatically, moving small-car-sized boulders and hundreds of tons of gravel.

*Although it's best to avoid the wash during periods of heavy rain, if you find yourself in the canyon during a rainstorm, head for higher ground and seek shelter.*

### ► Fewer Crowds

In part due to the more-difficult boulder hopping and short scrambles found in the canyon itself, the Gateway Canyon hike is less frequented than many others; a plus for those seeking an unspoiled experience.

However, on the Calico Basin side of Kraft Mountain, the trails are more popular and often used by horseback riders. Please use courtesy and remember: hikers yield to horses.

### ► Plants and Animals

The hike circumnavigates Kraft Mountain, which lies within the La Madre Mountain Wilderness Area. Despite its close proximity to the development of Calico Basin, the mountain is home to an amazingly diverse array of animal species.

It is common to see red-tailed hawks circling above, hear the hoot of great-horned owls at dusk, and spot Gambel's quail scurrying about. The south hillside of Kraft Mountain is also one of the best places at Red Rock to catch a glimpse of a Gila monster or a desert tortoise. Bighorn sheep sometimes visit the rocky hillsides of Kraft Mountain and require a careful eye to spot.

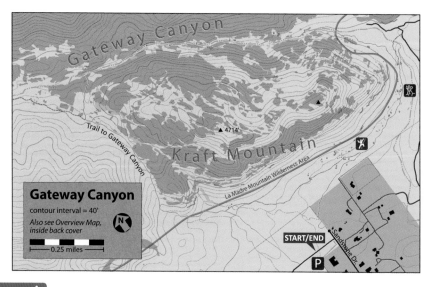

### ► Prehistoric Sites

Take time to stop at the Birthing Boulder (marked on the map), where one of the Native American petroglyphs resembles a pregnant woman. Please observe without touching or disturbing the petroglyphs or adjacent roasting pit. This area was likely used by Southern Paiutes, who harvested Utah agave locally and desert tortoise from the basin itself. See pages 11 and 26 for more information on Native American cultural resources and history.

### ► Directions

From the turnoff for Red Spring (see page 161), continue on Calico Drive and make an immediate left onto Assisi Canyon Avenue, which leads to a right turn onto Sandstone Drive. Follow Sandstone Drive for 0.5 miles to a cul-de-sac. Park in the dirt road adjacent to the cul-de-sac or along Sandstone Drive (observe parking signs, as ticketing frequently occurs).

From the cul-de-sac, there are two directions to hike the loop: clockwise or counter-clockwise. The clockwise direction is more popular, because it puts most of the strenuous hiking near the start and descends, rather than ascends, the wash. However, the counter-clockwise direction offers more viewpoints of Turtlehead Peak and is preferred by those with kids, because it can easily be done as an 'out-and-back' style hike.

***Clockwise Direction:*** An unmarked trail begins 250 yards from Sandstone Drive along the dirt road used for parking. Follow this trail north and aim slightly left of the sandstone (red and brown) cliffs. Although there are a number of social trails in the area, most lead to the correct trail. Follow the largest of the trails up a steep grade to the saddle west of Kraft Mountain where the sandstone meets the gray limestone. From the saddle, the trail meanders down

and left, then heads right at a trail junction, leading into the wash of Gateway Canyon. Follow the wash downstream for 1.1 miles until the trail can be found heading right, out of the wash. If you miss this turnoff, the wash makes a hard right and leads to a tall drop-off surrounded by deep-red Chinle Sandstone.

*Whether running or hiking, the fantastic shapes and colors of the rocks are sure to please.*

Once out of the wash, follow the trail as it swings south around the toe of Kraft Mountain. The trail leads through large boulders on the south side of Kraft Mountain and veers left through a vacant property, crossing a deep wash before rejoining the cul-de-sac of Sandstone Drive.

***Counter-clockwise Direction:*** From the cul-de-sac, head north towards Kraft Mountain, following a trail that immediately dips down through a wash, then leads right (northeast) through a vacant property into a boulderfield. Continue east through the boulderfield. When the boulders start to thin out, the trail heads north, then west, and drops into the wash of Gateway Canyon. Follow the wash for 1.1 miles and take a trail found near a prominent drainage that enters from the left. The trail heads uphill adjacent to the Aztec Sandstone to a saddle, then descends back to the parking area.

# MOENKOPI LOOP

Spectacular views, quick access, and casual terrain make the Moenkopi Loop a popular hike after touring the visitor center.

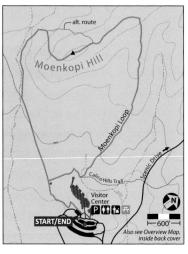

### ▶ A Pleasant Stroll

With gentle grades and a solid walking surface, the Moenkopi Loop is a good choice for those unsure of their hiking capabilities as well as those out for an enjoyable outing among family or friends. Indeed, a bench near the high point makes a nice spot to take in the scenery.

### ▶ Viewpoints

One of the most memorable aspects of this trail is the great views of the surrounding terrain. Moenkopi Hill is situated such that the Red Rock Escarpment and Calico Hills encircle it on many sides, creating a beautiful panorama.

### ▶ Noteworthy Rocks and Fossils

Along the ridge of Moenkopi Hill, the trail follows a band of Virgin Limestone that serves as a 250-million-year-old sidewalk. Underfoot, numerous snail (*Gastropoda*) and seashell (*Brachiopoda*) fossils can be found. The animals, however, were not flawlessly fossilized and take a keen eye to distinguish. See page 104 for fossil info.

### ▶ Interpretive Signs

Along the trail, the BLM has installed

*Once a seabed, now a 250-million-year-old sidewalk, the crest of Moenkopi Hill affords a wrap-around panorama of Red Rock.*

signs describing the sand dunes from which the Aztec Sandstone was formed, the Moenkopi Limestone (referenced in this book as Virgin Limestone), and the Keystone Thrust. A large, burned area roughly borders the trail to the north. This area was burned in the Loop Fire of July 2005 (see page 60 for more info on fires).

### ▶ Directions

The hike begins at the Red Rock Canyon Visitor Center. Described below is the more-popular counterclockwise manner of hiking the loop:

From the courtyard near the entrance to the visitor center, head left (west) past a group of picnic tables to a sign that marks the beginning of the trail. The trail leads down a slight hill, follows an old dirt track for about 70 yards, then makes a right after a weather-monitoring station. Follow the trail as it skirts around the visitor center, then head left at a junction with the Calico Hills Trail and climb a slight grade up to a band of gray rock. The trail follows this band of rock south to the high point of Moenkopi Hill. An alternate trail breaks off to the right to bypass the high point. The trails rejoin on the southwest side of the hill then head east towards the visitor center.

# CALICO HILLS TRAIL

3.2 MILES  2.5 HOURS  POINT TO POINT

Bordering the vivid sandstone of the Calico Hills, this trail winds through rolling hills of magnificent scenery, offering intriguing petroglyphs and glimpses of wildlife.

## Magnificent Scenery
With the intricate landscape of the Calico Hills seemingly an arm's reach away, nearly every turn of the trail is endowed with remarkable vistas.

## Moderately Strenuous
Lacking any scrambling or rock hopping, this hike appeals to many because of its gently sloping terrain, which allows for a leisurely walk or a scenic run if so desired.

## Plants and Animals
This hike illustrates well the differences between the blackbrush scrub, creosote bush, and wash plant communities. Along the wash, the soil is deeper, more organically rich, and supports a higher density of trees and shrubs, including honey mesquite, catclaw, silktassel bush, and the occasional pinyon pine.

Along the trail, some animals, such as white-tailed antelope squirrels, side-blotched lizards, and rock wrens, are commonly seen throughout the year. Many others come out only in certain seasons or times of the day. With luck, it's possible to spot a chuckwalla, gray fox, chukar, Southwestern speckled rattlesnake, or ringtail.

## Native American Rock Art
Two panels of petroglyphs can be found adjacent to the Calico Hills Trail about 0.4 miles past Calico II. Some of the glyphs are heavily varnished over, suggesting usage of the area for thousands of years. Others show atlatls, which continued in the rock art record long after the advent of the bow and arrow, circa AD 500. The flat panels and nature of the site suggest it may have been used by the Southern Paiutes as a starting point for a vision quest into the

mountains or as a 'healing place' where shamans could administer remedies.

*Please observe these irreplaceable artifacts with respect and do not touch or stand on the panels.*

## ▶ Directions
The hike begins at the visitor center (see page 137) and ends at the Sandstone Quarry (see map, inside back cover). The

trail passes close by the Calico I and Calico II parking areas, which allows each section, or a combination of sections, to be hiked.

After breaking right from the Moenkopi Loop, the trail continues northeast and crosses the Scenic Drive. It then veers left (northwest), remaining adjacent to the Scenic Drive until Calico I. From Calico I, hike down the wide trail and make a left before reaching the sandstone. The trail meanders northwesterly, always keeping the Calico Hills to the right, until the Sandstone Quarry is reached.

# CALICO TANKS TRAIL

 **2.3 MILES** **2 HOURS** **OUT AND BACK**

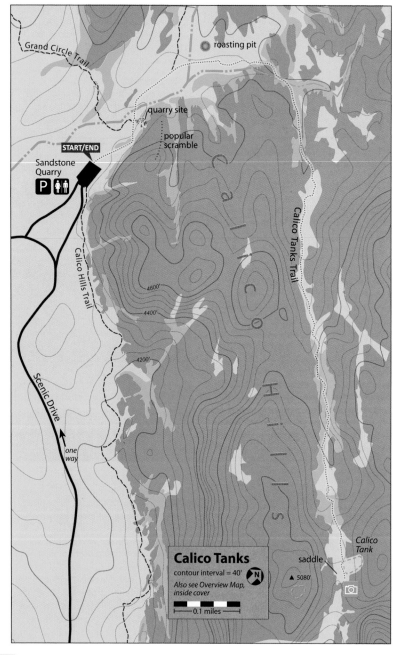

Grand Circle Trail

roasting pit

quarry site

popular scramble

**START/END**

Sandstone Quarry
P

Calico Hills Trail

Calico Tanks Trail

4600'
4400'
4200'

Scenic Drive

one way

Calico Hills

Calico Tank

saddle

5080'

**Calico Tanks**
contour interval = 40'
*Also see Overview Map, inside cover*

0.1 miles

This is one of the most popular hikes at Red Rock Canyon and with good reason. Over its entire length, the Calico Tanks Trail pleases visitors with breathtaking scenery, cultural history, amusing rocks to scramble, a diverse array of plants and animals, and to top it all off, a view of the Strip.

### ► Stunning Landscape
The Calico Tanks Trail leads through vast stretches of multi-colored, ornately-shaped rock formations. The second half of the hike allows visitors to experience sandstone underfoot and on all sides of the trail.

### ► Moderately Strenuous
Another plus to this hike is its length, which many find to be not too long nor too short. The terrain can be physical with a few sections of rock steps and small boulders to negotiate.

### ► Scrambling Side Trip
While not on the hike itself, a popular scramble begins behind (east of) the main quarry site and leads to a spectacular viewpoint. Be aware that there are many precipitous drop-offs in the area. Each year people are injured, and occasionally die, due to scrambling in the Calico Hills.

### ► Plants and Animals
In the first stretch of the hike, knee-high blackbrush is contrasted with the taller Mojave yucca and its head of stiff, pointed leaves. When crossing the wash, scrub oaks, California redbuds, and silktassel bushes are prevalent.

If the tank itself is filled, as is often the case in spring or after rains, look for small aquatic creatures, such as fairy, brine, and clam shrimp; water striders; and numerous other invertebrates along the edge and in the water. Occasionally, large mammals, such as mule deer and bighorn sheep, come to the tank for water.

### ► Prehistoric and Historic Sites
Evidence of Southern Paiutes and earlier Native Americans exists in the area; roasting pits are the most conspicuous. In these pits, agave hearts were roasted by limestone rocks which were heated by fires. The hearts were chewed for their sweet flesh and dried for later use.

In 1905, a stone quarry near the present-day parking area began operation. Over the span of seven years, a small amount of rock was extricated under three different owners who struggled to keep the business solvent. Much evidence of their activity remains, including many steel rods, bore holes, and quarried blocks (see page 45 for more details).

### ► Amazing Views
The saddle just past Calico Tank offers a gorgeous view east towards Calico Basin and the Las Vegas Valley. To reach the viewpoint, scramble around to the right of Calico Tank.

*The Calico Tank, one of the largest intermittent pools in the Calico Hills, supports many forms of life not commonly found in the Mojave Desert.*

### ► Directions
The hike begins at Sandstone Quarry, which is located at the third parking area on the Scenic Drive, 2.5 miles from the fee booth (see map, inside back cover).

From the parking area, a trail leads north past the restrooms. About 170 yards from the parking area, the trail passes the main quarry site, then crosses a large gravel wash. After 0.2 miles, the trail forks (signed); follow the right fork and pass a Native American roasting pit. Continue on the west bank of the wash until the trail crosses the wash and pokes through a dense growth of trees and shrubs at the mouth of a gully. The trail follows this gully for another 0.8 miles to the largest of the tanks, dubbed 'Calico Tank.'

# TURTLEHEAD PEAK

⭐ ⭐ ⭐

4.3 MILES | 4 HOURS | OUT AND BACK

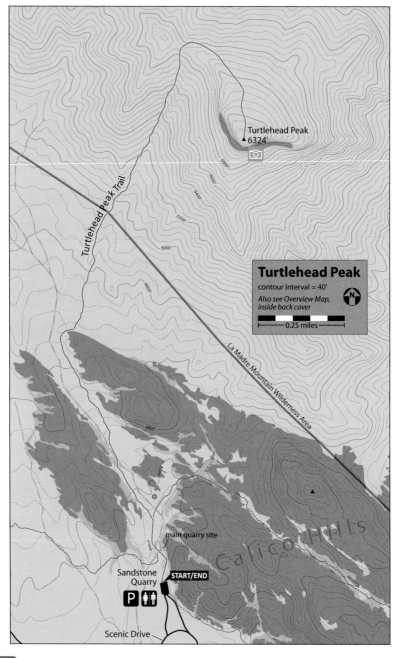

Turtlehead Peak
▲ 6324'

Turtlehead Peak Trail

**Turtlehead Peak**

contour interval = 40'

*Also see Overview Map, inside back cover*

N

0.25 miles

La Madre Mountain Wilderness Area

Calico Hills

main quarry site

Sandstone Quarry

START/END

P

Scenic Drive

With a distinct summit and one of the most dramatic views of Red Rock Canyon, Turtlehead Peak is a favorite hike for those in good shape.

### ▶ Commanding Views

Turtlehead Peak is well positioned for admiring the surrounding landscape that stretches out in all directions. Situated at the edge of a cliff, the dramatic summit commands breathtaking views—some of the best at Red Rock. The serrated ridge of the La Madre Mountains stretches north then east from the Red Rock Escarpment nearly to Las Vegas, framing Brownstone Canyon, Gateway Canyon, and Calico Basin to the east.

### ▶ Surreal Landscape

Like the Calico Tanks hike, which shares the first section of trail, this hike takes visitors around blobular sandstone formations that seem to grow from the desert floor.

The playful mood fades as the elevation increases. Higher up, limestone spires and gnarly, stunted trees impart a mystical feeling.

### ▶ Strenuous and Steep

Turtlehead peak is one of the more difficult hikes at Red Rock because of the steepness of the trail and the occasionally unstable terrain. Although the sections that require the use of hands are short, there are some spots where a fall could be serious. Despite the difficulty, most physically fit people enjoy the hike.

### ▶ Plants and Animals

After leaving the Sandstone Quarry parking area, the trail meanders through a large, gravel-filled wash that is populated by large shrubs, such as scrub oak, manzanita, desert willow, and California redbud. Here is the best place for spotting animals. Blue Western scrub-jays are fairly common and can often be identified by their loud, raspy calls. Avocado-sized white-tailed antelope squirrels and larger desert cottontails are nearly always present. Some of their predators, the red-tailed hawk, gray fox, and a number of snake species, are less-likely to be seen. After heading out of the wash, the trail climbs through a rising slope populated by the blackbrush scrub plant community. Look for strawberry hedgehog, spiny menodora, and other small, flowering shrubs. The higher, rocky terrain supports a sparse population of stunted pinyon pines and Utah juniper trees. In the late spring and early summer, the tall, beautiful flowering stalks of the Utah agave delight visitors in this area.

*Like a limestone fortress rising into the clouds above the Calico Hills, the stunning Turtlehead Peak is not to be missed.*

### ▶ Directions

The hike begins at Sandstone Quarry, which is located at the third parking area on the Scenic Drive, 2.5 miles from the fee booth (see map, inside back cover).

From the parking area, a trail leads north past the restrooms. About 170 yards from the parking area, the trail passes the main quarry site, then crosses a large gravel wash. After 0.2 miles, the trail forks (signed); follow the left fork, which heads northwest adjacent to a large wash. The trail exits the wash to the north (right) as the landscape ceases to be dominated by sandstone formations. The trail then climbs the rising slope, generally staying left of a prominent drainage. As elevation is gained, the trail becomes braided and poorly marked. It is best to follow the most well-traveled path. However, most paths lead to the saddle on the ridge above. From the saddle, follow braided paths southeast, generally staying close (about 10' to 40') to the edge of the cliff. A rock cairn marks the summit.

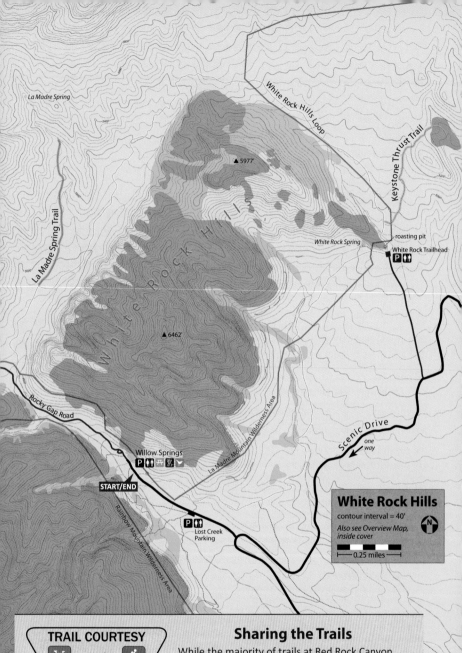

La Madre Spring

White Rock Hills Loop

Keystone Thrust Trail

▲ 5977'

La Madre Spring Trail

White Rock Spring

roasting pit

White Rock Trailhead

▲ 6462'

W h i t e   R o c k   H i l l s

Rocky Gap Road

Willow Springs

La Madre Mountain Wilderness Area

Scenic Drive

one way

START/END

Rainbow Mountain Wilderness Area

Lost Creek Parking

### White Rock Hills

contour interval = 40'

*Also see Overview Map, inside cover*

N

0.25 miles

## TRAIL COURTESY

YIELD TO

## Sharing the Trails

While the majority of trails at Red Rock Canyon are dedicated to foot traffic, a number of trails share usage with mountain bikes and/or horses. The common courtesy is for bikes to yield to horses and hikers, and for hikers to yield to horses. When yielding, move to the side of the trail; if it is necessary to step off the trail, select a spot with no vegetation to minimize environmental impacts.

# WHITE ROCK HILLS LOOP

A local favorite, this multi-hour excursion takes hikers through a lovely pinyon-juniper woodland, passes numerous Native American roasting pits, and offers striking views of the Keystone Thrust.

### ► Picture-perfect Country

This trail winds through the expansive woodlands found northwest of the White Rock Hills. The woodland is found in a picturesque valley bordered by the impressive La Madre Mountains to the north and west (see photo, page 22).

### ► A Wild Feel

The longer distance of this hike keeps the crowds away and rewards active hikers with solitude and seemingly unspoiled wilderness.

### ► Varying Plant Communities

With stops at White Rock Spring and Willow Spring, this hike allows visitors to experience pinyon-juniper woodlands, blackbrush scrub, wash, and riparian plant communities. Most of the hike travels through a transition zone between the blackbrush scrub and pinyon-juniper woodlands with numerous specimens of cliffrose, banana yucca, Mormon tea, and buckhorn cholla.

The White Rock Hills are a great place to spot bighorn sheep from the fall to spring. Look for them along the base of craggy hillsides. Smaller mammals, such as desert cottontails, black-tailed jackrabbits, and kangaroo rats, are also common.

Bird watchers enjoy Willow Spring and find numerous species near White Rock Spring as well.

### ► Native American Sites

In addition to the rock art sites at Willow Springs, there are a number of roasting pits along Rocky Gap Road and near the White Rock Trailhead. These areas were used extensively by people with ties to the Anasazi and Patayan peoples as far

back as AD 500. In more recent times, the Southern Paiutes likely made communal gatherings in this area during the spring when Utah agave hearts were ripe with sugar. The hearts, sometimes along with desert tortoises or other small animals, were roasted in these large-diameter pits. The limestone used to line the roasting pits lost its ability to hold heat after its first use and had to be discarded and changed out with each roasting. The used limestone was discarded adjacent to the pits, which gives the mounds a donut shape (see page 32).

*Please respect cultural resource sites; do not touch or walk on artifacts.*

### ► The Keystone Thrust

Through a long series of earthquakes, the Keystone Thrust event moved the older Paleozoic carbonate rocks, which initially rested below the Aztec Sandstone, to their current position above. The effects of the event are displayed on the northwest side of the White Rock Hills where the layered sandstone has been rolled upward like the edge of a carpet by the thrusting. For more information, see page 22.

### ► Directions

Follow the Scenic Drive (see map, inside back cover) for 7.1 miles from the fee booth, and make a right towards Willow Springs (signed). Follow this road for 0.5 miles to the Willow Springs parking area, just before the road turns to dirt.

Begin the hike by walking northwest up the dirt road (Rocky Gap Road). After 0.6 miles, the road crosses a wash. Then, after about 150 yards, a foot trail leads right (north), paralleling the wash. Follow this trail as it ascends a slope, passing a turnoff for the La Madre Spring Trail. The White Rock Hills Loop swings southeast near the northern tip of the White Rock Hills, then heads gradually downhill to the White Rock Trailhead. Pass through the trailhead parking area to the west and continue downhill. After crossing a wash, the trail ascends a slight mesa, then descends into the Willow Springs area and back to the parking area.

# KEYSTONE THRUST TRAIL

This concise hike leads to an awe-inspiring geologic feature and grand views of Red Rock and the La Madre Mountains.

### ▶ Views for Miles

The location of this hike, near the head of the valley, affords splendid views of the multi-colored sandstone of the Calico Hills, as well as the Red Rock Escarpment, which trends away from the viewer.

*The dramatic scenery of the La Madre Mountains adds to the awe of the earth-moving forces that created this place.*

### ▶ A Short Trek

With no technical rock hopping or scrambling and a moderate distance, this hike offers a fresh diversion from an auto tour of the Scenic Drive, especially when other areas are crowded.

### ▶ Plants and Animals

This hike traverses a transition zone where the blackbrush scrub of lower elevations grades into the pinyon-juniper woodlands commonly found at higher elevations. Expect to find numerous blackbrush, cliffrose, banana yucca, and the occasional buckhorn cholla or strawberry hedgehog. In late spring, look for the beautiful, bright-red flowers of the Mojave kingcup cactus, which are found only at higher elevations

at Red Rock.

### ▶ Ancient Barbecue

Just left of the trail, about 80 yards from the White Rock Trailhead, the remains of a roasting pit can be found. This pit and many others like it found at Red Rock were primarily used to roast the sugar-rich hearts of Utah agave. Although this pit has not been dated, many like it date to the time when Red Rock was used by people with ties to the Anasazi and Patayan peoples, circa AD 1000. See painting, page 32.

*Please respect cultural resource sites; do not touch or walk on the roasting pit.*

### ▶ The Keystone Thrust

One of Red Rock's most amazing geologic features, the Keystone Thrust is visible from many places in the area and described in detail in page 22. The great thing about this hike is that visitors can see and touch the thrust fault underfoot.

Roughly 65 million years ago, a long series of earthquakes pushed the older, gray limestone and dolomite above the younger Aztec Sandstone, which previously laid at the top. Since then, the limestone overlying the sandstone has been eroded away to re-expose the sandstone.

### ▶ Directions

*See map, page 170.*
From the fee booth, follow the Scenic Drive for 5.7 miles and make a right onto a dirt road that leads 0.5 miles to the White Rock Trailhead.

The Keystone Thrust Trail leaves the uphill side of the parking area, passes by a roasting pit and crosses a wash shortly thereafter. After the wash, the trail ascends gently to a trail junction with the White Rock Hills Loop. Take the right fork, which swings around a minor, gray-limestone-capped hill to the exposed fault.

# LA MADRE SPRING TRAIL

Despite the gorgeous scenery, interesting history, and access to a lush oasis, this hike is a relatively well-kept secret.

### ► A Picturesque Valley
This hike strolls through a pinyon-juniper woodland, nearly a forest by Red Rock standards, as it climbs up a valley bordered by the striking cliffs of the White Rock Hills and the sweeping ridge line of the La Madre Mountains (see photo, page 22).

### ► Well-Graded Trail
Although some find the climb to be a bit strenuous, the trail follows an old dirt track that is well-graded and has very few loose rocks to twist an ankle on. For those choosing to venture up the wash above the dam, be aware that the trail is not maintained and can be easily lost in the thick vegetation.

### ► Area of Special Biodiversity
The water from La Madre Spring courses down a wash for over half a mile. In this area, a lush oasis with a diverse array of plant species flourishes. Along the wash, look for thistles, desert paintbrush, and canyon grape. As the spring season turns to summer, the grapes take shape and more flowers appear alongside the small stream as it cascades down the wash. These include long-stemmed evening primrose, thistles, cardinalflower, and Nevada goldenrod. In addition to the perennial sedges, wiregrass, and common reed, the water provides habitat for Northern Pacific treefrogs that sing in the spring and summer.

### ► Historical Significance
The first documented use of La Madre Spring and its surroundings was in 1876 when mine shafts were blasted to follow a vein of silver on the hillside above the spring. The operation proved unprofitable, due to costs required to wagon-cart the ore to Los Angeles for smelting, and was abandoned in 1883.

In 1907, the mine was reopened by local Las Vegans. They were able to pack-mule the ore to horse-drawn carts and take it to the railroad in Las Vegas for shipment to LA. There, it was smelted for zinc and silver (see also page 43).

In the 1960s and early 70s, the Las Vegas Archery Club set up an extensive camp along the trail to the wash, which they dammed to produce a water supply.

*Western columbine flutter alongside a small waterfall in the wash below the spring.*

### ► Directions
*See map, page 170.*
From the fee booth, follow the Scenic Drive for 7.1 miles and turn right onto a road that leads 0.5 miles to the Willow Springs parking area. Low-clearance vehicles need to park here.

High-clearance vehicles can follow Rocky Gap Road (the rough gravel road past Willow Spring) for 0.7 miles to the La Madre Spring Trailhead (signed), which is found on the right. A two-car parking pullout is located left of the road.

From the trailhead, walk north up a slight grade following an old dirt track. About 0.5 miles from Rocky Gap Road, the trail forks, and the White Rock Hills Loop goes right. The La Madre Spring Trail goes left and passes several foundations from the archery club camp, then skirts up the hill to the dam-formed pond, the end of the official trail.

# WILLOW SPRINGS AREA

Tucked into a broad notch in the Red Rock Escarpment, Willow Springs provides friendly access to a diverse group of interesting sites and activities.

### ► Riparian Areas

The two springs here provide some of the most lush vegetation found at Red Rock Canyon. While the area immediately surrounding Willow Spring has been developed for picnicking, the Lost Creek Spring has remained closer to its natural state, thanks in part to a boardwalk that limits foot traffic in the sensitive area.

*The friendly hike to the Lost Creek Waterfall is popular with families. Along the way is a verdant spring, tall pine trees, a maze of boulders, and the chance to see remarkable wildlife.*

A visit to Lost Creek Spring is well worth the short hike. The area around the spring is remarkably cooler than the surrounding desert, and many visitors enjoy listening to the trickling water and chirping birds. The spring supports canyon grape, coffeeberry, numerous grasses, and rough angelica (*Angelica scabrida*), which is endemic to the Spring Mountains.

Each spring supports populations of tiny springsnails. Neither of the two species found here occur outside of southern Nevada. See page 101 for more information.

### ► Plants and Animals

Aside from the unique collections of life near the springs, the Red Rock Wash, which runs through Willow Springs, is home to California redbud trees, desert willows, shrub live oaks, and two species of pricklypears. Outside the wash, the drainages are choked with scrub oak, and the hillsides are dotted with cliffrose, banana yucca, and pinyon pine.

Bighorn sheep are occasionally spotted in the craggy areas surrounding Willow Springs. Other mammals that might make an appearance include the gray fox, black-tailed jackrabbit, or ringtail.

### ► Bird Watching

The easy access, combined with varied habitats, makes Willow Springs one of the most popular locations to view birds at Red Rock. In fact, more than 70 species have been recorded here. While ravens and jays are conspicuous, especially near picnic sites, the more observant might notice spotted towhees and white-throated swifts. With a bit of luck and a healthy dose of patience, ladder-backed woodpeckers, ash-throated flycatchers, hummingbirds, wrens, and warblers can sometimes be seen.

### ► Native American Heritage

Willow Springs is one of the most significant sites of Native American activity at Red Rock. Here, visitors can observe multiple roasting pits and rock art sites containing both pictographs and petroglyphs.

While many questions remain about the people who lived here, some aspects are known. For example, Willow Springs was unlikely to be a permanent settlement, but rather a seasonal camp used when Utah agave were ripe, or when other resources, like pine nuts, could be collected. The group that used Willow Springs when Europeans arrived were the Southern Paiutes. They understood life through the idea of *puha*, a dynamic energy force that flows through everything around us in varying intensities. Due to its geographic location, surrounded by high peaks, and endowed with flowing water, Willow Springs is speculated to have had a large amount of *puha* and could have been considered a spiritual place for this reason.

### ► Picnicking

The cooler temperatures and shade from nearby cottonwoods make the area a popular spot for casual picnics and barbecues. There are some 28 picnic tables and three grills; charcoal is not provided.

### ► Rock Climbing

Since the late 1960s, Willow Springs has been a popular area for experienced rock climbers to refine their techniques and to introduce beginners to the joys of moving over stone. If lacking a guide, check out the 'Brown Round Boulder' where it is possible to climb close to the ground without the need for ropes (see map, page 177).

### ► Lost Creek Falls Trail

This short (0.6 miles) out-and-back trail is a great addition to an auto tour around the Scenic Drive or an after-picnic stroll. The trailhead is located at the Lost Creek parking area. The trail takes visitors through numerous plant communities and niche environments where wildlife might be spotted.

After passing the boardwalk adjacent to Lost Creek Spring, the trail terminates at the Lost Creek Waterfall. Although often dry, if there has been even a small amount of precipitation, the waterfall forms, dropping water 50' past an overhang in the rock.

### ► Willow Springs Loop

This 1.5 mile loop is a memorable way to see the place and appreciate what life may have been like for Native Americans that lived in this area for thousands of years.

From the Willow Springs parking area, head east along a concrete path that leads to a large boulder with the 'Painted Hands' pictograph. Adjacent to the boulder is an ancient roasting pit (see painting, page 32).

*'Painted Hands' is thought to have been made by people with ties to the Anasazi and Patayan peoples roughly 1000 years ago or later, by Southern Paiutes. The pictograph is easily accessed via a paved path that leads a short distance from the parking area.*

The trail continues southeast, past the roasting pit, through a pinyon-juniper woodland, then turns southwest, crosses the road, and follows the trail towards Lost Creek Spring. Immediately after crossing the boardwalk, head right (the Lost Creek Waterfall can be found about 150 yards further up this trail). The Willow Springs Loop skirts below a band of Chinle Sandstone that was possibly used by Native Americans as a spiritual place for telling stories. A discussion of Native American history can be found beginning on page 26. The trail continues northwestward, meandering through pinyon pines and Utah junipers, then crosses the Red Rock Wash and heads towards the Willow Springs parking area.

### ► Directions

*See map, page 177.*
Follow the Scenic Dr. (see map, inside back cover) for 7.1 miles from the fee booth, and turn right towards Willow Springs. Follow this road for 0.2 miles to the Lost Creek parking area on the left, or continue another 0.3 miles to the Willow Springs parking area on both sides of the road.

# CHILDEREN'S DISCOVERY TRAIL

A n interpretive journey set up for kids, but appealing to all ages, this trail is a nice way to stretch the legs and get a sense of Red Rock Canyon.

### ► Great for Kids

As the name implies, this is a great trail to introduce kids to Red Rock. In fact, the Clark County School District often takes field trips here to give students an appreciation for the natural features of the area.

### ► The Trail

The well-graded trail is generally not too rocky, has a pleasant boardwalk near Lost Creek Spring, and makes a gentle climb about halfway through its loop.

### ► Points of Interest

The BLM has installed numbered signs along the trail at certain points of interest.

The slender, brown Carsonite signs correspond to a free, 15-page booklet that describes the natural features at each stop. The booklet is available at the information desk within the visitor center and on the internet at: www.blm.gov. Below are brief descriptions of the stops:

### ❶ The Wash

The rocks on the trail have been carried here by flash floods caused by rainfall. When it rains, much of the water cannot be absorbed into the ground and sometimes forms into torrents of water capable of transporting an enormous amount of soil and rock. This process has occurred for millions of years and slowly eroded the mountains seen around here.

### ❷ The Vegetation

A number of different plants grow in this area. Here, one can point out four that are well known at Red Rock: manzanita (page 118), a shrub with smooth, reddish bark;

*There are a number of stops along the trail that highlight a variety of interesting features. Here, visitors can view pictographs and imagine what life was like for Native Americans who frequented this place for many generations.*

grizzlybear pricklypear (page 112), a cactus with pads about the size of a child's hand; pinyon pine (page 114), a tree with needles that grow singularly; and Utah juniper (page 115), a tree with shaggy bark and scale-like leaves.

### ❸ Ancient Sugar - Utah Agave

With a careful eye, it is possible to spot Utah agave (page 109) by its low-growing dome of pointed leaves. For thousands of years, Native Americans collected the hearts of this plant and roasted them in earthen pits. The roasting brought out a molasses-like sugar, an important part of their diet.

### ❹ Rock Art

The area of Willow Springs has been used by a number of culturally-distinct groups of Native Americans. The rock art seen in this overhang was likely made by people with ties to Anasazi or by Southern Paiutes. Both groups could have used an overhang such as this for a temporary shelter or as a stage from which to tell stories and myths.

### ❺ Plant Communities

Notice the riparian, wash, and pinyon-juniper plant communities found here (page 66). Each one of these communities, even though only yards apart, are inhabited by distinctly different plants and animals.

### ❻ The Music of Nature

Take a moment to appreciate the sounds of the area: water flowing over rocks, birds chirping, wind in the trees. The symphony of nature has remained essentially unchanged since man's ancestors began walking on two legs.

### ❼ Old Growth Trees

The better watered, cooler spots in the canyons have allowed tall evergreens, called ponderosa pines (page 114), to take root. They grow to be 200' tall and live more than 450 years. The bark has a delightful aroma.

### ❽ Young Trees

Because flash floods occasionally uproot whatever is growing in their paths, the

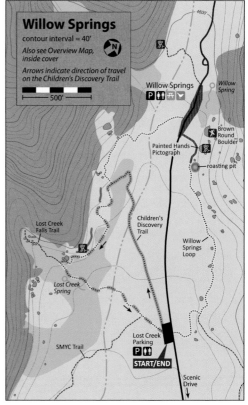

trees here are much younger than those above the embankment. Many of these trees have evolved to live in this area, and some require the abrasive force of a flash flood to break down protective sheaths that surround their seeds.

### ❾ Final Stop

A stop simply to enjoy the beauty of the surroundings and reflect on the importance of a place such as Red Rock Canyon National Conservation Area in our modern world.

### ▶ Directions

Follow the Scenic Drive (see map, inside back cover) for 7.1 miles from the fee booth, and make a right towards Willow Springs. Follow this road for 0.2 miles to the Lost Creek parking area on the left. The trail begins on the west side of the parking area and is marked with signs.

# ICE BOX CANYON

**2.2** MILES  **2.5** HOURS  **OUT AND BACK**

Great for warm days, this trail leads into a cool canyon within the Red Rock Escarpment and offers glimpses of towering cliffs, numerous plants and animals, and a seasonal waterfall.

### ▶ Inside a Deep Sandstone Canyon

This popular half-day hike leads visitors into a dramatic canyon within the Red Rock Escarpment. Inside the canyon, tall walls of sandstone loom overhead, blocking out direct sunlight. Cool air descends into the canyon, often creating chilled temperatures, hence the name. The main attraction of the hike is a waterfall found deep in the canyon. Formed by a cliff in the wash, the waterfall usually is dry in the summer and fall.

### ▶ Rock Hopping

This hike has a modest elevation gain (440') and is not aerobically strenuous. However, the first half is on a very rocky trail, and the second half requires some agile movement through the wash to reach the waterfall. Despite this, many visitors find it a good place to take kids if under a watchful eye.

### ▶ Multiple Plant Communities

The hike begins in a blackbrush scrub plant community dotted with Utah juniper. After crossing the broad Red Rock Wash, a good example of the wash plant community, the landscape adjacent to the trail transitions into a pinyon-juniper woodland at the mouth of the canyon. In spots along the wash, the mixed chaparral can be identified. Ponderosa pines, typically found at higher, wetter locations, can also be seen here.

Many animals prefer the pinyon-juniper woodlands at the mouth of the canyon area over the confined spaces of the canyon itself.

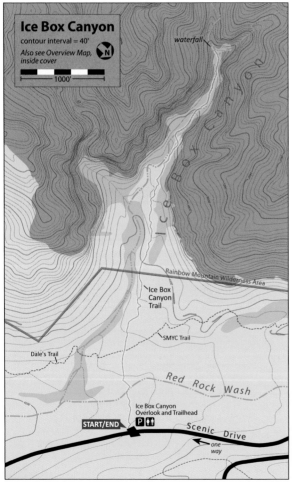

Ice Box Canyon
contour interval = 40'
Also see Overview Map, inside cover
1000'
waterfall
Ice Box Canyon
Rainbow Mountain Wilderness Area
Ice Box Canyon Trail
SMYC Trail
Dale's Trail
Red Rock Wash
Ice Box Canyon Overlook and Trailhead
START/END
Scenic Drive
one way

A notable exception are the bighorn sheep that use the steep terrain within the canyon as protection against predators, such as mountain lions, that are less agile in craggy surroundings. Birds, such as red-tailed hawks, peregrine falcons, white-throated swifts, and the occasional golden eagle, frequent the canyon for feeding and protection from predators.

### ► Geologic Processes

Ice Box Canyon provides a great opportunity to see the effects of two geologic processes: erosion and the formation of desert varnish.

As discussed on page 22, the Aztec Sandstone of the Red Rock Escarpment initially extended many miles eastward. At Ice Box Canyon, like the Grand Canyon, storm-water flows have carved their way through the layers of rock. Here at Red Rock, the process has been underway for some 65 million years since the earthquakes of the Keystone Thrust event.

In the geologic instant of hundreds to thousands of years, desert varnish can form on the Aztec Sandstone of Red Rock. This thin, dark-brown coating, found extensively in Ice Box Canyon, is caused by a process that is not completely understood, but involves the underlying rock, clay, water, sunlight, and possibly microbes.

### ► Directions

Follow the Scenic Drive for 7.6 miles from the fee booth to the Ice Box Canyon Overlook and Trailhead. From this parking area, located on both sides of the road, the Ice Box Canyon Trail heads southwest and crosses the Red Rock Wash. The well-

*After rainstorms or winter snow melt, Ice Box Canyon hosts a picture-perfect waterfall. In the summer or years of little precipitation, the feature typically is dry.*

trodden trail continues southwest along a flat area into the canyon. Although the trail is braided in spots, most paths lead back to the main trail, which heads for the prominent canyon.

After dropping down into the wash, the trail follows its boulder-filled course to the waterfall. If a section of wash seems impassable due to an obstruction, there is likely a hidden trail around it.

*Most people plan to avoid the Red Rock Wash and Ice Box Canyon during periods of heavy rain; if you find yourself in either spot during a rainstorm, head for higher ground, seek shelter, and enjoy the show.*

# BRIDGE MOUNTAIN

**6.4** MILES  **6** HOURS  OUT AND BACK

Views on par with the Grand Canyon, seen from a heavenly rock-scape, await for those capable of this rugged hike.

### ► Floating with the Clouds
The one-of-a-kind landscape found atop the Red Rock Escarpment is well worth the hike. The terrain, a rolling plateau seemingly thrust into the clouds, conjures images of a foreign planet mixed with earthly delights. On a clear day at the peak, views across the Colorado River into Arizona might draw your attention from the seemingly-vast Las Vegas Valley.

### ► Strenuous and Rewarding
The physical nature of this trek requires hikers to be of good fitness and comfortable using their hands and feet to move over rocky terrain, sometimes above precipitous cliffs where a fall could be life threatening. This being said, the exceptional surroundings and unique sights make for a gratifying experience.

### ► Plants and Animals
The trail starts out in a pleasant pinyon-juniper woodland populated with many Utah agave, and occasionally, red-barked manzanita, dagger-leaved banana yucca and fragrant mountain mahogany (*Cercocarpus* spp.).

Vegetation becomes sparse atop the Red Rock Escarpment where plants are found growing out of small cracks and fissures, and pinyon pines have been beautifully gnarled by decades of wind and weather. Peregrine falcons, white-throated swifts, and red-tailed hawks are commonly seen riding the air currents created by sheer cliffs adjacent to the trail.

Enclaves of vegetation exist where soil has collected in tanks and depressions. These pockets of life support a number of rare species, including the endemic Red Rock Canyon aster (*Ionactis caelestis*). Other tanks are filled by rainstorms and sometimes hold water year-round. In water tanks, tiny fairy shrimp and various invertebrates can be found.

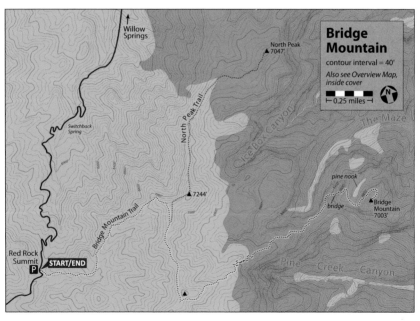

*There are many rain-filled tanks to be found in the rolling rock-scape seemingly thrust into the sky above the Las Vegas Valley. People in good shape find the Bridge Mountain hike to be one of the most rewarding southern Nevada has to offer.*

One of the most striking of these enclaves is adjacent to the trail, passed just before the final climb to the peak. Here, a group of tall ponderosa pines thrive in an unexpected nook tucked away high on the rocky peak.

*Please refrain from disturbing these special spots. They are irreplaceable ecological niches.*

### ► Geology Underfoot and Overhead

The first part of the hike winds its way up the west side of a Bonanza King Limestone (see pages 15 and 23) ridge that parallels the Red Rock Escarpment. This ridge extends to the north and south and sits atop the younger Aztec Sandstone of the escarpment. The reason for older rocks above younger is the Keystone Thrust, described on page 22. Take a moment, after crossing over the limestone ridge, to consider the awesome forces required to thrust these Paleozoic carbonate rocks up and over the sandstone.

Another amazing feature of this hike is the extraordinary sandstone shapes that have been created from tens of millions of years of weathering and erosion. The most prominent is an arch of sandstone some 35'

tall that the trail traverses under and from which Bridge Mountain receives its name. Surrounding the bridge are numerous tanks that collect rainwater. Some of these tanks can fill with water many feet deep.

### ► Directions

Follow the Scenic Drive (see map, inside back cover) for 7.1 miles from the fee booth, and make a right towards Willow Springs. Follow this road for 0.5 miles to the Willow Springs parking area where the Rocky Gap Road begins. Follow this rough dirt road (**high-clearance vehicle required**) for 4.7 miles to the Red Rock Summit, a small, dirt pullout left of the road at a scenic gap.

The well-traveled trail (not signed at the trailhead) begins on the east (uphill) side of the pullout. It heads east, switchbacking up a moderate grade. When it reaches the ridge, the trail heads south to swing around a minor peak, then continues east to the red and white sandstone. With sandstone underfoot, the trail is marked with small cairns and black paint blazes. It follows a peninsula of rock down, then steeply up, to the summit.

# PINE CREEK CANYON

**2.4** MILES   **2** HOURS   OUT AND BACK

**W**ith an abundance of life to be observed, Pine Creek Canyon is a naturalist's dream where spectacular cliffs drop down to a lush sanctuary in the midst of the Mojave Desert.

### ► Broad, Colorful Canyon
Considered by many to be one of the most beautiful canyons of Red Rock, Pine Creek has a large, relatively flat, lush area nestled against a backdrop of sheer cliffs and craggy buttes.

### ► Casual Promenade
Aside from the initial descent (which must be climbed to return to the parking), this hike follows gentle grades and involves no rock hopping or scrambling, allowing visitors to focus on the natural beauty of Pine Creek.

### ► Area of Special Biodiversity
While noteworthy plant communities are found in all the canyons of the Red Rock Escarpment, Pine Creek holds the most diverse array of species; a collection found nowhere else in the world. Such diversity is made possible by the availability of water, isolation from other areas, and a micro-climate created by the canyon itself.

The abundance of life is particularly apparent within the riparian plant communities found in the canyon. Here visitors can observe cardinalflowers, Nevada goldenrod, stream orchids, numerous types of ferns, Northern Pacific treefrogs, red racers, small mammals, and the occasional mule deer or bighorn sheep.

*Do not disturb these special spots. They are irreplaceable ecological niches that are constantly being monitored to ensure their health and longevity.*

### ► Bird Watching
Second in popularity only to Spring Mountain Ranch, Pine Creek offers bird watchers the opportunity to see golden eagles, red-tailed hawks, chukars, Gambel's

*A homestead was established near the mouth of Pine Creek Canyon in 1922. Today, only its foundation, shown here with Bridge Mountain in the background, remains.*

quail, ladder-backed woodpeckers, cactus wren, phainopepla, thrushes, thrashers, warblers, and many other songbirds.

Most find the grassy meadow adjacent to the Wilson homesite to be a good starting point.

### ▶ Historic Setting

In 1922, Horace and Glenna Wilson constructed a home at the mouth of Pine Creek Canyon. Using water from the nearby springs, they planted a small orchard of apple and apricot trees, some of which are still alive today. They also irrigated alfalfa, sweet potatoes, melons, wild grapes, and berries in the nearby meadow.

In the mid-20s, the homestead was a popular spot for their friends to spend the day, and cars would line the dirt access road. The Wilsons' occupation, however, was rather short. In 1933, the couple moved to Las Vegas, and in the following years the homestead fell into disrepair. A photo of the home, circa 1930, appears on page 48. Today, the foundation of their home can be found adjacent to the trail (marked on the map).

The 1968 film entitled *The Stalking Moon*, staring Gregory Peck, was filmed near the Wilson homesite. Throughout much of the movie, the landscape and rock formations of Pine Creek Canyon can be clearly identified.

### ▶ Directions

From the fee booth, follow the Scenic Drive for 10.2 miles to the Pine Creek Overlook and Trailhead (see map, inside back cover).

The hike begins on the west side of the parking area and immediately descends towards the wash. This is the steepest part of the hike and will need to be ascended to return to the parking area. At the base of the descent, the trail proceeds westward towards the canyon. A small side-loop, called the **Fire Ecology Trail**, visits the wash and offers benches and a picnic table under ponderosa pines.

The Pine Creek Canyon Trail passes Dale's Trail and continues towards the Wilson homesite, which is reached 0.8 miles from the parking area. Past the Wilson homesite, the trail enters a relatively flat area bordered by bright-red Chinle Sandstone. Although the well-developed trail ends when it meets this band of sandstone, it is possible to follow social trails deeper into the north and south forks of the canyon.

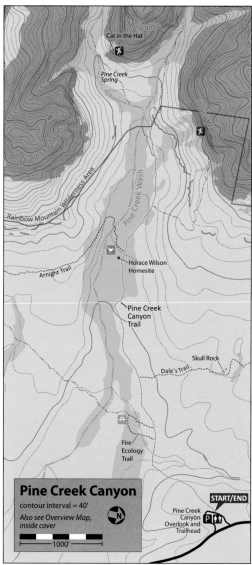

**Pine Creek Canyon**

contour interval = 40'

*Also see Overview Map, inside cover*

1000'

# OAK CREEK CANYON

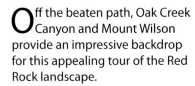

Off the beaten path, Oak Creek Canyon and Mount Wilson provide an impressive backdrop for this appealing tour of the Red Rock landscape.

## ► Awe-inspiring Topography

The towering bulk of Mount Wilson proudly pierces the sky and seems to rise as Oak Creek Canyon is approached. In fact, the craggy cliff faces of Mount Wilson rise nearly 3000' feet from the desert to its 7070' summit, making it one of the most dramatic formations at Red Rock Canyon.

Similarly, Rainbow Mountain, north of Oak Creek Canyon, delights visitors with its multi-colored bands of Aztec Sandstone.

Both mountains are popular with rock climbers. Look for them climbing the 'Solar Slab Wall' located just inside Oak Creek Canyon on the sunny, north side.

## ► A Flat Stroll

Many enjoy this hike because of the relatively flat grade, which makes for comfortable walking. However, the trail is often littered with rocks, a problem when a hiker's focus drifts to the impressive landscape.

After the official trail ends, it is possible to continue up the canyon following the wash. This requires some rock hopping and scrambling.

## ► Plants and Animals

The landscape surrounding most of this trail, from the parking area up to the mouth of the canyon, is covered with blackbrush scrub. As the trail enters the canyon, it crosses through a pinyon-juniper woodland that extends north below Rainbow Mountain. This woodland is a great place to find mule deer and coyotes in the winter. Bighorn sheep are occasionally spotted as they browse near the mouth of the canyon.

As its name implies, Oak Creek is endowed with numerous thickets of scrub oak. These hardy trees are found in the mixed chaparral plant community that lines the wash in and outside the canyon.

## ► Directions

From the fee booth, follow the Scenic Drive for 11.5 miles and make a right turn onto a dirt road signed 'Oak Creek Trailhead' (see map, inside back cover). After 0.7 miles on the dirt road, the parking area is reached.

From the parking area, take the Oak Creek Canyon Trail southwest. The trail leads into the mouth of the canyon and ends when it reaches the Oak Creek Wash. The adventurous may want to explore further up the wash.

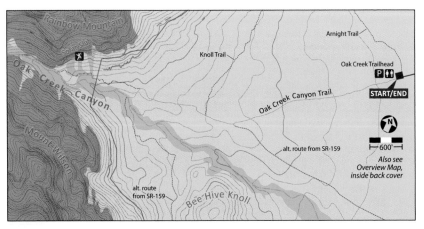

The impressive east face of Mount Wilson reaches into the sky above Oak Creek Canyon. This alternate route into the canyon was blazed by Tilghman Rhea to access the now-abandoned Rheastone Quarry, located in the mid-ground of the photo.

# FIRST CREEK CANYON

3.0 MILES | 2 HOURS | OUT AND BACK

This casual trail leads to a serene water hole and continues, with increasing difficulty, into a picturesque sandstone canyon.

### A Flat Stroll

Following a slight uphill grade, this trail makes for pleasant walking. It is well graded and seldom rocky. Kids who make the trek into the canyon enjoy exploring the playground-like scattering of boulders and trees along the wash.

The mouth of the canyon is a popular spot to bring a picnic, although no facilities are provided.

*Near the mouth of the canyon, the trail gets rocky but the scenery becomes more impressive.*

### An Idyllic Nook

A major point of interest is the First Creek Waterfall (see photo, page 67). While not quite the stature of Niagra Falls, this small drop usually has a nice little pool of water below it. The waterfall is tucked into a shady spot along the wash and is worth the effort to find it.

### Towering Cliffs

Those who choose to continue past the waterfall will find themselves at the bottom of a deep canyon with 2000'-tall cliffs rising on both sides. The canyon is broad enough to avoid feeling confined, but it is possible to lose the trail as it meanders through the wash. The thick brush of the mixed chaparral plant community will be the clue to return and find the proper trail. For an all-day adventure, fit hikers continue up the wash and swing back east to reach the summit of Mount Wilson.

### Plants and Animals

The trail begins in an area burned by the First Creek Fire of 2006. Many Joshua trees, blackbrush, and Mojave yuccas fell victim to the fire, but vegetation is recovering. Past the burned area, the trail traverses through blackbrush and Mojave yucca. This is prime territory to see jackrabbits, cottontails, and, at night, kangaroo rats.

The occasional cactus wren nest, built in the branches of buckhorn cholla, is visible from the trail.

At the waterfall, a wide variety of plants and animals are sometimes seen, including Northern Pacific treefrogs, songbirds, and with luck, a raptor, ringtail, or bobcat.

### Directions

From the junction of the CC-215 and W. Charleston Blvd., follow W. Charleston Blvd. (which becomes State Route 159) for 8.4 miles and turn right into a dirt pullout, signed 'First Creek.' The pullout is 2.1 miles past the exit of the Scenic Drive (see map, inside back cover).

The trail heads west from the parking area and immediately crosses a wash. To find the waterfall, continue on the trail for 1.0 miles and take a social trail that leads right, 130 yards to the well-vegetated nook. Because there are no signs and many social trails in the area, it is often difficult to find the proper trail on the first try. A good landmark is a red bank of the wash, located downstream of the waterfall. With a GPS device, the coordinates are: 36°4'49.95"N, 115°27'56.18"W.

To reach the canyon itself, continue on the largest of the trails until it descends into the wash at the mouth of the canyon. From there, the trail generally follows the wash.

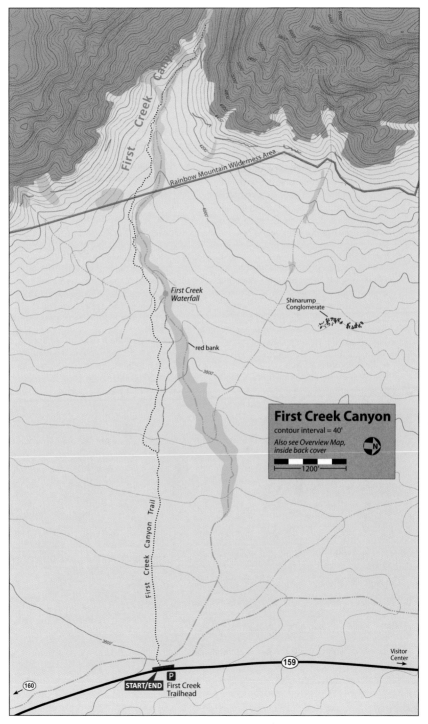

First Creek
Waterfall

Shinarump
Conglomerate

Rainbow Mountain Wilderness Area

First Creek Canyon

First Creek Canyon Trail

red bank

**First Creek Canyon**

contour interval = 40'

*Also see Overview Map, inside back cover*

1200'

159

160

Visitor
Center

START/END  P First Creek
Trailhead

# BLUE DIAMOND HILL TRAILS

Frequently overshadowed by Red Rock Canyon, Blue Diamond Hill offers a change of pace and a plenty of reasons to 'stop and smell the roses.'

### ► Great Views of Vegas and Red Rock
From nearly all points in this area, the Red Rock Escarpment provides an impressive panorama. At the crest of the hill, the Las Vegas Valley stretches out below, seemingly as far as the eye can see.

### ► Friendly Setting
Although at first glance there appears to be a maze of trails, the moderate slopes and open terrain make orienting and hiking in the area stress-free. There are, however, dramatic cliffs that pose a falling hazard, something to consider when bringing youngsters.

### ► Extraordinary Cacti
The plant community in this area is a mix of creosote bush scrub, blackbrush scrub, and Joshua tree woodlands. Blue Diamond Hill is a great place to view cacti: nearly all the species found at Red Rock inhabit the hill and often occur in rather dense populations.

### ► Geology
The prominent cliffs, visible from the parking area, are composed of limestone in the Kaibab Formation. This formation was usually deposited when the area was under a shallow sea. However, the sea receded intermittently, leaving seawater to evaporite, which caused the formation of gypsum. Useful in making sheetrock for buildings, the mineral was mined from the mid-1920s until the early 2000s immediately south of the hiking trails.

### ► Fossils
One of the best areas in all of Red Rock Canyon to see fossils is along the trails in this part of Blue Diamond Hill. The Kaibab Formation, exposed here, is characterized

*The Rock Garden Trail takes hikers through a delightful cactus sanctuary and provides exceptional views of Red Rock Canyon away from the crowds of the Scenic Drive.*

by dense patches of a brownish mineral called chert in which millions of animals have been fossilized. Expect to see seashells (*Brachiopoda*), especially rounded ones of the order *Productida*; moss animals (*Bryozoa*); sea lilies (*Crinoidea*); several types of sponges; and the occasional rugose coral. See page 104 for more information on fossils.

### ▶ Horseback Riding

The trail network on Blue Diamond Hill is a popular spot to take guided horseback riding tours, provided by Cowboy Trail Rides. For more information, see page 196.

### ▶ Mountain Biking

The trails in this area are a good alternative for experienced riders looking for terrain that is more technical than in Cottonwood Valley. However, the trails are awaiting BLM use designation. See page 191 for more details on mountain biking.

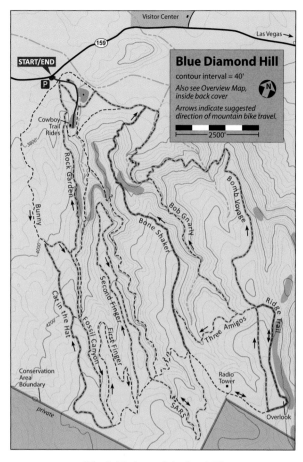

### ▶ Caving

Tucked into the limestone cliffs are a number of elaborate cave systems that are lined with fantastic rock formations. The caves support unique ecosystems and provide bat habitat. Because much vandalism of these caves has occurred in the recent past, many are gated. The Southern Nevada Grotto organization occasionally guides tours of the caves.

### ▶ Directions

From its crossing with the CC-215, follow W. Charleston Blvd./SR-159 6.3 miles to a dirt parking area on the left signed 'Horseback Riding' (see map, inside back cover). Park here for hiking or continue down the dirt road to the ranch house for horseback riding tours. Described below are two popular hikes; trails are not signed.

**Hike 1:** *Moderate, 2.4 miles, 1.5 hours.*

From the parking area, head southeast and climb a short hill to a rising mesa that runs to the right of the Cowboy Trail Rides ranch house; this is the Rock Garden Trail. Follow it until you reach a trail junction near a band of conglomerate rock; head right and return to the parking area via the Bunny Trail.

**Hike 2:** *Difficult, 6.9 miles, 4 hours.*

From the parking area, continue up the dirt road. Just past the ranch house, take a trail on the left that switchbacks through the wash and swings northeast around the hill. Follow this trail to the Bomb Voyage Trail, which leads to the overlook. Head down past the radio tower to the Bone Shaker Trail, which leads back to parking area.

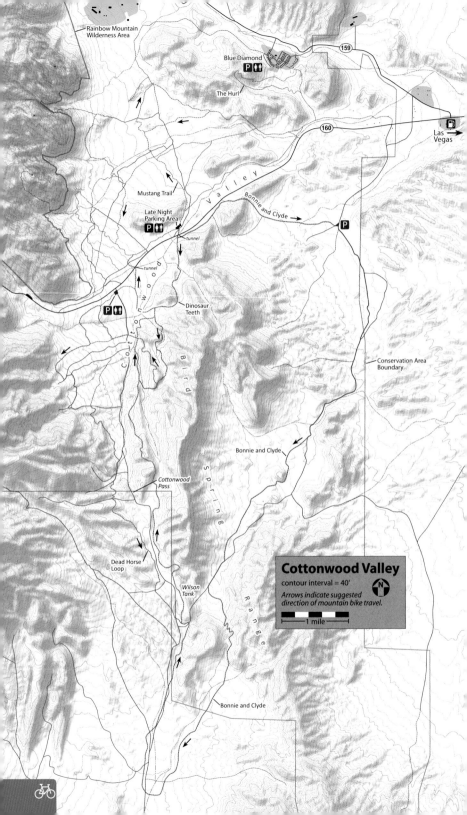

Rainbow Mountain
Wilderness Area

Blue Diamond
P 🚻

The Hurl

159

160

Las
Vegas

Valley

Mustang Trail

Bonnie and Clyde

Late Night
Parking Area
P 🚻

P

tunnel

tunnel

Cottonwood

Dinosaur
Teeth

P 🚻

Bird

Conservation Area
Boundary

Bonnie and Clyde

Spring

Cottonwood
Pass

Dead Horse
Loop

Wilson
Tank

Range

## Cottonwood Valley

contour interval = 40'

*Arrows indicate suggested
direction of mountain bike travel.*

1 mile

Bonnie and Clyde

🚲

# Bicycling
## at Red Rock Canyon

The extensive trail system, roadways considerate of bike traffic, and a stunning backdrop make bicycling at Red Rock a top choice for locals and visitors in the know.

### ► Road Biking

Thanks to the efforts of local groups and government officials, road biking at Red Rock Canyon has become much safer in recent years. In addition to the designation of dedicated bike lanes on many approach roads, the shoulder of SR-159 was widened to 7' and its speed limit reduced from 65 mph to 50 mph in 2006.

These improvements have opened the door for many to enjoy the fresh air and natural beauty of the area, be it from the cushy seat of a beach cruiser or while maintaining a machine-like cadence inside a peloton.

The **Scenic Drive** (see map, page 208) is likely the most popular ride at Red Rock Canyon, but not the easiest. Many cyclists park at the visitor center and make a loop back to their vehicles. Along the 14.7 mile ride (2.2 miles of which are on SR-159), expect a taxing climb of nearly 1000' before negotiating the curve-filled, downhill ride, which is followed by rolling hills.

Novice riders may prefer **SR-159**. It is common to start at the Vista Commons Shopping Plaza, located at Desert Foothills Drive and West Charleston Blvd., and head west on West Charleston Blvd. (which becomes SR-159). When tired, simply head back. Experienced cyclists often ride all of SR-159 and circumnavigate Blue Diamond Hill using bike paths or arterial streets east of the hill.

### ► Mountain Biking

With hundreds of miles of mountain bike trails winding their way through a gorgeous setting, Red Rock Canyon has become a premier Southwest destination for fat-tired peddle pushers. In fact, a number of professional riders call this place home and are occasionally featured in videos of the area.

The trails, however, appeal to all experience levels. Riders can find gentle grades on old wagon roads, moderate double tracks, tight curving singletracks

*Wider shoulders and lower speed limits on SR-159 have helped secure a thriving road-bike presence among the colorful sandstone at Red Rock Canyon.*

weaving through Joshua trees, and technical, rocky hills.

Mountain bikes are not allowed on many trails at Red Rock, including all trails west of SR-159 between Spring Mountain Ranch State Park and La Madre Mountain.

**Cottonwood Valley Trails:** This is the most extensive area for mountain biking at Red Rock. There are numerous trails that have been designated for mountain bikes; most are beginner-to-intermediate in difficulty and are well-marked with slender, brown Carsonite signs. See facing page for a map that shows popular rides. Due to the nature of the trail network, a multitude of combinations and variations can be

*With hundreds of miles of mountain-bike trails, Red Rock offers something for all ability levels. Here, LeAnna Conley and Adam Harrington recover on a scenic stretch of The Hurl, a difficult ride found south of Blue Diamond.*

made. Note that some trails in this area are designated for hiking only.

There are two trailheads commonly used to access the trails: The Blue Diamond Bike Outpost and the Late Night Parking Area. The **Blue Diamond Bike Outpost** is located in Blue Diamond village. Follow SR-159 north 3.0 miles from its junction with SR-160 and make a left onto Castalia Street. The bike shop is on the left after about 0.3 miles. For the four rides described below, most park at the **Late Night Parking Area**, which is found 4.7 miles west of the junction of SR-160 and SR-159 on the right side of SR-160.

*Mustang Trail:* Easy-to-moderate, 7.0 miles, mostly singletrack, also known as the Late Night Trail.

*Dinosaur Teeth:* Moderate, 6.0 miles, mostly singletrack.

*Dead Horse Loop:* Moderate-to-advanced, 14.0 miles, singletrack.

*Bonnie and Clyde:* Moderate-to-advanced, 25.0 miles, singletrack and dirt roads.

**Blue Diamond Hill Trails:** Although this area offers fewer trail-miles than the Cottonwood Valley Trails, it is favored by experienced riders for the more strenuous and technical terrain. See page 189 for a map of the area and directions.

It is important to note that these trails have not yet been designated for certain user groups. Stay on the established trails and be considerate of other users.

**Twilight Zone Trails:** Offering 21 miles of singletrack trails and dirt roads designated for mountain bike use, the Twilight Zone is an area of increasing popularity. The trails begin from either side of a dirt parking lot found on the right side of the Kyle Canyon Road (SR-157), 8.7 miles from US-95.

*Left: The Cottonwood Valley Trails are periodically marked with Carsonite signs showing designated user groups. Remember: bikes yield to hikers and horses.*

### ► Local Organizations

A great way to meet other riders and find out about special events is through local clubs that host group rides, promote bicycle safety, and receive discounts at local bike shops.

The two largest clubs in Las Vegas are the Green Valley Cyclists (www. greenvalleycyclists.org) and the Las Vegas Valley Bicycle Club (www.lasvegasbikeclub.org). BikingLasVegas.com is a cycling-advocacy website that promotes cycling, provides rides, events, and information on cycling in Las Vegas.

### ► Guide Services and Bike Rental

The two most active companies permitted by the BLM to provide bike tours at Red Rock Canyon are described below.

Founded in 1992, **Escape Adventures** is committed to reducing their environmental impact through the use of solar and wind powered facilities, vegetable-oil-fueled vehicles, and other programs. The Las Vegas-based company has a staff of friendly guides well-versed in the finer points of riding at Red Rock Canyon where they provide mountain and road biking tours.

Tours include shuttles to and from Las Vegas, bike rental, a helmet, gloves, water, and a tour guide. Half-day tours start at $110 and are offered in the morning and afternoon. Full-day tours, from 8:00 am until 3:00 pm, start at $160 and include lunch. Multi-day and multi-activity packages are also available.

Bike-only rentals are $45 to $75 per day depending on the model. Pick-up and drop-off of rentals is at Las Vegas Cyclery, located in Las Vegas at 10575 Discovery Drive.

**www.escapeadventures.com • info@escapeadventures.com • (800) 596-2953**

Conveniently located in the village of Blue Diamond, the **McGhie's Blue Diamond Bike Outpost** is a full-service bike shop that offers mountain-bike tours and rentals. With access to the extensive Cottonwood Valley Trails, the bike outpost is a popular meeting spot and hang for local cyclists. Their friendly staff have helped point countless pedal pushers in the right direction and fixed thousands of bikes.

Mountain bike tours include a professional guide, bike, helmet, water, and transportation to and from Las Vegas locations. Tour length, location, and difficulty are tailored for each group. Prices start at $119 per person. Tours are booked through www.mcghies.com.

Many types of mountain bikes are available for rent, including women's bikes, youth sizes, standard bikes, as well as the latest designs. Day-rates are $40 to $65 depending on the model and include pedal options, a helmet, and water. Road bikes can be rented from McGhie's main shop at 4035 S. Fort Apache Road in Las Vegas.

The bike outpost is open from 7:00 am to 3:00 pm, but closed Mondays, Tuesdays, and certain holidays.

**www.mcghies.com • sales@mcghies.com • (702) 875-4820**

# Rock Climbing
## *at Red Rock Canyon*

Each year thousands of people from all over the world come to climb on the dramatic sandstone formations of Red Rock Canyon. While many visitors are content to watch these vertical gymnasts, participants find the activity to be safe and gratifying.

### ▶ For All Skill Levels

The well-featured sandstone of Red Rock is ideal terrain for beginners to experience the fundamentals of rock climbing. It also provides a range of options: small 'boulder problems' that do not require ropes, an extensive collection of single-pitch sport and traditional cragging, and day-long adventure routes that challenge the body and mind.

### ▶ Where to Go

While most will want to consult guidebooks, such as *Red Rocks: A Climber's Guide*, *Fun Climbs Red Rocks: Topropes and Moderates*, and *Southern Nevada Bouldering*, which are dedicated to the thousands of routes in the area, listed below are a few spots that are great to get a taste of what Red Rock has to offer:

For multi-pitch climbing, try *Cat in the Hat*, a 5.6 first climbed in 1976 that takes a prominent line up the striking Mescalito formation in Pine Creek Canyon (page 182). Another multi-pitch classic is *Crimson Chrysalis*, located in Juniper Canyon. At 5.8, this airy crack-and-face climb is a must-do for those new to the area.

For single-pitch climbing, some nice first-stops include the *Black Corridor*, *Magic Bus*, and the *Gallery*. While the first two are great beginner areas, the latter features a handful of steeper, more-difficult routes. In the winter, the *Brass Wall*, located on the north side of Pine Creek Canyon, is a popular spot for single-pitch traditional routes from 5.6 to 5.12.

The popularity of bouldering has blossomed in recent years. This activity allows beginners, as well as experts, a method to practice the art of moving on rock without the need for ropes or complicated safety systems. Two great spots to check out are the Kraft Boulders (page 162), and Willow Springs (map, page 177).

*Although exhilarating, the world-class rock climbing at Red Rock can be safely enjoyed by visitors of all ability levels. Here, expert climber Audrey Sniezek climbs Choad Warrior in the Calico Hills.*

► **Professional Guide Services**

One of the best ways to safely enjoy this activity is to hire a guide. There are a number of guide services, listed below, that have permits to operate at Red Rock. Most offer a wide range of services, including half-day and full-day outings to suit their clients' needs. Specialized safety equipment is provided. It's best to make reservations in advance, but last-minute bookings are sometimes available.

Locally managed, **Jackson Hole Mountain Guides** has been operating at Red Rock since 1985. They offer trips and instruction for all experience levels and group sizes. Additionally, they provide guided hiking tours in several of the beautiful canyons like Oak Creek, Pine Creek, and Juniper. Reservations are suggested, especially during the busy fall and spring seasons.

**www.jhmg.com • redrock@jhmg.com • (702) 254-0885**

**Mountain Skills** has 15 years of experience guiding beginner, intermediate, and expert climbers at Red Rock. Some of their guides are Red Rock pioneers who have helped make the climbing area what it is today. They can accommodate groups up to 10 people as well as provide one-on-one service for any crag or route at Red Rock Canyon.

**www.climbingschoolusa.com**
**climb@climbingschoolusa.com • (575) 776-2222**

Operating from September 1st until mid-May, **American Alpine Institute** specializes in private ascents and skill-specific courses such as Aid Climbing and Big Wall Technique, Basic Rock Camp, Learn to Lead, and the Warrior's Way Falling and Commitment Camp. They even offer a 'First Ascent' program where clients can team up to climb a new route. Guides are American Mountain Guides Association certified.

**www.alpineinstitute.com • info@aai.cc • (360) 671-1505**

Managed by the local climbing gym, **Red Rock Climbing Center Outdoor Guide Service** focuses on group and team-building rock climbing events. They also have a wide range of youth programs geared towards Las Vegans, such as a junior climbing team, a scout merit badge program, summer climbing camps, and birthday or special-event parties.

**www.redrockclimbingcenter.com**
**sales@redrockclimbingcenter.com • (702) 254-5604**

Each spring, the **Red Rock Rendezvous** is held at Spring Mountain Ranch. The weekend-long event attracts professional instructors who lead clinics on various rock-climbing-related topics. The event is hosted by Mountain Gear, an online retailer. Companies set up booths to show off their gear. The atmosphere is casual—beer and slide shows in the evenings and pancake breakfasts before the clinics.

**www.redrockrendezvous.com • redrock@mountaingear.com**

# Horseback Riding
## *at Red Rock Canyon*

For those who have never seen a horse as well as those raised on a ranch, there are fantastic horseback riding opportunities at Red Rock Canyon.

### ► Guided Trips

Convenient and friendly, guided horseback riding tours allow everyone to engage with nature, connect with a gentle beast, and experience a bit of the romantic Wild West.

There are two outfits that provide horseback riding tours at Red Rock: Cowboy Trail Rides and the Red Rock Riding Stables at Bonnie Springs.

**Red Rock Riding Stables** is situated at the base of Mustang Canyon and commands stunning views up and down the Red Rock Escarpment. Tours are given at regular intervals during the day and range in price from $60.00 to $140.00. Breakfast, lunch, and dinner rides, complete with meals served at the Bonnie Springs Restaurant, begin at 9:00 am, 11:30 am, and 2:00 pm in the winter; with an additional 4:30 pm in the summer. Reservations are required for scheduled tours. All riders must be under 250 pounds, wear closed-toe shoes, and be over the age of six. For kids under five, pony rides are available. Call (702) 875-4191 or email info@bonniesprings.com for details.

For over 18 years, Big Jim Sage's **Cowboy Trail Rides** has been operating at the base of Blue Diamond Hill, an area of dramatic, narrow limestone canyons overlooking nearly all of Red Rock and certain rides provide views out across the entire Las Vegas Valley. Over the years, they have refined the art of giving guests an 'Old West' experience, complete with cowboy hospitality.

Guests can choose from six rides: the *Coyote Canyon Ride* is the shortest at one hour, and the *Wow Ride* is the longest, with five hours of saddle time. For the full experience, take the popular *Sunset Trail Ride* in the early evening and enjoy a Western-style BBQ followed by cowboy entertainment and marshmallow roasting.

*Big Jim Sage and his company, Cowboy Trail Rides, have been refining the art of giving horseback-riding tours for over 18 years at Red Rock. Here, Big Jim leads the Canyon Rim Ride, which laces its way along the top of dramatic cliffs and through terrain studded with beautiful cacti set against a backdrop of the Red Rock Escarpment.*

Rides are offered throughout the day, mainly in the morning and afternoon. Reservations are strongly recommended. Cowboy Trail Rides maintains a large number of horses, some of which have been purchased from BLM horse auctions (see page 71). The horses are gentle, well-broken, and come in many sizes to suit people of all shapes and statures. Rides range from $69.00 to $329.00 per person. Transportation pick-up and drop-off can be arranged. Discounts are available for locals. Group packages, complete with rodeo-style activities, are available on request. Visit www.cowboytrailrides.com, call (702) 387-2457, or email sales@cowboytrailrides.com for more details.

### ► Private Stock Use

The scenic beauty, numerous trails, and proximity to Las Vegas make Red Rock Canyon a favorite spot for back-country horseback riding in southern Nevada. An array of trails, from single-file-only to wide dirt tracks, traverse the terrain, which varies from rolling hills to rocky, technical slopes.

The Bristlecone Chapter of the Back Country Horsemen of Nevada works to maintain and expand the great access that horseback riders currently enjoy in the conservation area. This non-profit organization coordinates with the BLM to maintain trails, educate horse owners about the area, and perpetuate the common-sense use of horses in the back country. They can be reached at (702) 278-3566 and crzyhrsldy@gmail.com.

For visitors planning to be in the area for an extended period, the Red Rock Riding Stables offers horse boarding at an ideal location, surrounded on all sides by the conservation area.

### ► Private Stock - Where to Go

Horseback riding is limited to designated trails at Red Rock; therefore no cross-country use is allowed. The trails designated for horseback riding are the White Rock Hills Loop, Keystone Thrust Trail, Oak Creek trails (from SR-159 and the Scenic Drive), trail from Willow Springs to the visitor center, Knoll Trail, First Creek Trail, trails around the exit of the Scenic Drive, and Cottonwood Valley Trails.

The best staging areas for gearing up are the parking lot at the exit of the Scenic Drive, the Wheeler Camp Spring parking area, and the Late Night Parking Area adjacent to SR-160 (see map, inside back cover).

### ► Environmental Considerations

In addition to the ethical guidelines of Leave No Trace presented on page 13, owners are required to stay on designated trails and clean up after their horses and pack animals at all staging areas. The use of weed-free hay is suggested to limit the spread of nonnative grasses.

Springs and riparian areas are fragile environments and can be severely damaged by horse traffic. Horse owners should water their animals away from areas of sensitive vegetation and fragile soils.

### ► Directions

*See map, inside back cover.*
To reach **Cowboy Trail Rides**: From its crossing with CC-215, follow W. Charleston Blvd./SR-159 for 6.3 miles to a dirt parking area on the left of the road marked with a sign for 'Horseback Riding.' (This is 0.9 miles past the visitor center.) Continue down the dirt road to the ranch house where tours begin.

To reach the **Red Rock Riding Stables**: follow SR-159 (the extension of W. Charleston Blvd.) for 3.4 miles past the exit of the Red Rock Canyon Scenic Drive. Turn right onto Bonnie Springs Road, passing under the 'Bonnie Springs Ranch' sign. After 1.1 miles, the road leads to Bonnie Springs where the friendly staff can direct you to the stables.

**Private-stock Staging Areas**: The **Late Night Parking Area** is located 4.7 miles west of the junction of SR-160 and SR-159, on the right side of SR-160. The **Wheeler Camp Spring parking area** is located 3.8 miles north of the junction of SR-160 and SR-159, on the left side of SR-159. The **Scenic Drive exit parking area** is located 7.4 miles from the junction of W. Charleston Blvd. (SR-159) and the CC-215, on the right side of SR-159.

# Further Resources

Below is a list of selected references for learning more about the region. A complete list of references can be found at www.snellpress.com/rrcvg/references.

Ahlstrom, Richard V.N. *Desert Oasis: The Prehistory of Clark County Wetlands Park, Henderson, Nevada*. Report prepared for the U.S. Bureau of Reclamation, 2005.

Baldridge, W. Scott. *Geology of the American Southwest: A Journey through Two Billion Years of Plate-Tectonic History*. Cambridge: Cambridge University Press, 2004.

Baldwin, Bruce G., et al. *The Jepson Desert Manual: Vascular Plants of Southeastern California*. Berkeley, CA: University of California Press, 2002.

Beffort, Brian. *Afoot and Afield: Las Vegas and Southern Nevada: A Comprehensive Hiking Guide*. Birmingham, AL: Wilderness Press, 2010.

*Birdandhike.com*. Boone, Jim. Desert Wildlife Consultants, LLC. Accessed 28 May 2012. <http://www.birdandhike.com/>

Blythin, Evan. *Vanishing Village: The Struggle for Community in the New West*. Las Vegas, NV: City Life Books-Stephens Press, 2010.

*Butterflies and Moths of North America*. Big Sky Institute at Montana State University. Accessed 28 May 2012. <http://www.butterfliesandmoths.org/>

*California Herps: A Guide to the Amphibians and Reptiles of California*. Nafis, Gary. Accessed 28 May 2012. <http://www.californiaherps.com/>

Chan, Marjorie A., and William T. Parry. *Rainbow of Rocks: Mysteries of Sandstone Colors and Concretions in Colorado Plateau Canyon Country*. *Utah Geological Survey* Public Information Series 77 (n.d.).

Clinesmith, Larry, and Elsie Sellars. *Red Rock Canyon Plants*. Las Vegas, NV: Red Rock Canyon Interpretive Association, 2001.

Cordell, Linda. *Archaeology of the Southwest*. 2nd ed. San Diego, CA: Academic Press, 1997.

Fiero, Bill. *Geology of the Great Basin*. Reno, NV: University of Nevada Press, 1986.

Findley, Tim. *Special Report Mustang: Legends and Myths. Faith, Hope and Charity*. *Range Magazine* (Winter 2011): M1-M24.

Fischer, Pierre C. *70 Common Cacti of the Southwest*. Tucson, AZ: Southwest Parks and Monuments Association, 1989.

Floyd, Ted, Chris S. Elphick, and Graham Chisholm. *Atlas of the Breeding Birds of Nevada*. Reno, NV: University of Nevada Press, 2007.

Fowler, Catherine S., and Don, eds. *The Great Basin: People and Place in Ancient Times*. Santa Fe, NM: School for Advanced Research Press, 2008.

Grayson, Donald K. *The Desert's Past: A Natural Prehistory of the Great Basin*. Washington, DC: Smithsonian Institution Press, 1993.

Grater, Russell K. *Snakes Lizards and Turtles of the Lake Mead Region*. Tucson, AZ: Southwest Parks and Monuments Association, 1981.

Hafen, Leroy R., and Ann W. Hafen. *Old Spanish Trail: Santa Fé to Los Angeles: with Extracts from Contemporary Records and Including Diaries of Antonio Armijo and Orville Pratt*. Lincoln, NB and London: University of Nebraska Press, 1993.

Hall, Raymond E. *Mammals of Nevada*. Reno, NV: University of Nevada Press, 1995.

Inter-Tribal Council of Nevada. *Nuwuvi: A Southern Paiute History*. Sparks, NV: Inter-Tribal Council of Nevada, 1976.

Justice, Noel D. *Stone Age Spear and Arrow Points of California and the Great Basin*. Bloomington, IN: Indiana University Press, 2002.

Kelly, Ralph Aubry *Liberty's Last Stand*. Ed. Floyd Bilyeu. San Francisco: Pioneer Publishing Company, 1932.

Knack, Martha C. *Boundaries Between: The Southern Paiutes, 1775-1995*. Lincoln, NE: University of Nebraska Press, 2001.

Laird, Carobeth. *The Chemehuevis*. Banning, CA: Malki Musuem Press, 1976.

Lockley, M. G., Adrian P. Hunt. *Dinosaur Tracks: And other Fossil Footprints of the Western United States*. New York: Columbia University Press, 1999.

Longwell, C.R., et al. *Geology and Mineral Deposits of Clark County, Nevada*. Nevada Bureau of Mines and Geology Bulletin 62, 1965.

Martin, Jason, D. *Fun Climbs Red Rocks: Topropes and Moderates*. Boulder, CO: Sharp End Publishing, 2009.

Martineau, LaVan. *Southern Paiutes, Legends, Lore, Language, and Lineage*. Wickenburg, AZ: KC Publications, 1992.

—. *The Rocks Begin to Speak*. Las Vegas, NV: KC Publications, 1990.

MacKay, Pam. *Mojave Desert Wildflowers: A Field Guide to Wildflowers, Trees, and Shrubs of the Mojave Desert, Including the Mojave National Preserve, Death Valley National Park, and Joshua Tree National Park*. Guilford, CT: Falcon-Globe Pequot, 2003.

Moehring, Eugene P., and Michael S. Green. *Las Vegas: A Centennial History*. Reno, NV: University of Nevada Press, 2005.

Moulin, Tom. *Southern Nevada Bouldering*. Las Vegas, NV: Snell Press, 2010.

Myhrer, Keith, William G. White, and Stanton Rolf. *Contributions to the Study of Cultural Resources: Archaeology of the Old Spanish Trail/Mormon Road from Las Vegas, Nevada to the California Border*. Technical Report No. 17. Report prepared for the U.S. Bureau of Land Management, 1990.

Niles, Wesley, and Patrick Leary. *Mentzelia: Annotated Checklist of the Vascular Plants of the Spring Mountains Clark and Nye Counties, Nevada*. Las Vegas, NV: Nevada Native Plant Society, 2007.

Page, William R., et al. *Geologic and Geophysical Maps of the Las Vegas 30′ × 60′ Quadrangle, Clark and Nye Counties, Nevada, and Inyo County, California*. U.S. Geological Survey. Scientific Investigations Map 2814 and accompanying pamphlet, 2005.

Paher, Stanley W. *Las Vegas: As it Began - As it Grew*. Reno, NV: Nevada Publications, 1971.

Rafferty, Kevin A. *Cultural Resources Overview of the Las Vegas Valley*. Technical Report No. 13. Report prepared for the U.S. Bureau of Land Management, 1984.

—. *"Sandstone Quarry: A Site Complex in the Spring Mountains of Nevada."* Nevada Archaeologist 4.2 (1984): 25-39.

Rhode, David. *Native Plants of Southern Nevada: An Ethnobotany*. Salt Lake City, UT: University of Utah Press, 2002.

Ryser Jr., Fred A. *Birds of the Great Basin: A Natural History*. Reno, NV: University of Nevada Press, 1985.

Schaafsma, Polly. *Indian Rock Art of the Southwest*. Santa Fe, NM: School of American Research, 1980.

Shutler, Richard, Jr., et al. Wormington, H. M. and Dorothy Ellis, eds. *Pleistocene Studies in Southern Nevada*. Anthropological Papers No. 13. Carson City, NV: Nevada State Museum, 1967.

Sibley, David Allen. *The Sibley Guide to Bird Life and Behavior*. New York: Alfred A. Knopf, Inc., 2001.

Simms, Steven R. *Ancient Peoples of the Great Basin and Colorado Plateau*. Walnut Creek, CA: Left Coast Press, Inc., 2008.

Stoffle, Richard W., Fletcher P. Chmara-Huff, Kathleen A. Van Vlack, and Rebecca S. Toupal. *Puha Flows from It: The Cultural Landscape Study of the Spring Mountains.* Report prepared for the U.S. Forest Service Humboldt Toiyabe National Forest Spring Mountains National Recreation Area, 2004.

Stokes, Donald and Lillian. *The Stokes Guide to the Birds of North America*. New York: Little Brown and Company-Hachette Book Group, 2010.

Tingley, Joseph, et al. *Geologic Tours in the Las Vegas Area*. Nevada Bureau of Mines and Geology Special Publication 16. Reno, NV: University of Nevada Press, 2001.

United States Department of the Interior Bureau of Land Management. *Spring Mountains Herd Management Complex – Preliminary Population Management Plan and Environmental Assessment NV-052-2007-50*. Las Vegas Field Office. November 2006.

Warren, Elizabeth von Till. *Armijo's Trace Revisited: A New Interpretation of the Impact of the Antonio Armijo Route of 1829-1830 on the Development of the Old Spanish Trail*. MA Thesis. Department of Anthropology, University of Nevada, Las Vegas, 1974.

Weatherly, Megan Sharp. *Transforming Space into Place: Development, Rock Climbing, and Interpretation at Red Rock Canyon National Conservation Area, 1960-2010*. MA Thesis. Department of History, University of Nevada, Las Vegas, 2010.

White, William G. *Adits, Shafts, and Glory Holes: An Inventory of 380 Hazardous Mine Features in the Alunite, Charleston, Cresent, Eldorado, Goodsprings, and Searchlight Mining Districts, Clark County, Nevada*. Technical Report No. 17-20. Report prepared for the U.S. Army Corps of Engineers, the U.S. Bureau of Land Management, the U.S. National Park Service, and the U.S. Forest Service, 2008.

Whitley, David S. *A Guide to Rock Art Sites: Southern California and Southern Nevada*. Missoula, MT: Mountain Press Publishing Company, 1996.

Wilson, Don E., and Sue Ruff, eds. *The Smithsonian Book of North American Mammals*. Vancouver: University of British Columbia Press, 1999.

# Glossary

**alluvial fan:** Sediment deposited in a fan shape when a swift-moving water course is suddenly slowed. An alluvial fan typically forms where a water course pours out from a steep canyon onto a flat plain.

**basal:** Located at or near the base of a plant stem, typically at ground-level.

**basal rosette:** A circular arrangement of leaves around the stem of a plant near its base.

**braided trail:** A trail that is comprised of a number of poorly defined paths, which typically lead to the same location.

**bract:** A leaf-like or scale-like plant part, sometimes brightly colored, and usually located immediately below a flower.

**burro:** A small donkey. The term can refer to a feral donkey or a pack animal.

**caliche:** A hard layer of soil cemented together with calcium carbonate occurring in arid or semiarid regions.

**canid:** Carnivorous mammals of the family *Canidae*, which include coyotes, wolves, foxes, and domestic dogs.

**carbonate:** Any rock or mineral containing $CO_3$, such as calcium carbonate ($CaCO_3$) in limestone and calcium magnesium carbonate ($CaMg(CO_3)_2$) in dolomite.

**carrion:** Dead and decaying flesh.

**Carsonite:** A company that manufactures slender, flexible signs, such as the one shown on page 192.

**chert:** A hard, brittle form of silica ($SiO_2$) often found locally in reddish-brown or dark layers and nodules within limestone and dolomite.

**compound leaf:** A leaf that is composed of two or more leaflets on a common stalk, such as the leaves of a walnut tree.

**conglomerate:** A sedimentary rock that consists of rounded cobbles, pebbles, and/or gravel embedded in a finer matrix.

**conifer:** A tree or shrub, such as pine, juniper, and fir, that typically has cones and evergreen leaves.

**detritus:** The organic debris resulting from the decay of plants and animals.

**diurnal:** Occurring or active during the daytime.

**dolomite:** A sedimentary rock resembling limestone but consisting principally of the magnesia-rich mineral calcium magnesium carbonate ($CaMg(CO_3)_2$).

**donkey:** A domestic beast of burden descended from the African wild ass.

**drought deciduous:** A term used to describe a plant that loses its leaves during periods of dryness.

**endemic:** Present only within a specific region and not occurring naturally anywhere else.

**gape:** The length of the space between the open mouth pieces of a vertebrate animal.

**glochids:** Minute barbed hairs or bristles often found where spines meet the stem of a cactus.

**granite:** A common type of rock that has a visibly crystalline texture and is generally

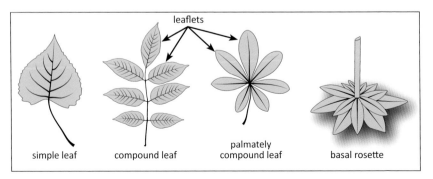

leaflets

simple leaf          compound leaf          palmately compound leaf          basal rosette

composed chiefly of quartz. It is formed by slow, underground cooling of magma.

**hindwings:** The two back wings of a four-winged insect.

**intaglio:** A figure or design made by removing and arranging soil and rocks on the surface of the ground.

**limestone:** A sedimentary rock consisting mainly of calcium carbonate ($CaCO_3$) derived from the remains of marine animals or precipitated from the ocean.

**mantle:** The layer of the earth between the crust and the outer core.

**megafauna:** Exceptionally large, typically land-dwelling animals, especially of the Pleistocene Epoch.

**mule:** The sterile offspring of a male donkey and a female horse.

**overwinter:** To live through the winter.

**palmately compound:** A term used to describe leaves with leaflets that number greater than three and attach at a single point on the stem of the leaf.

**petal:** One of the modified, often brightly-colored leaves surrounding the reproductive organs of a flower.

**pueblo:** A permanent village or community consisting of a cluster of stone or adobe dwellings.

**raptor:** A bird of prey, such as an eagle, hawk, vulture, owl, or falcon.

**rift:** A gap made by cleaving or splitting, as in a fault zone, that results from tensional stress on the earth's crust.

**riparian:** Relating to or inhabiting the banks of a spring or running water.

**sandstone:** A sedimentary rock consisting of fine-to-coarse sand grains compacted or cemented together by other minerals.

**scrape:** A bird nest consisting of a shallow depression in the soil sometimes lined with vegetation, stones, or feathers.

**sedimentary rock:** A type of rock formed by deposition of sediments such as silt, sand, gravel, and other minerals. Sediments are typically transported by water or wind and deposited on the surface of the earth or within bodies of water.

**sepals:** The usually green parts found below the flower that enclose the petals.

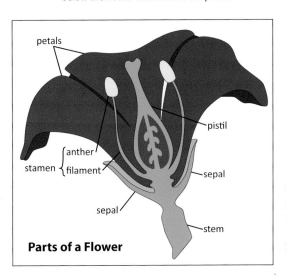

**Parts of a Flower**

**shale:** A sedimentary rock formed by compression of clay, silt, or mud layers. Unlike siltstone, this rock is characterized by having thin layers that often separate from each another.

**siltstone:** A sedimentary rock consisting of compacted and hardened silt.

**simple leaf:** A leaf that is not divided into parts. See also compound leaf.

**social trail:** An unplanned trail that has developed from human and/or animal traffic but is not officially recognized.

**stamen:** The pollen-producing reproductive organ of a flower, usually located at its center, and surrounded by petals.

**subduction:** A geologic process in which one edge of a crustal plate is forced below the edge of another, typically resulting in earthquakes and volcanic activity.

**understory:** The low-growing plants that exist below a taller collection of trees and/or shrubs.

# Index

## Artwork and Photo Credits

*All photos and illustrations are by the author unless noted. When noted, unless in the public domain, the copyright belongs to the photographer, artist, or organization that loaned the image(s) for use in this book.*
p.16: photograph by Jeanette McGregor, courtesy Nevada State Museum (NSM), Carson City. p.17 and 18: paleogeographic maps by Dr. Ronald C. Blakey, Northern Arizona University. p.19: painting by Ariel Milani Martine. p.23: geologic map adapted from Page, William R., et al, 2005. p.25: painting by Bradley W. Giles. p.26: figure 1 adapted from Cordell, 1997; and Justice, 2002. p.27: painting by Jay Matternes courtesy of the National Geographic Stock. p.28: figure 3 adapted from Fowler and Fowler, 2008; mano and metate from the archives of the NSM, Las Vegas. p.29: photo from the collection of the Lost City Museum. p.32: painting by Bradley W. Giles; quids from the archives of the NSM, Las Vegas. p.33: figure 9 adapted from Cordell, 1997. p. 34: turquoise from the archives of the NSM, Las Vegas. p.35: photo courtesy of the National Museum of the American Indian, Smithsonian Institution. p. 36: winnowing tray from the archives of the NSM, Las Vegas. p.37: photo courtesy of the National Archives, Archival Research Catalog (ARC ID # 517728). p.38: painting by Mervin Corning courtesy of the University of Nevada, Las Vegas (UNLV) Special Collections. p.39: painting by Cameron Bragg. p.40: lithograph by Frédéric Lehnert after a drawing by Carl Nebel, 1836. p.41: *Los Angeles Trail* drawing by William Henry Jackson courtesy of Scotts Bluff National Monument. p.42: photo courtesy of the Utah State Historical Society. p.43: photo courtesy of the UNLV Special Collections. p.45: Sandstone Quarry photo courtesy of the UNLV Special Collections. p.46: unknown photographer. p.47: photo courtesy of Spring Mountain Ranch State Park (SMRSP). p.48: unknown photographer(s). p.49: photo courtesy of UNLV Special Collections. p.50 and 51: photos of early Blue Diamond, homes atop the bluff, and loading ore are courtesy of the Blue Diamond Historical Committee (BDHC). p.53: photo courtesy of Faye Rhea Porter. p.56: Bells of San Angelo distributed by Republic Pictures, Electric Horseman sceenshot courtesy of Universal Pictures. p.57: Fear and Loathing in Las Vegas poster and sceenshot courtesy of Universal Pictures, Las Vegas Lady screenshot courtesy of Crown International Pictures, Inc. p.58: photo of the pistol from The Mexican courtesy of Profiles in History, Megaforce © Galaxy Films, Inc. p.59 Rain Man screenshot courtesy of MGM Media Licensing, Mission: Africa produced by A.T.F. Studios Inc. p.72: gray fox photo courtesy of James Marvin Phelps/JMP Photography, kit fox photo courtesy of Tim Smith. p.73: all photos courtesy of Phillip Colla/Oceanlight.com. p.74: ringtail photo courtesy of Lynn Chamberlain/cameraoutdoors. com. p.76: long-tailed pocket mouse photo courtesy of Dr. Jim Boone/birdandhike.com. p.77: bat photos courtesy of Michael Durham/Durmphoto.com. p.78 and 79: all photos courtesy of Tom Lindner. p.80: Steller's jay, Western scrub jay, great-horned owl, and burrowing owl photos courtesy of Tom Lindner; pinyon jay photo courtesy of Dr. Jim Boone/birdandhike.com. p.82: lesser nighthawk photo courtesy of Dr. Jim Boone/birdandhike.com; ladder-backed woodpecker, northern flicker, and white-throated swift photos courtesy of Tom Lindner. p.83 and 84: all photos courtesy of Tom Lindner. p.85: bushtit, Bewick's wren, and canyon wren photos courtesy of Tom Lindner. p.86: ruby-crowned kinglet, blue-gray gnatcatcher, black-tailed gnatcatcher, and mountain bluebird photos courtesy of Tom Lindner. p.87: phainopepla, yellow-rumped warbler, common yellowthroat, yellow warbler, and orange-crowned warbler photos courtesy of Tom Lindner. p.88 and 89: all photos courtesy of Tom Lindner. p.92: all photos courtesy of Adam Harrington. p.93, 94, and 95: all photos courtesy of Dr. Josh Parker. p.98: tarantula hawk photo courtesy of David Horner. p.99: giant hairy scorpion and black widow spider photos courtesy of Dr. Josh Parker, Jerusalem cricket photo courtesy of Alex Wild. p.100: tick photo courtesy of Dr. Josh Parker. p.101: white-lined sphinx moth photo courtesy of David Horner, yucca moth photo courtesy of Sherwin Carlquist, tadpole shrimp photo courtesy of Dr. Josh Parker. p.102: indra swallowtail, orange sulphur, and gray hairstreak photos courtesy of David Horner. p.103: Western pygmy blue and sagebrush checkerspot photos courtesy of David Horner. p. 104: fossil of *Amphipora* sp. from the UNLV archives. p. 105: fossils of trilobites from the archives of the NSM, Las Vegas; fossils of *Foraminifera* and *Maclurites* sp. from the UNLV archives. p.106: fossils of *Caninia* sp., *Syringopora* sp., and *Spirifer* sp. from the UNLV archives. p.107: *Grallator*, *Octopodichnus*, and *Brasilichnium* photos courtesy of Dr. Stephen Rowland; manganese dendrite sample courtesy of the UNLV archives. p.139: Pahrump poolfish painting by Joseph Tomelleri. p.140, 141, and 142: photos courtesy of SMRSP. p.146: train inauguration photo courtesy of Bonnie Springs Ranch. p.149: photo courtesy of Scoot City Tours. p.167: photo courtesy of Jared McMillen. p.179 photo courtesy of Luke Olson. p.207: photo courtesy of Norah S. Siller.

## Acknowledgements

A book of this scope relies on the expertise of many people. I would like to thank the following people for their guidance and assistance in tasks big and small.

*Any errors made in this book are the fault of the author and the following people, who have been kind enough to help, are not responsible.*

**General Information and Assistance**: Kathy August and Kirsten Cannon, BLM; Steve Gould; Jerry Handren; Anne Nasher, Elements Gift Shop; Jody Pedaline; and Chad Umbel.

**Information on Specific Organizations**: Karin Marie Bell, Bonnie Springs; Blaine Benedict, RRCIA; David Bert and Big Jim Sage, Cowboy Trail Rides; Lisa Caterbone, BikingLasVegas,com; Jared and Heather Fisher, Escape Adventures; Jim Gianoulakis, Las Vegas Astronomical Society; Mary Sue Kunz, Bristlecone Chapter of the Back Country Horsemen of America; Mark Limage, Jackson Hole Mountain Guides; Randy McGhie, McGhie's Ski, Bike & Board; Bill McLemore, Red Rock Climbing Center; and Tim Page, American Alpine Institute.

**Geology**: Dr. Joshua Bonde, Dr. Jean Cline, Dr. Stephen Rowland, and Dr. Mandy Williams, UNLV; and Nick Saines.

**History**: Kenny Anderson and Clara Belle Jim, Las Vegas Paiute Tribe; Pat Van Betten; George Bogdanovich, Angie Bogdanovich DeLong, Linda McCollum, Faye Rhea Porter, Sophie Bogdanovich Romans, Gretchen Schroeder, and Nina Bogdanovich Wolters, BDHC; Pauline Van Betten; Paul Carson, Dennis McBride, Sali Underwood, and Crystal Van Dee, NSM; James Cribbs, BLM; Dr. Catherine S. Fowler, University of Nevada, Reno; Max Heeman; Mandy Keefer, Richard and Jan Keller, and Mike Ward, SMRSP; Dr. Isabel T. Kelly (1906-1982); Harold Larson and Chuck Williams, Friends of Red Rock Canyon; Bonnie Levinson; Lalovi Miller, Moapa Band of Paiutes; Ian Pohowsky; Angus Quinlan, Nevada Rock Art Foundation; Kevin Rafferty, College of Southern Nevada (CSN); Heidi Roberts, HRA Inc.; Danette Tull, Nevada Film Office; Joanne Urioste; Dr. Elizabeth von Till Warren; Megan Sharp-Weatherly; Jeff Wedding; and William White.

**Plants and Animals**: Dr. Lois Alexander, CSN; Dr. Jim Boone, Desert Wildlife Consultants; Dr. Josh Parker, Clayton State University; and Sue Parsons. A special thanks go to Tom Lindner for lending an extensive collection of bird photographs.

**Photos**: Allison Bonanno; LeAnna Conley; Will Dameron; Ryan Deegan; Mike Doyle; Lisa Fernandes; Travis Graves; Pauline Goodwin; Adam Harrington; Jaci Lynn Jones; Jacob and Emma Keller; Jen and Alex Kruleski; Sarah McCrea; Mike, Lisa, and Noah Lorenzo; Jody Pedaline; Bill and Faye Rhea Porter; Heather Robinson; Matt Robinson; Big Jim Sage; Audrey Sniezek; Maximina Snyder; Joe Tasso and the cast at Old Nevada; Mike, Michele, and Nicholas Michael Ward; Chris Weidner; and Seth and Emma Zeigler.

**Review/Editing**: Dr. Jim Boone, Desert Wildlife Cons.; Pat Van Betten and Linda McCollum, BDHC; Dr. Jean Cline, UNLV; Sandy Martin; Dr. Claude Warren; and Dr. Elizabeth von Till Warren.

## About the Author

Growing up in rural Maine, Tom Moulin gained an appreciation for the outdoors at an early age. At 15, he skipped a semester of high school and hiked the Appalachian Trail from Georgia to Maine. In lieu of schoolwork, he was assigned to observe, identify, and write about the species of plants he encountered along the trail.

The practice of careful observation has continued into his adult life and mixes with a healthy dose of patience and attention to detail, traits he needed for the long hours of studying required to receive above average marks in college, since he was not an especially gifted student. In 2002, he received a Bachelor of Science degree in Civil Engineering and came to Las Vegas for an engineering job, knowing that Red Rock, a world-class rock climbing destination, was only minutes away. After working for a few years, he decided that rock climbing was of more interest than engineering and pursued other job options that allowed him free time to explore Red Rock. During these years of exploration, he stumbled upon traces of history, learned about the plants and animals, came to know the geology, and asked plenty of questions.

This book is a product of those explorations and questions. The author hopes it will enhance others' appreciation of the natural treasure we have so close to Las Vegas.

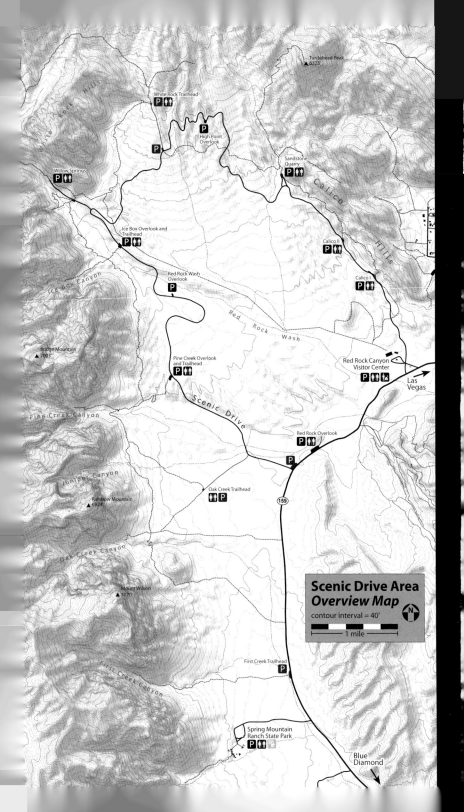

Turtlehead Peak
▲ 6323

White Rock Trailhead
🅿 🚻

High Point
Overlook
🅿

🅿

Sandstone
Quarry
🅿 🚻

Willow Springs
🅿 🚻

White Rock Hills

Calico Hills

Ice Box Overlook and
Trailhead
🅿 🚻

Calico II
🅿 🚻

Red Rock Wash
Overlook
🅿

Calico I
🅿 🚻

Ice Box Canyon

Red Rock Wash

Bridge Mountain
▲ 7003'

Pine Creek Overlook
and Trailhead
🅿 🚻

Red Rock Canyon
Visitor Center
🅿 🚻 🚻

Las
Vegas

Pine Creek Canyon

Scenic Drive

Juniper Canyon

Red Rock Overlook
🅿 🚻

🅿

Rainbow Mountain
▲ 6924'

Oak Creek Trailhead
🚻 🅿

159

Oak Creek Canyon

Mount Wilson
▲ 7070'

## Scenic Drive Area
### *Overview Map*

contour interval = 40'

N

▬▬ 1 mile ▬▬

First Creek Canyon

First Creek Trailhead
🅿

Spring Mountain
Ranch State Park
🅿 🚻 🏛

Blue
Diamond